*Praise for* BRAVE, GENERO

"Fierce like a lioness to benefit beings, dedicated Dharma teacher Barbara Du Bois took to heart the *37 Practices of the Bodhisattva*. Her profound commentary marries the precision of Dharma instructions for conduct with the highest view of spacious mind. Like an arrow to the heart, her clarity pierces our habit of self-absorption. Her delightful earthy humor and contemporary take on applications for our time and culture guide us unerringly towards the ultimate."

–Khenmo Konchog Nyima Drolma, Abbess, Vajra Dakini Nunnery

"Barbara Du Bois has done us all a great service in bringing forth her commentary on Tokme's *37 Bodhisattva Practices*, one of the most loved and revered texts in the Tibetan tradition of Buddhism. Simple and direct, *Brave, Generous, & Undefended* covers all the essential points of Mahayana Buddhism, and Dr. Du Bois' commentary guides the dedicated reader to a deeper appreciation of this wonderful teaching."

–Ken McLeod, author of *A Trackless Path* and *Reflections on Silver River*

"*Brave, Generous, & Undefended* is an honest, brilliant, and precise guide in the most profound process of dissecting what love and wisdom really are and how to free oneself to realize them. Anyone with a genuine yearning to wake up will greatly benefit from Barbara Du Bois' altruistic laboratory of lifetime practice, penetrating understanding, and integration of Dharma. Her book is an invaluable resource of precious, detailed insight into how to unlock and make manifest our ultimate birthright and purpose for being human."

–Christina Lundberg, award-winning American creator of films with a Buddhist focus, including *For the Benefit Of All Beings: The Extraordinary Life of Garchen Triptrul Rinpoche, On The Road Home, Discovering Buddhism, Maitreya Project,* and *Mystic Tibet*

"Making the Dharma real and immediate in daily life, getting down in there with us and teaching from that poignant place, is the treasure Barbara Du Bois offers. Here you have a vibrant distillation of the decades she has given and honed these teachings on Ngulchu Tokme Zangpo's magnificent work, and may it be an excellent elixir for you."

–Trisha Lamb, retreatant, former Director of the Garchen Buddhist Institute

# BRAVE,
# GENEROUS,&
# UNDEFENDED

Foreword by His Eminence Garchen Triptrul Rinpoche

# BRAVE, GENEROUS, & UNDEFENDED

## Heart Teachings on the
## *37 Bodhisattva Practices*

## Barbara Du Bois

Hohm Press
Chino Valley, Arizona

ISBN: 978-1-942493-88-4
Ebook: 978-1-942493-89-1


Hohm Press
PO Box 4410
Chino Valley, AZ 86323
800-381-2700
http://www.hohmpress.com


Printed in the United States of America

Library of Congress Control Number: 2022952361

MIX
Paper from
responsible sources
FSC® C011935
FSC
www.fsc.org

*For*

*His Eminence Garchen Triptrul Rinpoche*

# CONTENTS

His Eminence Garchen Triptrul Rinpoche

Portrait by Pema, Taiwan Garchen Dharma Institute;
kindly provided by Juanita McCarron

২ অবহ্নিঞ্জ্ভূষ্ণৰ্দ্ধিবিজ্

## His Eminence D. K. Garchen Rinpoche

Tashi Delek!

Lopon Barbara's first guru was Dudjom Rinpoche, before meeting me some years later.
Now, we have been close friends for many years. The 37 Bodhisattva Practices, the root of all Dharma,
are all I really know. Lopon Barbara has trained in these practices for over thirty years.
Having studied, contemplated, practiced, and discussed their meaning with me over the years,
she has now completed this commentary on the Bodhisattva practices. In this book you will find
instructions that come straight from the heart and are based on direct experience, so it is not
an ordinary academic piece of literature. Her mind and my mind are one; whatever I know,
she knows. Her experiential instructions are based on the practice-blessing lineage
and are suitable for anyone who wishes to engage in practice. For this reason, this book
is truly very precious. Anyone will surely benefit from it, and in particular, I am asking all my
friends to make sure you read this precious book.

His Eminence Garchen Triptrul Rinpoche
22 June 2018

# INTRODUCTION

I bow to His Eminence Garchen Rinpoche, great bodhisattva and beloved spiritual friend to countless beings, through lifetimes dedicated to the benefit of all.

Living through the period when his country, Tibet, was taken over by the Chinese government, Garchen Rinpoche was imprisoned for twenty years in a labor camp, where he met his root teacher, Khenpo Munsel.[1] The prisoners paid a high price if discovered engaging in Dharma, so Garchen Rinpoche contemplated and practiced the lama's instructions secretly. His inner practice included the wisdom teachings of the renowned 14th century bodhisattva, Gyalse Tokme Zangpo, who composed the noble text we hold in our hands right now: *The 37 Bodhisattva Practices*, essence of the entire Buddhadharma. Garchen Rinpoche says of these precious, profound verses, "This is all I know," and gives them to all he meets, in words and in the example of his life.

Many years ago, my mind troubled by itself, I found myself silently calling out to Rinpoche in my heart, day after day, "Lama, please help me become like you." I never said it to him in person. Then one day, in a meeting where I was displaying my negativity about someone else's negativity, Rinpoche abruptly halted the flow of my complaint, reached across the table with *The 37 Bodhisattva Practices*, looked me in the eye and said, "Barbara, if you want to become like me, this is how I became the way I am. Study these

---

1. Khenpo Munsel (1916-1993). See biography by Samten Chhosphel at https://treasury-oflives.org.

1

teachings. Take them literally. Practice every day what is contained in this small book and you will accomplish what I have accomplished."

Great teachers normally do not proclaim their great qualities. For example, once when Tenzin Gyatso, His Holiness the 14th Dalai Lama, was teaching on *A Guide to the Bodhisattva's Way of Life*—Shantideva's quintessential treatise on compassion—he said to us, "I myself have not developed any compassion, so I really have to study this text."[2] A sigh ran through the large audience: tender love for this magnificent being whose tender compassion for us brings our minds together in such a natural way: Oh, of course I need to study, as you do, so let us simply proceed. Thus, when a great master does acknowledge something about her or his realization it is rare and precious to hear, itself a confirmation of path: we are walking in the footprints, still warm, of those who have walked and are even now walking before us. When Garchen Rinpoche promised that I could accomplish what he has accomplished he was acknowledging the realization we see in him and with utter kindness placing in our hands and minds the very means upon which he himself relies, the thirty-seven core practices of the bodhisattva: "This is how I became the way I am." This was an act devoid of self—pure generosity—to give us courage and confidence on the way.

Deep in the prison camp, with privation and torture, without books or notes, working with his lama's secret instructions and with his own mind, Gar Rinpoche distilled the essence of every teaching he received and practiced on that. His essence practice opened to him the profound meanings of the entire Dharma. This is his heart teaching also to me, his pith instruction: Whatever teaching or practice you receive, distill the essence and practice on that.

The times and circumstances appear different: 14th-century Tibet would seem to contrast in every way with our lives in the 21st century—but the mind of sentient beings is not different. We want meaning yet pursue the trivial; we confuse virtue and nonvirtue

2. Tucson, Arizona, 2005, recollection of the author.

and so misunderstand the causes of our own unhappiness; we yearn to help others and grieve the harm we do; we experience the anguish of separation from truth and love while in every moment indissolubly one with them. We, too, urgently and deeply need unmistaken, undeceiving wisdom in our own times and places. Gar Rinpoche's prison cell became his holy retreat hut, where he took his ultimate freedom, while we, so rich in worldly freedoms, are still held in the prison of our confusion and suffering. *The 37 Bodhisattva Practices* will break open the lock.

## What is a bodhisattva?

A bodhisattva is one who makes the highest altruistic commitment: to free all beings from ignorance and suffering and into ultimate wisdom. This intention, followed lifetime to lifetime, is *bodhicitta*, "enlightenment mind." We can also describe the bodhisattva very simply as one who has a good heart, and bodhicitta as love and compassion.

Bodhisattvas exist throughout time and in all worlds. While traditions of Buddhadharma beautifully and profoundly elucidate the concept of bodhisattva, its meaning refers to universal potentials of consciousness, awareness, love, and power. We don't have to be Buddhists or even human beings to become bodhisattvas; a bodhisattva can take any form or act in any manner needed to bring benefit.

We can speak of three kinds of bodhisattva motivations: the motivation of the king, proclaiming, "In order to lead all to enlightenment, I must attain enlightenment first"; that of the ship captain, who affirms, "As we sail across the ocean of samsara, I must captain well this great ship so that we all attain enlightenment together"; and that of the shepherd: "Let all the flock go first." We can find ourselves in one or the other state of motivation at different times. All good. And if you think you have no bodhisattva motivation at all, or if this is the first you are even hearing about this possibility, then what you are, in this lifetime, is a person fresh and new on the bodhisattva path. Wonderful!

That any being might generate the bodhisattva intention is so rare and precious it is often likened to a flash of lightning in the dark of night. Simply to hear of bodhicitta stirs its potential within us: love-compassion, radiance of our true nature. Nothing can destroy this; everything else comes and goes, while our true nature is present beyond all coming and going. Hearing this we might think, "But if this is my true nature, why don't I see it? Why do I suffer and cause others to suffer? Why am I craving, angry, sad, selfish?" We are of the nature of perfection and we create and experience everything that obscures it from our sight. Perfect. This is what gives rise to spiritual longing and seeking and what brings forth compassion for others, and eventually for all: bodhicitta, the good heart of the bodhisattva.

## Gyalse Tokme Zangpo and his teaching

The cook whose heart is filled with love can't keep love out of the pudding. I have heard that Buddha Shakyamuni first declined to teach others because what he had realized was so simple no one would believe it—and of course every teaching he did give pointed to that inexpressible simplicity of ultimate truth. And so it is with Tokme Zangpo. This humble bodhisattva, a learned scholar and great teacher, was a profound practitioner who sat in retreat for over twenty years in the Precious Cave of Ngulchu.[3] *The 37 Bodhisattva Practices* are alive with his learning and realization, his compassionate wisdom.

Tokme Zangpo's text is not a theoretical or philosophical treatise. It is to be studied, plumbed, and practiced in the actual circumstances of your life and mind, to liberate that which is ever within and beyond circumstance. These radical teachings penetrate to the root of our confusion, turning our conventional conditioning and habits on their heads. They are also accessible to

---

3. Tokme Zangpo is also referred to as Gyalse Tokme (or Thogme) and Ngulchu Tokme. His dates are given as 1295-1369 (sometimes 1297-1371). See Samten Chhosphel, treasuryoflives.org. Dilgo Khyentse Rinpoche includes a beautiful biography of Tokme Zangpo in *Heart of Compassion*, 9-26.

each of us, and readily applicable. No initiations, secret teachings, or famous teachers are required in order to take these precepts literally, to understand and use them. They are our guidebook for the path of awakening, a training manual for becoming a bodhisattva, for abandoning the prison of self, for becoming truly able to care about others and eventually to love and liberate all.

These are also inner teachings, pointing to the absolute. These verses speak to the intellect that is necessary for knowledge and understanding in our present existence, while at the same time reminding us that absolute wisdom nature is the very essence of this existent reality. The highest view pervades these teachings. Be aware that you have innately the capacity to work with their meanings at both levels, for you have conventional intellect and you are of the nature of the ultimate.

The Buddhadharma can be described as holographic, each part revealing the whole; this is true also of *The 37 Bodhisattva Practices*. To study and contemplate this succinct wisdom compendium, to comprehend what each of these verses teaches and how to practice it, is to gain access to the meanings of both the simplest teachings and the most profound wisdom you may receive from the great spiritual masters. This eases our minds; we now have no reason to doubt that we will find the teachings we need. They are in our hands right now.

Tokme's penetrating, concise treatise illumines the complete path, giving us the core principles of the three vehicles (the three *yanas*) of the Buddhadharma: identifying and abandoning non-virtue, the cause of suffering (Hinayana, Sutrayana, the vehicle of individual liberation); generating the great compassion of the bodhisattva, to benefit and liberate all beings from suffering and its causes (Mahayana, Bodhisattvayana); and pure view, opening to the nondual, to the ultimate (the transformational Vajrayana, the Diamond Vehicle). The great Dilgo Khyentse Rinpoche calls *The 37 Bodhisattva Practices* the "most direct and profound Mahayana teaching on attaining enlightenment. . . . If you practice according to these precepts, all concern for yourself will be dispelled and you will find it easy to turn all your efforts toward benefiting others."[4] This is the heart of the bodhisattva path.

## About the commentary

No scholar here, nor any kind of meditation master, just a lover of the fine Dharma and the recipient, beyond fortunate, of lineage blessings and guidance from true teachers, vessels of love and compassion for all beings. My purpose for this writing is to give you what they have given me.

Tokme Zangpo's root text immediately follows this Introduction. I encourage you to read it in full before embarking on the commentary—and then every day of your life from now on.

In preparing this work I have relied especially on over twenty years of teachings and training with H. E. Garchen Rinpoche, since he first came to the United States in 1997. I sat with him that summer in a geodesic dome packed hip to knee with a grateful, happy collection of longtime practitioners and newcomers to Dharma, yoginis and yogis, holy fools and quiet inquirers, all agog in our good fortune. In the time since Rinpoche left Tibet and began teaching throughout the world, many have enjoyed deep, recurring contact with him. His presence with us in personal interactions as well as in large gatherings has been warm and radiant with an intimate, tender, penetrating, unwavering love that has profoundly inspired and nurtured us as aspiring bodhisattvas. He is an ocean of bodhicitta and we are little cups; the elixir is the same in each.

Gar Rinpoche elucidates so gracefully how to understand and actualize in the ever-changing present the subtle, vast teachings of the Dharma. As my mind is awed by his profound explanations it is also opening effortlessly to their precision, which makes readable and walkable the path ahead. I am exultant, wanting to shout out, "This is it! This is how it works, this is how we do it! Let's go, let's go!" Joyous confidence arises for those in the care of this holy bodhisattva, and he is present in these pages.

---

4. Dilgo Khyentse, *Heart of Compassion*, 198.

To share with you some of the teachings and instructions I have received from Rinpoche I have relied on memory and on my notes; on unedited, unpublished summaries and transcripts of his teachings; and on explanations and instructions that Rinpoche has given me privately. I have also drawn on the two main commentaries I have used in giving teachings on this material over the years: Dilgo Khyentse Rinpoche's luminous explanations of *The 37 Bodhisattva Practices* and the clear, thorough expositions of Geshe Jampa Tegchok—as well as several related works, but not many, for this is not a scholarly commentary but rather the testimony and heart teachings of an ordinary practitioner who has been taken in hand by extraordinary beings.

Meeting with Dharma friends, students, and practitioners, I have found that Tokme's pith instructions quite naturally provide a basis and framework for our life and practice. Together, we have recited and contemplated them; analyzed, reflected, and meditated upon each verse; discussed and wrestled with the teachings and their implications, sometimes calmly and sometimes not; and probed profound commentaries and our own life experiences in the light of the teachings and practices. *Sangha* friends (sangha is, broadly, the community of students, practitioners, teachers) have posed excellent questions arising from their direct experience as they confronted the possibility of actually living the ideals of unconditional compassion and love. Much of that body of teachings is in this book, edited and amplified, including some of our lively interchanges, which were often laced with tears and laughter. The Dharma points out our follies so vividly and clarifies them so briskly that often the response is simply to burst out laughing. We did a lot of that.[5]

You will find some repetition here. We need to hear, reflect, and practice on the teachings over and over, to penetrate confusion,

---

5. The teachings were given over a period of some ten years or more, mainly in Arizona, California, and Utah, and briefly also in Sweden and Mexico. I have edited and amplified the transcribed material from those teachings. No living participants are identified.

correct mistaken conceptions, and to elucidate deeper layers of meaning—so I sometimes say again what I've already said, just as I want to hear again from my lama what I have already heard from him. Never knowing if we will meet again in this life, I want to pour it all out in every meeting, the essence of all I have heard and understood.

A few words about words: Mind, consciousness, and awareness are tricky words for English speakers because we can use them to mean both the same and different things, or what we take to be the same or different. When we speak of these matters we are using concepts to communicate both that which is familiar, conventional, and that which transcends it—and which, being nondual, can be neither communicated nor comprehended through concepts. In the commentary, *consciousness* refers to conventional mind: mind that thinks, posits, explores, takes apart, constructs, and that can be aware of itself. I use *awareness* and *true nature* to point through or beyond consciousness to that which is ever present, luminous, awake; this is sometimes called pristine mind or wisdom mind, primordial awareness, and also the ultimate or absolute. I most frequently speak of it as the *true nature*. It is the nature of the absolute and also of conventional mind, of emptiness and of phenomenal appearances. Dudjom Rinpoche once said, "I don't know why we speak of the nature of mind: it's the nature of absolutely everything." Conditioned mind appears like waves on water, and takes itself for what is rising and falling, coming and going, while the absolute, the unchanging, is like the water itself.

## The Two Truths

Absolute and relative both are. We already are what we aspire to become: we are templates of truth, to be laid bare by love. The laying bare is the spiritual work, and love, inseparable from truth, is its ground, its path, and its result. To be what we already are only two things are required of us: to love and to know—to love completely all beings and all existence and to know directly the true nature of reality. These two are not two. Thus, you will find herein a rhythm, a steady pulse: relative and absolute dancing together. This is the heartbeat of this work, the work of these teachings and the great work of the bodhisattva. Where one is invoked the other also appears. A primordial, indissoluble union, the nondual Two Truths are the way of bodhisattva being.

•

I am confident that you will find trustworthy guidance for your life and your spiritual path in this book because it contains the teachings of holy bodhisattvas and the pristine Dharma. You will also find here my own considerable limitations of understanding and expression, errors and muddled thinking, and explanations that are wordy because my mastery is shallow. May all my evident impediments impel you to your own deep study and practice!

So often I have heard teachers say, in giving a teaching or practice, "This is the only teaching, the only practice you need." The best, highest, most profound teaching or practice is the one that works for you. In reading this book, please have this simple, profound instruction in mind. If you are touched, stirred, awakened by one teaching, practice on that one. If one practice reveals to you the clear light of wisdom or the infinite love of bodhicitta, follow that one. In this way confidence will naturally grow and you will live and practice with gladness. Take up what speaks to you and contemplate and practice on that to attain certainty—and then continue, for the benefit of all beings.

Thank you.

# THE ROOT TEXT
## *37 Practices of a Bodhisattva's Way of Life*
### by Gyalse Tokme Zangpo[1]

Namo Lokeshvaraya!

While seeing that all phenomena neither come nor go, you strive solely for the sake of all beings. Supreme guru and protector Chenrezig, at all times, I respectfully pay homage to you with my body, speech, and mind!

The perfect buddhas—source of all well-being and ultimate peace—arise from having accomplished the true Dharma, and since that depends on knowing the practices, I shall explain the way of the bodhisattvas.

1. Having now gained this great ship of freedom and fortune—so difficult to find—in order to free yourself and others from the ocean of cyclic existence, listen, reflect, and meditate day and night without distraction. This is the way of a bodhisattva.

2. Attachment to loved ones churns like water. Hatred for enemies rages like fire. In the darkness of ignorance, one forgets what to adopt and what to avoid. Abandon your homeland. This is the way of a bodhisattva.

1. English translation © 2017 by Ina Dhargye (Ina Trinley Wangmo), used with her kind permission. Inquiries about obtaining copies, translation rights, etc., may be addressed to the Garchen Buddhist Institute: 928-925-1237, questions@garchen.net, P.O. Box 4318, Chino Valley, Arizona 86323, www.garchen.net.

3. When negative places are abandoned, disturbing emotions will gradually decline. Without distractions, attention to virtue naturally grows. When the mind becomes clear, certainty in the Dharma arises. Live alone in seclusion. This is the way of a bodhisattva.

4. Family and longtime companions will part from each other. Possessions gained with effort will be left behind. Consciousness, a guest, will leave the guesthouse of the body. Let go of all worldly concerns. This is the way of a bodhisattva.

5. In bad company, the three poisons grow stronger. The activities of learning, reflecting, and meditating decline, and love and compassion are lost. Give up such companions. This is the way of a bodhisattva.

6. When one follows a true spiritual friend, faults will dissolve and good qualities will grow like a waxing moon. Consider this friend more dear than your own body. This is the way of a bodhisattva.

7. Who can worldly gods, themselves imprisoned in samsara, protect? Therefore, seek refuge in the Three Jewels, the undeceiving source of refuge. This is the way of a bodhisattva.

8. The Buddha taught that all the unbearable suffering of the lower realms is caused by wrongdoing. Therefore, never do wrong, even at the cost of your life. This is the way of a bodhisattva.

9. Like a dewdrop on a blade of grass, the happiness of the three worlds vanishes in but an instant. Strive for the supreme state of never-changing liberation. This is the way of a bodhisattva.

10. When mothers who have loved you since beginningless time are suffering, what good is your own happiness? Therefore, give

rise to bodhicitta in order to liberate infinite sentient beings. This is the way of a bodhisattva.

11. All suffering without exception comes from seeking your own happiness. The perfect buddhas are born from the altruistic mind. Therefore, truly exchange your own happiness for the suffering of others. This is the way of a bodhisattva.

12. Even if someone driven by great desire steals all your wealth or lets others steal it, dedicate to them your body, possessions, and all virtue of the three times. This is the way of a bodhisattva.

13. Even if someone cuts off your head when you haven't done anything wrong, take all their negative deeds upon yourself through the power of compassion. This is the way of a bodhisattva.

14. Even if others slander you throughout a billion worlds, in return, speak with a loving mind of their good qualities. This is the way of a bodhisattva.

15. Even if someone exposes your hidden faults and insults you in front of others, view that person as a teacher and bow with respect. This is the way of a bodhisattva.

16. Even if someone you have cared for as dearly as your own child regards you as an enemy, love that person even more, as a mother would her ailing child. This is the way of a bodhisattva.

17. Even if someone of equal or lower status, driven by pride, treats you with disdain, respectfully place them on your crown as your teacher. This is the way of a bodhisattva.

18. Though you may be impoverished, always disparaged, gripped by disease, and tormented by spirits, never lose courage

but take on the pain and misdeeds of all beings. This is the way of a bodhisattva.

19. Though you may be famous and admired by many who bow to you, and as rich as the Wealth God himself, having seen that worldly fortune is without essence, do not be proud. This is the way of a bodhisattva.

20. If the enemy—your own anger—is not tamed, subduing outer enemies will only make them increase. Therefore, subdue your own mind with the army of love and compassion. This is the way of a bodhisattva.

21. Sensory pleasures are like salt water: the more you drink, the greater your thirst. Abandon at once all things that bring forth clinging attachment. This is the way of a bodhisattva.

22. The way things appear is your own mind. Mind itself primordially transcends fabricated extremes. Knowing just this, do not create concepts of subject and object. This is the way of a bodhisattva.

23. When you come across things that attract you, like beautiful rainbows in summertime, do not regard them as real and abandon clinging attachment. This is the way of a bodhisattva.

24. All suffering is like the death of your child in a dream. How exhausting it is to hold illusory appearances as real! Therefore, when you meet with difficult circumstances, see them as illusory. This is the way of a bodhisattva.

25. When even one's body must be given up when aspiring for enlightenment, what need is there to mention material things? Therefore, practice generosity, without hope of reward or karmic results. This is the way of a bodhisattva.

26. If you lack moral discipline, you cannot accomplish even your own purpose, so wanting to achieve the purpose of others is truly absurd. Therefore, protect your discipline without concern for worldly existence. This is the way of a bodhisattva.

27. For bodhisattvas who desire a wealth of virtue, all harm is like a precious treasure. Therefore, without hostility, be patient with everyone. This is the way of a bodhisattva.

28. Even hearers or solitary realizers, who accomplish only their own purpose, strive as if putting out a fire on their head. Seeing this, practice with diligence—the source of good qualities—for the sake of all beings. This is the way of a bodhisattva.

29. Disturbing emotions are destroyed by insight grounded in calm abiding. Knowing this, cultivate meditative concentration that purely transcends the four formless absorptions. This is the way of a bodhisattva.

30. Without wisdom, the other five perfections alone are not enough to reach complete enlightenment. Thus, combined with skillful means, develop the wisdom that does not distinguish among the three spheres. This is the way of a bodhisattva.

31. Unless you examine your own confused ideas, you might look like a practitioner but not be acting like one. Therefore, always examine yourself and abandon confusion. This is the way of a bodhisattva.

32. If you are driven by disturbing emotions and talk about another bodhisattva's faults, it is actually to your own detriment. So, don't mention the faults of those who have entered the Great Vehicle. This is the way of a bodhisattva.

33. Concern for gain and respect causes conflict and a decline in the activities of learning, reflecting, and meditating. So abandon attachment to your circle of friends, relations, and benefactors. This is the way of a bodhisattva.

34. Harsh words disturb others' minds and thus diminish the practice of a bodhisattva. Therefore, abandon harsh speech, which is unpleasant to others. This is the way of a bodhisattva.

35. When disturbing emotions become habitual, it is difficult to reverse them with antidotes. Thus, the soldier of mindfulness wields antidotes as weapons and destroys disturbing emotions such as attachment the moment they start to arise. This is the way of a bodhisattva.

36. In brief, wherever you are and whatever you are doing, always examine the state of your mind. Act to accomplish the purpose of others through constant mindfulness and awareness. This is the way of a bodhisattva.

37. With the wisdom of threefold purity, dedicate all the virtue gained from having made such effort toward enlightenment. Dedicate it to clear away the suffering of infinite beings. This is the way of a bodhisattva.

In accordance with the words of the holy ones regarding the meaning of the sutras, tantras, and their commentaries, I have written these thirty-seven verses on the ways of a bodhisattva for those who wish to train on the bodhisattva's path.

This composition will not be admired by the learned because my intellect is poor and my education is limited. However, I have followed the sutras and the words of holy ones, so I believe these ways of a bodhisattva are not mistaken.

Still, because the vast deeds of bodhisattvas are difficult to grasp by simple-minded beings like myself, I beg the forgiveness of the holy ones for the mass of my errors such as contradictions and inconsistencies.

By the virtue arising from this, may all beings give rise to relative and ultimate bodhicitta and thereby become like the Protector Chenrezig, who does not abide in the extremes of existence or peace.

*The monk Tokme, a proponent of scripture and reasoning, composed these verses in the Precious Cave of Ngulchu, for his own and others' benefit.*

# CHAPTER ONE

# HOMAGE TO BODHICITTA: THE OPENING VERSES

Namo Lokeshvaraya! While seeing that all phenomena neither come nor go, you strive solely for the sake of all beings. Supreme guru and protector Chenrezig, at all times, I respectfully pay homage to you with my body, speech, and mind!

The perfect buddhas—source of all well-being and ultimate peace—arise from having accomplished the true Dharma, and since that depends on knowing the practices, I shall explain the way of the bodhisattvas.

The thirty-seven practices of the bodhisattva way are the distilled nectar of bodhicitta, heart essence of the bodhisattva's aspiration and attainment. This is signaled instantly as our teacher, Tokme Zangpo, begins with homage to Lokeshvara (Avalokiteshvara, Skt.; Chenrezig, Tib.), Buddhist deity of compassion. Homage to great compassion, he proclaims—meaning its full, complete, faultless, absolute realization, and its seed of potential ever present within, source of both aspiration and accomplishment. Homage to compassion tells us precisely what this text is and what it is for.

To compassion's exemplar Tokme first says, "While seeing that all phenomena neither come nor go, you strive solely for the sake of all beings." This line stirs me deeply, standing as my inspiration and instruction for the entire path.

One who realizes the true nature of reality perceives directly the union of being and existence, ultimate and relative, the changeless and the ever-changing—and this direct realization instantaneously, spontaneously, irresistibly gives rise to the limitless compassion, the infinite love, that would bring all beings to this realization and its absolute freedom.

In our conventional minds all phenomena, including material appearances and inner experiences, appear constantly to be coming and going. What sees this phantasmagorical display? It is primordial awareness, changeless natural wisdom, which recognizes both our temporary, ever changing condition of mind and its true nature, awake and unmoving.

Is the arising, dancing, subsiding wave other than the water in which it momentarily swells and disappears? In our natural mind, appearances likewise continually arise and dissolve, so what can be said to have come, what to have gone? Yet something does *appear* to happen, and we sentient beings are those who fixate to appearances: Something came, I'm happy; something went, I'm sad. Something came, I'm sad; something went, I'm happy. And therein lies the cycle of samsara. The "I" and the "something"—subject, object, with grasping and aversion: this is what gives rise to the illusion-like display.

Although there is no solidity or endurance, no inherent existence, to this phenomenal display in which we are sporting and also caught, those who have penetrated this illusion witness and participate in it for our benefit, as bodhisattvas seen or unseen. For our sake the compassionate ones strive to show the way to wellbeing and happiness and to liberate all from ignorance, confusion, and suffering.

Tokme acknowledges this vast, profound, potent compassion and love with deep gratitude and respect: "at all times, I respectfully pay homage to you with my body, speech, and mind." In our ordinary lives, we, too, can practice this homage. The physical homage can be expressed through gesture of hand or head or by the whole body taking us to the ground, softening the stiff neck of pride. The verbal homage is our speech, giving reverence, praise, and devotion in formalities or in our own sincere, spontaneous words or sounds. The supreme homage is mind in its natural state, continuously one with love and compassion—never separate from bodhicitta.

The essence of *The 37 Bodhisattva Practices* is bodhicitta, so we will be learning about bodhicitta in virtually every verse. Here at the beginning of our study together, then, a very brief explanation:

Bodhicitta is the pinnacle of altruism: others-before-self, caring concern for all, for their wellbeing and for their ultimate liberation from ignorance and suffering. In the realms of existence, bodhicitta arising in the mind of a sentient being is transforming, illuminating, and rare. Mind realizing the absolute, the true nature of beings and all created appearances, is naturally radiant and powerful with ultimate bodhicitta, truth-love. Bodhicitta, the seed that has come to fruition as vast, profound, absolute love-wisdom in all buddhas, is the same seed, the *same* seed, in us. If we water it, how can we fail?

Perhaps you have noticed, when with your teachers, that in speaking of bodhicitta they sometimes weep. They mist. That is bodhicitta stirring. The weeping or misting is not because they are emotionally moved in a personal way; the tears in the eyes when we witness, think, or hear of bodhicitta, that *is* bodhicitta, moistening, softening, opening. I have heard that His Holiness the 14th Dalai Lama, speaking to a large audience in Europe, suddenly burst into tears, covered his face with his hands, and wept—then lifted his head up, smiled in his radiant way, and simply went on with his teaching, like the sun giving full light when the little rain ceases. As our awareness opens to bodhicitta, every sign of bodhicitta that we see or hear of, that we notice or taste in the world, in others and ourselves, stirs and quickens that seed within ourselves.

The second introductory verse goes on to say "the perfect buddhas—source of all wellbeing and ultimate peace—arise from accomplishing the true Dharma." Accomplishing the true Dharma, or what is often called enlightenment, can be spoken of in many sublime ways, all pointing to this: all confusion and negative potentials cleared away and all positive potentials expanded and fulfilled.[1] We only need to clear away the obscurations to reveal the intrinsic perfection. This is what "purification" means in Buddhadharma: the process by which already and always existing perfection is revealed. It's not like scrubbing a greasy cooking pot; it's more like washing a mirror so you can clearly see your own face.

And what is the wellbeing and ultimate peace for which the perfect buddhas are our source? Absolute truth, beyond concept and change: our true nature and the true nature of all phenomena, all appearances, from which we are never separate and which each of us must reveal within. Our teachers and unfailing spiritual friends are its mirrors, ever shedding blessings and grace to help us realize it. Thus they are the source of our ultimate benefit and happiness by enabling us, too, to secure the happiness of all, by becoming bodhisattvas and buddhas ourselves—thus accomplishing the "two purposes," the enlightenment of ourselves and others.

Finally, Tokme Zangpo says that in order to accomplish the Dharma we have to know the Dharma practices. For his explanations, generations and centuries of practitioners bow to him in homage and gratitude. Tokme is spoken of and written about with profound love and respect as a great bodhisattva. His teaching in *The 37 Bodhisattva Practices* gives the entire Buddhadharma, accessible and practical at the outer level while also imbued with and pointing to the profound inner meaning. Receiving his jewel-like spiritual legacy, we take this text as our roadmap for the bodhisattva way.

What you place your mind upon, that you will become. Never remove your mind from bodhicitta: always keep your mind in bodhicitta, always keep bodhicitta in your mind. It is your most precious possession, your lifeline. Hanging from a cliff high over the sea of samsara, you cannot fall: on bodhicitta belay you are safe.

---

1. H. E. Garchen Rinpoche, oral explanation to author.

# Discussion: Phenomena, bodhicitta, attachment

*What is meant by "phenomena"?*

A phenomenon is anything that can be said to happen, to occur. Phenomena arise from causes and depend upon conditions; they change with changing conditions and cease to exist when their causes are exhausted. Without exception, then, all phenomena are impermanent and interdependent. This is what is being pointed to in the teaching that phenomena are "empty." It doesn't mean phenomena don't exist; it means they exist relatively but not absolutely—relative to causes and conditions but not inherently, in and of themselves.[2]

There are inner and outer phenomena. An outer phenomenon is that we are sitting together in a group; an inner phenomenon is a question arising in your mind. We sometimes refer to phenomena as "arisings," registering in consciousness as emotion, image, memory, and so on. This is what is happening with our conventional, conditioned mind, which is also habitually perceiving and grasping to phenomena, inner and outer, as solid, real, inherently existent—while the fact that the phenomenal display is constantly changing is an immediately understandable demonstration of its emptiness. Even as all phenomena come and go, what recognizes this display is vast, primordial awareness, which neither comes nor goes. Each phenomenon has a cause, while awareness that sees phenomena, within or without, is uncaused, always already here, as luminosity-presence. We tend to involve ourselves instantly and endlessly with our thoughts and other phenomena; when we refrain from engaging with our mind's display we gradually become familiar with and able to rest in awareness itself.

---

2. "This does not mean that nothing exists; phenomena, both inner and outer, do exist—just not in the way we think they do. To consider that there is nothing is the error of nihilism; to consider that what there is possesses or is possessed of some inherent self-nature is the error of eternalism. In Buddhadharma these are referred to as the two extremes. The teaching of the Two Truths cuts through these errors: absolute (or ultimate) truth is the truth of emptiness, while relative (or phenomenal) truth is the truth of apparent existence. The two truths are completely interpenetrating, nondual . . . " Barbara Du Bois, *Light Years*, 92, n.51.

*I'm unclear what bodhicitta is.*

Bodhicitta, sometimes called enlightenment mind, is the altruistic intention, the peak of intentions—to liberate all beings, past, present, and future, from suffering and the causes of suffering, and to establish all in happiness and the causes of happiness. It includes, therefore, the intention to purify, to clear away, all causes of confusion and ignorance in one's own mind and to establish oneself in buddha mind—*in order to liberate others.*

Absolute bodhicitta is buddha nature itself, our true nature, present and perfect in every being as primordial wisdom essence and potential, while relative bodhicitta is its reflection and expression in the realms of existence. Its conventional appearance is what we know as relative love and compassion, so we have a reference point for bodhicitta in our ordinary human experience, because we've all experienced love and compassion, both in receiving and in giving. All-pervading, like the rays of the sun, ultimate love and compassion are vast, without limit and without reference, rather than being aroused by a particular condition, person, or circumstance. At this time our love and compassion are wavering and conditional, tending to arise for those close to us and whom we care about, or the suffering that we might hear about that stirs our fellow-feeling. We don't need to "develop" ultimate bodhicitta, for the ultimate is completeness itself. Our work is to sweep away that which obscures its natural expression, and this we do by actively generating relative bodhicitta, right here in relative reality, where we are ceaselessly rubbing and bumping and scraping up against beings and circumstances that challenge—and thus help us develop—our capacities for love and compassion.

It is our compelling habits and blinding afflictions rooted in the false notion of "self" which prevent us from recognizing and manifesting bodhicitta. Cultivating caring concern, compassion, and love for others diminishes this self-grasping—so take this now as an essential point for your bodhisattva training: In moments when you experience sincere love and compassion for the particular, the few, extend it—vividly, intensely, spaciously, powerfully—to the many. When you think of one, think instantly of all. Imagine and intend that someday you will effortlessly desire and act for the happiness of all beings. This simple practice expands your attention and your intention: your relative bodhicitta.

Of relative bodhicitta, also, there are two kinds: aspiring bodhicitta and acting bodhicitta. We could say that bodhicitta is inspired by hearing about and seeing examples of bodhicitta in holy gurus, in what seem like ordinary beings, in visual images like paintings and statues, and in natural displays in land, sea, and sky. We aspire to generate all-encompassing, universal love and compassion and we train in that by thinking and acting in ways that place others before self—ultimately revealing original pristine mind, in which duality of self and other is not. Undertaking the trainings that relax our self-grasping, that calm our afflictions and confusions, and that express naturally in the ways bodhisattvas actually live: this is the bodhicitta of action, of application—what we do in mind, speech, and activities to develop, for the benefit of all, our bodhicitta potential.

So now you know how to bring forth love and compassion: inspiration, aspiration, and perspiration. You would not have asked this question if you did not have the seed of bodhicitta already alive within. We don't even aspire to become bodhisattvas and buddhas unless we have that potential within us, already beginning to whisper, "Wake up, wake up!" And we begin to pay attention: Oh, there's a possibility of waking up? Okay, then!

*How is compassion different from emotion with attachment?*

Emotion with attachment is self-referential, in some degree for and about ourselves, as all attachment is, while compassion and love are for others—with some admixture of self-reference and partiality, in our present state. We start where we are. As we cultivate love and compassion our self-concern and self-grasping diminish, ultimately revealing no I, no other.

Love and compassion are not really emotions; they are aspects or qualities of our true nature. In our relative, conditioned state we experience them emotionally, with all that this implies about self-reference. Emotion with attachment, whether we call it love or compassion, because it is self-referential is also conditional: it will change when conditions change, which they constantly do and always will. And it is partial: it applies to this circumstance and not that one, to this being and not that one—as with the kind rescuer of animals who feels compassion for suffering animals and hatred for the humans who harm them. Also, love or compassion with attachment is wavering and unsteady; it will arise and then change or subside: we will care warmly and then cool, champion and then attack.

Our ordinary love and compassion shine in our experience as the radiance of the absolute. As the butter is already in the milk, the bodhicitta is already in the love. We already are what we aspire to become.

*You spoke of misting and tears that can occur as bodhicitta is being stirred; doesn't that bring bodhicitta back to the level of emotion with attachment?*

It can, if we react to it as a personality phenomenon, as in "Oh, I'm crying, how embarrassing," or as in reaching over to console someone weeping in the temple. In conventional situations, if someone is weeping you may want to offer comfort and that person may want to be comforted, but in a teaching or practice situation it may be wiser to let your friend weep—because conventional attention, however kindly meant, can distract, bringing mind touching the sublime back to personality level, to self-reference. It is not something conventional happening when that melting is occurring; it is bodhicitta stirring. We don't want to snatch it back to the limited, limiting emotional reaction: "Oh, I'm so sorry, you're weeping," or even "Oh, how wonderful, you're experiencing bodhicitta." In the privacy of your own mind simply rejoice in bodhicitta.

Conventional behavior keeps us tied to convention. Spiritual aspiration and practice are not about convention. Tokme's noble text is not about convention. It will turn your life on its head. And your heart inside out.

*I'm confused now about the list we keep of specific beings who have requested our prayers; isn't it limiting to be thinking of a particular person rather than of all sentient beings?*

Think of it as both-and, not either-or. Are you embedding your prayers for a particular individual always in the vast intention that this one *and* all beings may be released from suffering and established in happiness? Whatever prayer you are making, for whatever being or situation, is the point from which you generate the vast intention—so how can it be limiting?

*Because it tends to bring my mind back to me. Even though I can say it's really all who are suffering, when I think of a specific person's name it brings me back to the personal.*

It is this one *and* all others—including you. No contradiction. On the path of the great love, we are learning how to love the one in the many and the many in the one. The back-and-forth from individual to all and from all to individual: this is a training ground for us. There are many consciousnesses, so there can be many experiences of suffering, but there is only one true nature.

Your excellent question also points to why, in the prayer requests that are sent to practitioners, there is no information about the circumstance—because doesn't our mind just grasp hold of the drama? Person committed suicide, dog has cancer, friend's mother lost her job. It would be like reading the temporal tabloids, the *Samsaric Times*. Our thoughts of good and bad limit our mind's ability to see things as they are. That is why the prayer requests are sent out with no details—just the name, arising momentarily like a wave in the clear waters of mind and swiftly dissolving, leaving no trace.

*Can relative compassion be too discouraging?*

Well, we can experience it that way—although it is actually not the relative compassion but our self-grasping that gives rise to discouragement. Relative compassion, because it is still involved with self, is subject to all the kinds of emotions and thoughts that anything tied to self is going to provoke. In relative compassion, you may be exerting yourself greatly to be of help to others, but if there is a thought of "I" in there anywhere, afflictive emotions are there, too, even if very subtle.

It is also usually the case that in our conventional pursuits we are attached to an outcome, but attachment to outcome blocks the free flow to accomplishment; we are crimping the water hose and wondering why the garden is wilting. On the bodhisattva way, aspiring to realize truth and liberate all beings from suffering, we might not see the intended outcome this very week. Sometimes it is hard to keep on keeping on, with relative goals or sublime ones, but to one motivated by bodhicitta, obstacles eventually become *siddhis*, spiritual accomplishments. Attachment makes even a sublime goal into a worldly enterprise, because attachment to sublime outcome is still attachment. "Why, since I'm praying so hard, is there still fighting in Afghanistan? It's obviously not working, I think I'll stop praying and take up arms." It is not grandiose to want your prayers to end a war: that is how bodhisattvas think. But it is grandiose to cling to it being *your* prayers that achieve the desired result, and it is ignorance of karmic cause and consequence that makes us fixate on *our* desired outcome. Therein lie delusion and pride; therein lies discouragement. Instead, seeing the wars continuing, redouble your efforts: your prayers and actions for peace *and* your free offering, over and over again, of all your mind, voice, and body for the liberation of all.

This is a timeless project we're engaged in. We and the world, we and all beings, are timelessly one with truth and yet we waver between worldly and sublime, between confusion and clarity. With even the highest of intentions and the best of efforts, we are probably not going to go to bed tonight and wake up as fully realized buddhas tomorrow. Although it could happen; suddenly, effortlessly, the apparent fog of apparent illusion can apparently part to reveal directly the nature of reality, face to face, in an instant, with no apparent cause. But there is a cause, and perhaps a circumstance, too: perhaps your teacher says something and you suddenly understand, or you drop something, it breaks, and your mind opens. It can happen like that. So there may be a circumstance—but the cause? The cause of buddhahood is buddha nature, your true nature, always already here. Truth is the only source of truth.

To resolve discouragement, abandon self in love and devotion for all beings throughout the three times, past, present, and future. This is the training of *The 37 Bodhisattva Practices*—the training we have now begun.

# CHAPTER TWO

# ENGAGING
# THE BODHISATTVA WAY
# (VERSES 1-7)

In the Dharma the preliminaries are considered to be more important than the main body of the teachings, as they prepare the mind by clearing away confusion and establishing correct motivation. I often heard from one of my first lamas, Tsewang Dongyal Rinpoche, "Look innerly, always look innerly"—for in our mind's condition and our motivation in each moment lie the seeds which will ripen in our actual experience when the conditions for ripening arise. This is karmic causation, determined first and foremost by motivation. In the Dharma context, the motivation of love and compassion is the very meaning of virtue, so even if we don't see the specific circumstantial effects of our actions we can know that ultimately virtue will always bring forth benefit and nonvirtue will always bring forth harm.

As I approached spiritual study and practice in the Dharma, I found even the very first teachings beginning to clarify pathways of understanding and intention in my mind, in the way that one gentles and trains a horse, turning her head and her attention in the desired direction, making it simpler for her to choose. In a natural ordering process, the preliminaries in these next seven verses—the instructions that turn our minds and behavior toward aspiring and acting for the good of all—are strengthening our wisdom of discrimination and discernment, defining the basis for clear seeing and wise choosing. In clarity we see the purpose of a human life and how to fulfill it: what is to be abandoned and what is to be cultivated. These teachings are for our particular life, right now in the present, and for the future that will be karmically conditioned by causes we are setting now.

All the teachings in Tokme Zangpo's profound, practical text point to both our need and our potential to expand our natural love and compassion to include all beings, and to cultivate universal love and compassion at the levels of body, speech, and mind—especially mind. These preliminaries help us begin to recognize what presently obscures the indwelling bodhicitta and clearly point out *how* to abandon those habitual patterns of thought and behavior. First addressing the factors that are relatively apparent to us, Tokme guides us also to understand the obscurations and misconceptions arising from the more profound confusions of mind that we all experience, and the specific ways they play out for us as individuals.

**Verse 1.** Having now gained this great ship of freedom and fortune—so difficult to find—in order to free yourself and others from the ocean of cyclic existence, listen, reflect, and meditate day and night without distraction. This is the way of a bodhisattva.

It is through conscious intention and action that a given lifetime becomes spiritually precious—a great ship that can carry oneself and others across the samsaric sea of unknowing, illusion, and suffering to freedom's shore. Thus Tokme Zangpo's first instruction to us is about the rarity of this human birth and how to use it for its highest purpose.

Buddhadharma teaches that due to our actions and their consequences, our karma, we live countless lives in myriads of forms in the different realms of existence, and that in this process it is goodness that brings us into life as a human being. This human life, difficult to attain and precious in potential, can be understood and lived as a spiritual opportunity or as an ordinary human life. But it is not ordinary, this lifetime in which we begin to recognize the predicament of sentient beings and seek to resolve it, for ourselves and for others. In this very lifetime, in this very body, our altruistic aspirations and love can flower in bodhicitta. And you don't have to be convinced about rebirth in order to understand the uniqueness and value of the particular, specific human life you are living right now. It will not be repeated. So whatever may be your highest spiritual aspiration, this is the lifetime in which to bring it to its fullest possible fruition.

If we do think about a succession of rebirths, we are likely to think that we have always been and always will be humans, and perhaps even that one life follows another in an elegant chain of increasing wisdom. "Rebirth is marvelous! Although this time I have been very busy, next time I'll be able to make greater spiritual progress," and so on. But next time you might be an ant. There is no guarantee that you'll be reborn a human.

This may be theoretical and abstract to us at the moment, fixed as we are in our notions of self and reality, but it becomes more plausible and even urgent as we consider the traditional Dharma teachings on the freedoms and endowments of the precious human life. We are free because we were not born in conditions that make spiritual work exceedingly difficult or impossible, such as in hellish realms of unremitting suffering or among beings of primitive character; tormented mentally and physically by insatiable need, or animalistic, ruled by instinct; as someone elevated, powerful, and at leisure but ignoring virtue; with mistaken views or impairments that limit capacity for spiritual understanding and practice; or in a realm "without a buddha," without those who point us to truth. The endowments that make this life conducive to spiritual practice are that we are human, with intact sense faculties, with faith in the teachings, in a setting where Dharma flourishes and a way of life that doesn't conflict with it. In this era, also, a buddha has appeared in the world and given the Dharma, which still remains, and we have entered the Dharma and been accepted by a spiritual teacher.[1] These freedoms and advantages are ours now, in this very lifetime. How auspicious this is for us, and how critical this very lifetime is, this unrepeatable opportunity.

Our teachers all say, emphatically, that we must contemplate deeply and regularly these freedoms and fortunes, the benefits and the precariousness of the precious human rebirth, with an understanding of the other kinds of rebirth that are possible. This is the basis for developing at least a working knowledge of karma: cause and consequence. Without this foundation, you will really not take hold of the Dharma. You'll see no reason to. You'll just be moving along as best you can, sometimes up, sometimes down— and next lifetime, in whatever form, in some realm of existence, you will again find yourself with the confusions, afflictions, and predispositions universal to sentient beings, expressing in the unerring karmic vocabulary unique to you.

So yes, let's generate a healthy alarm about our predicament, to penetrate our illusions about this relative reality that we call samsara. And yes, life is not just painful and confusing but often lovely, wondrous, joyously fulsome. The beauty, fragrance, and delight, as well as the pain and confusion, are real to us as appearances and experiences—but pleasing or horrific, all appearances are always changing, arising and dissolving, coming and going. We grasp at what pleases us, thrust away what disgusts, and make up stories, identities, entire fabrics of "reality" to ward off panic and despair at this utter lack of reliability or solidity. There is nothing wrong here, though; this is just the cycle of existence: causes giving rise to appearances, appearances dissolving, our reactions setting causes anew. It is sometimes called the chain of delusion; we can also call it the dreamlike nature of phenomenal reality, experienced as real in the dreaming, recognized as a dream when we wake up.

The teachings in Tokme Zangpo's pith text are our alarm clock. Let's disable the snooze button. Middling motivation and desultory

---

1. For further study of the freedoms and endowments of the precious human rebirth, see the thorough explanations of Jampa Tegchok in his *Transforming the Heart*, 33-46. See also Khandro Rinpoche's excellent elucidation in *This Precious Life*.

effort may get us started on the path to awakening but they won't hold us steady and true to the end. I hear Garchen Rinpoche whispering in my ear, "You will only become free from the cycle of existence, the ocean of suffering, if your whole heart wants to become free."

•

*Wholehearted. I had been studying and practicing Dharma for some years when a friend brought me a gift from India: a small saffron-colored cotton panel printed with a simple line drawing of the Bhavachakra, the Wheel of Existence, graphically depicting the conditions of beings in the six realms of samsara. In this cosmology, the three lower realms are the hells, manifesting the afflictions of anger-hatred; animals, manifesting instinct-based existence; and the realms of hungry ghosts or insatiable spirits, manifesting craving, grasping, miserliness. The three higher realms are humans, who have choice and therefore also doubt; demi-gods, tormented by jealousy; and gods, whose virtuous karma has brought circumstances of great ease and pleasure but along with it moral laziness; no longer accumulating virtue, eventually they must fall. Extremes of suffering characterize the lower realms, but suffering pervades them all.*

*In my daily practice I had been contemplating the realms and the causes of their sufferings, but in a rather perfunctory way; my comprehension shallow and my compassion therefore abstract, my fleeting moments of urgency were basically about me. Though intense and intent, I was not wholehearted.*

*Then, as I opened a long solo retreat, I placed that humble cotton cloth on my little practice table; it became the first and last thing I saw as I took my seat and rose from it. Daily, I began to place myself in each realm of existence, one after the other, confronting those beings' specific ordeals and sufferings, and probing my ordinary, habitual mind and behavior to find the kinds of thoughts and actions that cause each kind of confusion* and suffering. They weren't hard to find, though it was hard to bear the anguish of seeing them so starkly and experiencing them in such a raw, undefended way there in my snowbound mountain solitude. When I saw in my own mind how anger, for example, is an actual realm of hellish experience as I live it here and now, it was no stretch at all to understand how anger-hatred as a habitual reaction pattern becomes a powerful predisposition of mind and behavior, sowing more seeds of itself with each episode, now and for the future. It became first acutely painful and then an immense relief to understand that this is simply the dynamic interplay of cause and consequence that we call karma. In my own mind and conduct are to be found the seeds of every kind of misfortune and confusion I experience. The six samsaric realms exist in my own mundane experience, my own mind. This gives me insight every single day into the condition of myself and others, and into how, for the benefit of others and myself, I can directly address specific causes of specific kinds of suffering and continuous rebirth—including the moment-to-moment birth and rebirth of confused states of mind.

This intense labor birthed in me an unbearable compassion for beings in every condition of existence, surging forth as the profound, implacable, consuming desire and intention to liberate us all. That little rough cloth on my practice table became the physical and moral base, the very ethical ground, of my reflections and practice throughout the day, throughout that retreat, and throughout my life since then. Relying upon them broke my heart. Open. Watered with my tears for all beings, my relatives in the circle of life, the bodhi seed began to grow.

At that small table, hour upon hour, day after day, month after month, I was literally leaning upon the sufferings of all beings for the liberation of this one. Now the Wheel of Existence is inscribed on my heart bone. Now I call upon all suffering beings to rely upon this one.

•

The Dharma teaches that, among beings, humans have the most powerful potential for generating virtue *and* nonvirtue, both for waking up and for falling more deeply asleep. This human realm is also the most promising for spiritual progress, for we have the perfect balance of suffering and freedom—enough suffering to catch our attention and enough freedom and opportunity to do something about it. So this lifetime can be either a path through confusion and ignorance or a path deeper into them. In every moment that choice is ours, and only ours. Am I going to recognize the arising of confusion as an opportunity to see through it, to transform it, or am I going to elaborate it, keep it going as explanation, as narrative, as my script to follow?

Our connection to Dharma is like a miracle: so improbable to be born a human, in an era and a world where there are beings of vast wisdom and love, receive teachings from such beings, and actually come into the care of a living buddha. Even rarer is the birth of bodhicitta, the altruistic intention, lighting up the dark of mind, the dark of existence. This is the transformational event that opens the door to freedom.

Beings overwhelmed by the results of their negative karma are not free to choose their own destinies, to relieve their own suffering, much less to think of freeing others—but in the Bhavachakra image we see in each of the realms, even in the lowest hell, a bodhisattva pointing the way to release. Always remember: in an instant one can wake up.

Positive karma and negative karma both exhaust themselves. The beings, the realms, and their pain dissolve with the exhaustion of their karmic causes. But while the experience of each realm is temporary, the dynamic is cyclical: as one karmic result comes to an end another begins. This is why our movement among the realms is called transmigration; for as long as there is karmic cause not yet exhausted or purified, we and other beings are transmigrating within, not out of, samsara, the realms of existence and of ignorance, and therefore of suffering.

Now, right here in this moment, you may perhaps recognize subtle wavelets of reaction moving in your mind, relating to your past associations with ideas of heavens and hells and hierarchies of beings—but consider that what these cosmological constructs offer you are some ways to understand this lifetime's experiences of mind, emotions, behavior, and events, and their causes. You may think of the samsaric realms as actual domains where beings exist, as conditions of your own mind, or as allegory or metaphor. You might also take the realms as something to believe in or reject, but belief or disbelief is not really pertinent, for in fact we already have direct experience of these realms, their causes, and their sufferings, as I began to understand in my snowy retreat. Likely every day, if not every moment, each of us frequently, repetitively experiences grasping, aggression, and confusion. We know, directly, what these states feel like and how easily they arise in our experience, seemingly out of nowhere and often seemingly beyond our control. We also know that the full, direct experience of any one of these states, and especially some admixture of them, means disturbance of mind and emotion. Mind fixates, emotions roil, physical sensations upset equanimity and equilibrium, words erupt, relationships are shaken. Confusion and desirous craving can submerge or carry away the mind, subverting good intention, while anger threatens not only our good works but also our relative bodhicitta. We know that a tiny spark can burn down a forest, so perceiving the slightest sign of anger-hatred arising in the mind is one of the most powerful practices, and one of the most difficult. Our teachers urge us to vigilance on this point. Gar Rinpoche once told of a student who claimed his slow progress in mastering anger was because he didn't have enough time to practice. Rinpoche's reply: "What? You didn't have time not to get angry?"

We can easily formulate a general intention to liberate ourselves and others, and even be uplifted and focused by it—but aren't we challenged and even confounded by the call to listen, reflect, and meditate day and night without distraction? What this instruction means is that once we understand the purpose of a human life we should *use it completely for that purpose.* Our intellectual and sensory faculties as humans allow us to take in, understand, and actually to practice spiritual teachings, to exercise active responsibility for our relationship to spiritual purpose. However, even many who have had the good fortune to meet authentic teachings aren't engaging them as if this is the *precious* human life, rare to achieve, easy to lose. So few actually take up study and practice, and of those even fewer bring their practice to fruition. Many will say, "Well, for now I'll study and think about things a bit and I'll practice when I have a little more leisure." What would that look like, a little more leisure? More hours in the day, fewer thoughts in the head, body free to run unfettered toward its grave?

If you place first what is most important to you, where to place other elements becomes clear, but if you don't place first what is most important it will always tend to fall back. Gotta do this, wanna do that, and the day goes by. I speak from experience here, obviously, and not to chastise but to highlight how even those of us who are deeply committed to our spiritual purpose and practice don't always place it first. There is an excellent French expression—*si j'avais su*, if only I had known. At the time of death, with shock and regret: if only I had known what was important while I was alive. If only I had known how valuable and how easy it was to practice when I was young, my body strong, my health good. *Si j'avais su*. I began to understand this difficult lesson, at least a bit, when I had cancer at age forty-seven and understood that the physically easy practice years were already behind me. Now, aging with grace if not gracefully, I can barely manage to sit on my cushion. *Si j'avais su!*

All day, all week, all twelve months of the year, in every decade, life offers us countless important, delightful things to do and experience. Dear friends, please include among those things the activities and experiences that will liberate your mind. And when you do all those other things, the conventional things that are either delightful or painful, literally do them for the benefit of all. Make that dedication, explicitly: "I offer this delicious meal, this frightening disease, this earthquake for the liberation of all." This stabilizes the mind in bodhicitta, the great freedom.

There is a universe of wisdom, understanding, and skillful action available to us once our mind is stable in motivation, but while the motivation is not yet stable everything, both outer and inner, can be a distraction. You don't need any more incentive than a given week in world news to understand the importance of dealing swiftly and decisively with the confusions and poisons of mind that create suffering for us and others.

Careful attention and effort are required here, to turn the ship of intention away from the submerged sandbars of laziness. Our misconceptions and burdened emotions don't shrivel from being ignored: they tend to proliferate, feeding on each other, and the karmic habit of indulging them becomes a heavy, dangerous weight when we are in strong currents, our own and the world's. It is not enough that there is a buddha sitting in the room with you and it's not enough that you fall in love with the Dharma. You have to practice it, put it into effect. No one can do this for us. You must *lift your life*, your actual living, into the Dharma. Otherwise this is not the precious human rebirth but an ordinary human rebirth, with some graceful decorations.

A serious student once said to me, "When I met the Dharma I thought I shouldn't be married, shouldn't have a job, should give up living a life." No, no, no. We're here. Our lives are to be lived. *How* we live them is the point to ascertain. Some feel they are always busy, working day and night, as the saying goes, and thus have little time to practice, but I think that every time I have heard Garchen Rinpoche teach he has said something like this: "If you are really working day and night your practice time is especially long!"— because consciously and intentionally offering all our activities for others' benefit we are practicing, no matter what it might look like. Rinpoche tells us over and over that even when engaged in the most tedious or most compelling activities to earn your living, raise your children, and so on, your mind doesn't have to be completely caught up in that worldly activity; it can be free, relaxed, and happy in a state of compassion. You can be percolating one simple teaching or generating aspirations for all those you know or hear of, including our motherly planet. And meditating doesn't necessarily mean sitting on the cushion all day, or even on a rock, like Milarepa, consummate yogi saint of Tibet.[2] In essence, to be ceaselessly practicing is to be ceaselessly aware of your mind: looking within, recognizing your condition, always generating compassion and love, limitless as the open, empty sky—and in moments of stress, tension, or distraction, allowing your mind simply and easily to rest in its true nature, even for an instant, just as your gaze can, for an instant, rest in the sky. In this way, ceaselessly hearing, reflecting, and meditating naturally becomes the bodhisattva's way of life.

For the aspiring bodhisattva who intends to sustain continuous practice, when you wake up at night, in that very instant, practice. You don't need to light a candle or sit on your cushion; just turn your mind within, think of your teacher, remember love and compassion. Maybe you'll fall asleep again the following second; it doesn't matter. When you wake up, practice; when you think of practicing, practice. This is not hard. What is initially hard is to remember to do it, and then to begin doing it regularly. The habit of "Oh, I want to go back to sleep" is very ingrained. Think about that as a metaphor for this precious human life: wake up or go back to sleep!

When it seems impossible to bring your attention and activities into a mind of practice, or even a mind of compassion, in that very moment dedicate the entire display to the enlightenment of all beings. The same with great suffering that seems to overwhelm not just body or emotions but mind itself; dedicate that suffering of yours to the wellbeing of all. "To free all from their suffering, may mine be sufficient." As you make bread, in the kneading of the dough: "May the minds of all beings become workable, like this good dough." Weeding the garden: "These weeds of passion, aggression, and ignorance, I pull them from the garden of my mind, for the freedom of all." As you groan with pain, groan "I offer my pain for the liberation of all."

The motivation is always key. If the motivation is to love and liberate all, every activity is that, no matter how worldly, trivial, marvelous, or challenging it may appear to be. Garchen Rinpoche

---

2. Milarepa (1052-1135). See Lobsang Lhalungpa, *The Life of Milarepa* and Garma C.C. Chang, ed., *The Hundred Thousand Songs of Milarepa*.

emerged victorious from twenty years in a Chinese prison camp, where severe punishment came for every visible act of Dharma— so the lama learned to practice within, invisibly and profoundly, day and night, on the *essence* of the teachings and practices he had received. Let us take this as inspiration for high aspiration. Astonishing and beyond imagining though it may seem in this moment, let us say to ourselves, and really know: "If he can do it, I can do it—and if I can, I must, and if I must, I shall."

## Discussion: Practice; the altruistic paradox

*What is "practice?"*

Remembering. Remembering love and compassion, remembering your highest aspiration, remembering what is to be taken up and what is to be put down. Practice is remembering what is true even when one is momentarily caught up in what is false—even remembering that there *is* something true when one is caught up in the false. Practice is any activity that expresses the mind's intention to liberate self and others from ignorance and suffering. Practice is ceaselessly cultivating love and compassion. Whatever it may look like, that is the heart of practice.

*I would say I'm at least seventy percent committed to mindfulness, but it seems that it's almost entirely for selfish purposes, for the sense of freedom, relaxation, and comfort I feel when I'm mindful, even in unpleasant circumstances—but I never remember to wish that for others, for every being.*

You will now, though, because now you see what has been missing. Bodhicitta. And remember that you're not separate from others. There may be many apparently discrete, distinct consciousnesses, but there is one true nature. As your mind relaxes, know it is relaxing for all, and make this your explicit intention. That will ease your mind even more. The altruistic paradox: the more altruistic we become, the happier we become.

**Verse 2.** Attachment to loved ones churns like water. Hatred for enemies rages like fire. In the darkness of ignorance, one forgets what to adopt and what to avoid. Abandon your homeland. This is the way of a bodhisattva.

Why does Tokme speak of attachment, hatred, and ignorance and then exhort us to abandon our homeland? Inner or outer, literal or figurative, the homeland is terrain so familiar that we lean back on habit. In the outer homeland the circumstances and relationships are all customary, and more important, our mental and emotional associations and reaction patterns are customary, too, so we continue to deepen attachment, aversion, and ignorance. It's like small-town syndrome: we know where everything is, what to expect from everyone we meet. We know everything, which means we know nothing. Looking through the lenses of established experience and expectations and following well-worn narratives of cause, meaning, value, and so on, we are unable to see things as they are. With our outer circumstances continually reinforcing our opinions, mental structures, and mental habits, on the inner plane we will be burrowing deeper and deeper into the familiar nest in which we continue to sleep and dream, when what we say we want, as aspiring bodhisattvas, is to be waking up.

At the outer level—place, people, activity—if the homeland needs to be abandoned, abandon it. Some of us have been confronted with that imperative, when our circumstances overwhelmed our ability even to cope, not to mention using them for insight, developing strength, and cultivating compassion. Better not to stay in a situation where, despite your intention and effort, your love and compassion are diminishing, your bodhicitta is deteriorating. In the earlier stages of training and practice, we need at least a minimally supportive environment where we are not continually unseated by the mental and emotional disturbances we haven't yet learned how to tame, abandon, transform, or liberate. When motivation and mind further clarify and stabilize, circumstances that were impossible or damaging at an earlier stage become the jewels of our practice. Stable in bodhicitta, the more difficult your circumstance the more powerful your practice. The sharp knife cuts clean. But at the beginning our minds are not that strong, so don't stay where you are getting worse. If you cannot leave, if you must stay, then you must also learn to master the inner abandoning, your doorway to freedom.

The inner abandoning is the inner meaning of this teaching, and the most important; examining the inner meaning here will help us orient to the inner meaning of all these teachings. They can all be taken on the outer level, and we need to understand them at that level, which can redirect our perceptions and behavior—but the inner meaning redirects our mind.

Our conditioned mind's disturbed and disturbing emotions and compulsive, deluded thinking, together with their causes: this is the inner homeland that must be abandoned. Nothing is more familiar to us than our disturbed emotions. In fact, they're so familiar to us that we hardly recognize them as afflictions. We think they are circumstances, people, feelings, and sensations that are luscious, necessary, inconvenient, irritating, irresistible, frightening, or wounding. But they are not: they are our emotional and mental afflictions: passion, aggression, and ignorance (also called grasping, aversion, and confusion). These are the principal vectors of suffering for sentient beings, all reflecting mind caught in grasping to "self" and its interests.[3]

---

3. A note on self-grasping: Absolute reality is primordially pristine, open, all-pervading. Within the boundless, a point of reference is taken by a sentient being: the perception of its own existing. And with this comes instantly the attribution of "I," and instantly, innocently, with "I" there is "other," each experienced as solid, having inherent selfness. On this mistaken ground, the original dualistic delusion, arise all the torments of attachment, aversion, and confusion, with their mistaken notions of love-hate, peace-war, good-bad, and so on. This is self-grasping: clinging to the false notion of an inherently existing self and the false solidity, the selfness, of all beings, appearances, and phenomena. On this basis we reach for and cling to what we want, recoil and push away from what we think we hate, and spin in confusion when we can't reliably impose our own narratives on appearances. Geshe Jampa says that this original ignorance is at the root of cyclic existence as "an inborn or innate self-grasping, not one which is intellectually acquired.... It is an ignorance which emerges spontaneously...." (Jampa Tegchok, *Transforming the Heart*, 239). For precise explication of these dynamics and their resolution, see Bhaka Tulku and Steven Goodman, "The Prayer of Kuntuzangpo."

We mistake these afflictive emotions and what to do with them. Confusing virtue and vice, we take up what is harmful and abandon what is good, whether in confusion, by habit, or by intent. And we cling to our disturbed mental and emotional states as if they are real or solid, though certainly we see over and over again how our emotions and thoughts come and go, by turns wavering and obdurate, searing and icy. For attachment we juice up more attachment, for aversion we stoke aversion. And with regard to confusion: it truly does mean ignorance—the state, of a moment or a lifetime, in which we do not know what is and is not real or true, what is wholesome or damaging, what is virtuous or malign. This confusion gives rise to fear, panic, aggression, and clinging. We cling to self and other, to objects and grievances and plans, to emotions and notions, and we cling to our suffering and to our clinging. We attribute these painful states to outer conditions, events, people, and so on—in other words, to circumstances.[4] But the causes of your afflictive mental and emotional states are to be sought and found in your own mindstream. That is where they have always been, and unless you are working to clarify your own mind that is where they will remain—and proliferate. The afflictive emotions give rise to our habitual ways of seeing, interpreting, thinking, feeling, reacting, and behaving; these and their roots in self-grasping are what is to be abandoned.

Things and beings, including us, do exist, and we do experience them, but they arise, abide, and fall away based on causes and conditions—so they cannot be said to have *intrinsic* existence. They appear, like the rainbow: vivid, yet without substance. Understanding this, to cling to our mental and emotional states and productions, to hate them, or to elaborate thought or action based on them, is to behave as if deluded. One in a state of delusion,

---

4. Circumstances: always changing, coming and going, impermanent and unreliable. In themselves circumstances have no meaning; they are simply temporary arrangements of karma, time, and appearances, lacking inherent existence. Their greatest potential gift is to sharpen your dissatisfaction like a spur—urging you to seek that which is unchanging.

whether it's momentarily a happy delusion or a sad delusion, is experiencing what in the Dharma is called suffering. Altruistic love and compassion, bodhicitta, will melt away this delusion, revealing illusion-like suffering as the dreamchild of illusion-like self.

## Discussion: Afflictive emotions; suffering and compassion

*I have a super-beginner novice question: What does "afflictive emotion" mean?*

I love this question; happy is the sangha with super-beginner novices posing questions.

Passion, aggression, and ignorance (or attachment, aversion, and confusion) are the three principal afflictive emotions, and when expanded to five they are passion, aggression, ignorance, pride, and jealousy. We recognize these as afflictions because, in their arising, abiding, and ceasing, suffering is experienced, whether mild or extreme, and because they obscure our ability to recognize the naturally spacious mind of clarity and love, reducing perception to the pinhole vision of I-me-mine. Everything from mild interest to global rapacity would be in the basket of attachment-passion-grasping, and in the basket of hatred-repulsion-aversion would be everything from mild annoyance to roaring rage, hatred, and murderous consequences. Ignorance is actually the root of them all. All the afflictions, all the confusions arise from misapprehending the true nature of reality—open and unimpeded, devoid of permanence or solidity, even while vividly displaying appearances of phenomena, beings, and so on, all of which, too, are empty of any intrinsic selfness of their own. All beings and all phenomena are of one nature: the true nature of reality. This is what is meant by the phrase "one taste."

*If I know others are suffering, how to sit with that in mindfulness but not actually experience the suffering myself?*

Why don't you want to experience the suffering yourself? [Long pause] This question is really at the heart of what it means to practice compassion. When we have bodhicitta, selfless compassion, we feel the sufferings of others as if they are our own; their sufferings naturally come to us, as Garchen Rinpoche says. And that is what the word compassion actually means: to suffer with. When we ourselves are suffering we usually want the suffering to cease, and it is a natural extension of our fellow-feeling and altruistic caring to desire for others the same freedom from suffering that we desire for ourselves. This is the Dharma meaning of compassion: the desire that others be free of suffering. [5]

In altruistic compassion there is objectivity, a caring concern for the being and its suffering with minimal contamination from our own self-interest, be it of attachment, aversion, or confusion. I'm sure that many of us have experienced the compassionate impulse that is suffused with the glow of self-approval, or mixed with attachment for our own particular outcomes. This kind of entanglement is arising simply from self-reference, distorting our relationship to the sufferings of others and limiting the ultimate benefit of our compassionate action. Caught up in our own emotional reactivity to another's suffering, we are like one who can't swim jumping into the water to save one who's fallen from the boat. Two will drown. As self-clinging gradually diminishes in the warmth of love and compassion, increasingly we experience altruistic compassion rather than an emotion we call compassion but which is often more akin to sympathy or pity, or even to over-identification. With altruistic motivation, compassion is impartial, non-preferential, even non-referential. This compassion

---

5. Yes, we usually want the suffering to cease—unless we understand karma so well that we are grateful, knowing our suffering is purifying our ignorance and karmic propensities, liberating us not just from suffering but from its actual causes, to become liberators of all.

is objective, not devoid of caring but free of subjective self-interest.

The English word "suffering" we usually take to mean misery, acute anguish, or torment, but in the Dharma suffering also refers to the general and pervasive unsatisfactoriness of existence. It seems as if things are working out nicely in the immediate; your major needs and desires are met, your excellent plans come to fruition—and then it falls apart. The apple has a worm in it. This is simply existence, relative reality, in which everything exists relative to everything else, interdependently and impermanently. Things are coming and going. In appearance. In absolute reality nothing is actually coming or going, but in the realm of phenomena—that is, in our experience—everything is in flux, conditional, always birthing, changing, and dying. We must clearly understand this. Whatever appears to come is going to appear to go: if you want it, that's sad, if you don't want it, that's pleasing, and if it is ambiguous and you are confused, that is disturbing and possibly alarming. These self-referencing reactions of attachment, aversion, and ignorance are what keep the whole samsaric engine running.

Pain is part of being able to feel, part of being alive. Life hurts; being in a body hurts. But suffering is largely what we bring to that with our mind. If we have pain, in body, emotions, mind, we could simply experience it, allowing it to arise and then dissolve again— which it will, because no experience or attention can be sustained without interruption. It's moment by moment by moment: the experience of pain comes and then it goes, it goes and then it comes again. We can breathe in the spaces between, but if we clutch or rail at the pain and tell ourselves, "This is terrible, it's not fair, I can't stand it, I don't want it!" we're making something of it, and that creates suffering in the mind. It means we are saying no to what is, no to present reality, pushing it away. That refusal is aversion and aversion is suffering. And if we're enjoying an experience, grabbing for it, then we're creating the suffering of attachment, for when that nice experience ends, as it will, we will have the suffering of change and loss. The pain can happen without the aversion and the pleasure can happen without the grasping; we can *be with* ignorance, confusion, desire, sorrow, anger, our disturbed emotions or thoughts, without elaborating them. Elaboration functions to shore up our confidence in the continuity of experience, life, and time: the illusion-like solidity of existence. What it is really doing is forging link after link in the chain of delusion.

We can live, and live more fully and deeply, more simply and authentically, when we are not generating afflictive emotional thoughts that obscure what simply is. That is practicing innocence.

As compassionate beings, let us be both comprehensive and discerning. Let us commit to freeing all beings from suffering—without regard to outcome. That means without regard to our own conceptions and emotions regarding what we ourselves might deem desirable or correct, what that might look like, when it might occur, and so on. When we cultivate compassion free of self-grasping or self-reference our compassionate motivation and activity arise not in the murk of emotional reaction and confusion but in the clear light of altruistic intention. That is the bodhisattva's way.

*The hardest part for me is "attachment to loved ones churns like water." My reaction to the suffering of my child and husband is quite different than my reaction to the suffering of a client or friend.*

What is the difference?

*Some beliefs about what one does when one really loves someone, what one should do. The wish to alleviate their suffering or to have them be happy is more urgent.*

Excellent—for now you have the basis very clear in your mind for how to generate compassion for all beings. On the basis of these two, husband and child, with imagination and effort you now generate compassion for all. You take the attachment relationship—in which you care strongly that someone is suffering—and you use that as the focal point from which you expand waves of caring, that same devoted, urgent concern for others that you feel for your husband and child. Over and over and over again you expand your loving concern, your compassion, out from that center. You know what it feels like to care intensely about the suffering of others: two others. Now you go for three, and then four, five, eventually to fill space with countless others. This is a profound practice.[6] This expanded heart, this mind of compassionate concern for beings, is the mind of the bodhisattva. Caring about all beings with the same urgent, active love that you have for your dearest—imagine the power in that. Imagine also how keenly you will feel the sufferings of others when the heart is that willing, that dedicated. Sometimes people fear that the heart, the actual physical organ, will burst from such intense compassion. I don't think we need to worry about that quite yet; first let's go from two to three.

The gradual process of expanding love starts with where we genuinely experience love and compassion, where it is vital for us, dynamic, truly energized. This is not an academic exercise. We are bodhisattvas in training: we ardently desire and aspire to realize this vast and profound love and compassion for all. And gradually, as we develop this capacity, we also develop the capacity to recognize that when the heart is breaking for the suffering of beings it is breaking *open*—to love without limit.

So we can ask ourselves again, now with heightened awareness: why would we *not* want to feel the suffering of other beings?

**Verse 3.** When negative places are abandoned, disturbing emotions will gradually decline. Without distractions, attention to virtue naturally grows. When the mind becomes clear, certainty in the Dharma arises. Live alone in seclusion. This is the way of a bodhisattva.

We have looked at what it means to abandon the inner and outer homelands of the afflictive emotions and their causes; now we

---

6. Equanimity practice, a method by which we transform the conventional self-referencing, like-dislike mind to mind that holds all in love; it is detailed in Verse II.

consider creating conditions that are actually conducive to profound, liberating practice for clarity and love.

Our inner distractions are the disturbed, disturbing mental conceptions and afflictive emotions in our mindstreams. Outer distractions are their mirrors. Seeking distraction, inner or outer, is to divert our mind from its momentary condition, whatever that may be. In a simple way we could say it's a tolerance problem, an inability or unwillingness to tolerate our own mental-emotional state. Mind seeking distraction from itself? Like water sizzling and jumping on a hot surface: agitated, frantic, disordered. Simple presence, meaning simply *being with* our present state, is relative non-distraction, while simply *being* is ultimate non-distraction: abiding in the natural state. We can cultivate this simplicity in any circumstance, with the inward attention that discerns mind's movements and the willingness and clarity to recognize them without engaging—gradually ripening into the ability to rest in the true nature of mind. This is the inner and ultimate secluded place.

In our conventional lives, though, we tend actively to cultivate the mind that seeks distraction. It is that habit, that tendency of mind, which gives any external distraction its power. Even to recognize this tendency is to shake one's servitude to it, but initially it may not be easy to see in the context of our ordinary lives. To step away from the clutter, activity, disturbances, enticements, and confusions of the usual, to allow the waves of emotions and thoughts to arise and naturally subside, and to turn one's mind to cultivating the inward attention, it is taught in many traditions that the aspiring practitioner should seek solitude. Dilgo Khyentse Rinpoche tells us that for the sincere practitioner "Even a single month in a quiet and lonely place will be enough for your animosity to be replaced by a wish to benefit others, and your attachment to friends by a strong feeling of impermanence and impending death." Turn your mind inward, he says; "identify your defects, rid yourself of them, and develop all your inherent good qualities . . . .

[G]o to a secluded place and put the instructions you have received from your teacher into practice."[7]

I will add: *don't wait*. If your foundation of practice is strong, go for retreat in solitude; it can be isolated and extended, but it doesn't have to be. If you are not yet an experienced practitioner, you can simply begin with a half-day or a day given to study, reflection, and contemplation in seclusion within your own home, and gradually increase the length; your teacher's guidance will be helpful here. Don't wait for what you imagine might be the ideal conditions for the ideal practitioner to become the ideal retreatant. Create a corner in your home, even in a closet; make strong, fervent prayers of supplication for blessings and guidance; practice sincerely, humbly, and confidently the instructions you have received from your teacher; and dismiss all concern with outcome. Spiritual practice is an offering, so give it freely, without wanting something back or checking your results. In that secluded place, approach and enter the secluded place of your mind. It is this that Gar Rinpoche calls the true secluded place: the concentered mind of awareness and the qualities arising from it.

At the conventional level there is a certain amount of abandoning of harmful companions and places that does need to be attended to, as we have discussed. Regardless of circumstances, however, distraction is always available—because distraction is an impulse of the mind. At its root I think that the motive of distraction is to turn away from the boundless. To keep moving and doing and thinking and speaking, not to be still, is to shield ourselves from what inner stillness requires and from what it gives: it requires radical patience and courage, and it gives insight into the nature of reality, the impermanent, ever changing, void and luminous nature of appearances. It is this that we will come to recognize, this for which we will take fearless responsibility.

Our spiritual intention and practice can be overwhelmed, particularly in the early stages, by conditions and influences both

---

7. Dilgo Khyentse, *Heart of Compassion*, 66-67.

inner and outer. For example, love and compassion can be easily swamped by a tendency toward anger, so practicing to cultivate bodhicitta in circumstances where we keep being drawn into that negative pathway can be like poking a hole in our bodhicitta bucket. In such a circumstance, it is wise to part from that condition, that place, or those people, at least from time to time, to recover balance and clarity. Another example might be a difficult family situation in which you are responsible; you're not going to abandon a child who is still in the care of a partner with whom you're having difficulties, and so you decide to stay, even though the situation is sorrowful and tense for you. As you make the decision not to abandon the circumstance, make also the concomitant decision: ". . . and I'm going to practice on it *continuously*." Then you will find your ways to practice on it continuously, drawing on your teacher's instructions for you, your sincere study of teachings, your commitment to generating compassion and love, your personal need for balance and confidence, and your own spontaneously inventive, creative play—that relaxed readiness to see things from an unexpected angle and to allow the tension of self-focus to release in even a momentary remembrance of the empty, luminous nature of appearances.

The inner method of continuous practice is to draw the mind within itself, over and over again, gently and often. Rely not on the fluctuating thoughts and emotions but on what you *know* to be true: the reliable, generative truths of compassion and kindness and the underlying truths of impermanence, interdependence, karma, and aspiration. For the outer methods, we need to be practical. In overwhelming negative circumstances you can momentarily lose your practice mind, but you can also momentarily step back out into the clarity of your purpose and practice, over and over again. No afflictive or obscured state of mind can be held unmoving. When you lose clarity, you can find it anew. It can be as simple as a glance into the sky or a glance within: an instant of rest in your natural mind, just as it is in that particular moment. Or even something as practical as bathroom retreat. Bathroom retreat? Yes, a very handy method of resorting to secluded places. In your workplace or your home, go into the bathroom and shut the door; maybe it's just a toilet stall: click it shut; your feet may show, but only you will see your mind. Use that moment to recollect yourself, to reorient to your clear intention as a practitioner of truth and love, and flush away the momentary confusion.

In our material, sensory enmeshment, we focus on condition and circumstance as being the reality, seen as either the problem or the solution, in endless rotation. We do this about ourselves, the world, other beings, remembered histories, anticipated futures, and so on. In material emergencies and times of great trial and suffering, often we must indeed try to change the circumstances, sometimes urgently, for ourselves or others—but always remember that bodhisattva outer activity to benefit beings moves in alignment with bodhisattva inner practice: continuous attention and effort to abandoning our erroneous conceptions and afflictive emotions and to generating compassion and love.

This is the radical teaching of the Buddhadharma, and an example of what is meant by "extracting the essence." As I have mentioned, the loving lama, Gar Rinpoche, gave me this pith instruction for my entire path: "From every teaching you receive and from every practice you do, distill the essence and practice on that." Extracting the essence of each of these verses is the way to take them into your continuous attention and practice, the inner seclusion that frees the mind. This means asking yourself—and really working to discern—what is the one teaching or practice here that *must* be cultivated? What is the one element here that I *must* understand and master? Distill the essence and practice on that. This is certainty in the Dharma.

As humans with free choice and therefore also doubt, if we aren't cultivating certainty as we go along, instead of ceaselessly practicing we might be among those ceaselessly chasing after more teachings, more practices, more great teachers, more profound books, and so on and on—more! better! other! next! This is the ceaseless round of samsaric activity, apparently devoted to

Dharma but still arising, at least in part, from doubt, grasping, and attachment. In the interim between now and full awakening we will use some attachment to keep us moving forward on the path—but it is still attachment, and eventually it has to go.[8]

As students and practitioners, we are advised to take ourselves as the sick patient, the teacher as the doctor, and the Dharma as the medicine. It is also taught that there is no universal remedy: each individual's karma is that individual's karma, so each individual's condition of mind and potentials is unique in its particular combination of confusion and insight, of causes and their consequences. However, there is a universal remedy at the level of essence: bodhicitta, the all-pervading, causeless radiance of emptiness. For self-grasping, thrown up by basic ignorance and the cause of every suffering, bodhicitta is the medicine, and this seed is within us right now. Gar Rinpoche: "The only cause of true happiness is love." Into the state of love, secluded from all harm, we invite all beings.

## Discussion: Cultivating bodhicitta in seclusion

*How do I cultivate and maintain great compassion for beings suffering in samsara while I am in a secluded retreat place, enjoying the luxury of time and space for practice? Should I ask people to send me news of the catastrophes and disasters that are happening in the world so I can be reminded of what sentient beings are experiencing?*

Astute question, because it reflects how important it is to keep in mind the central purpose of practice on the bodhisattva path. Cultivating bodhicitta is the principal means by which we clear away our own afflictions so we can see things as they are. In seclusion,

---

8. You don't get to keep anything held with attachment, but as you release attachment it doesn't matter so much what stays and what goes. Once you've given everything up and realized the essence, the true, empty nature of reality, it also seems you get everything back if you want it, and sometimes even if you don't. If you don't want it and you have the karma for it, you'll get it anyway, and if you do want it and you don't have the karma you won't get it anyway. So relax—there's nothing to worry about. Truly.

absent the usual exterior distractions, as you take silence and non-action, immersing in study, practice, contemplation, and meditation, your mind gradually recognizes and relaxes its habits of grasping to self and of grasping for distraction, and disturbing emotions gradually decline, as our verse says. So then, as your own agitation calms, how to remain awake to the suffering of others? How to remain vitally tuned to the ultimate purpose: to liberate all? A subscription to the daily *Samsaric Times* might be interesting—but tell me, do you actually need more information about samsara?

*Well, no, probably not.*

It can sometimes be useful to be reminded of the ordinary and dramatic catastrophes of samsara, as a spur to generating compassion. But remember this: the samsaric dramas on the outer plane arise from seeds and tendencies that are also within the mind of the secluded meditator. My solitary practice vividly reveals to me that the confusion, iniquity, or suffering of others is truly a mirror in which to see such seeds in my own mindstream. That is where our work is.

Always remember that any particular individual or group represents *all* sentient beings, whom we aspire to liberate from suffering into ultimate freedom. Why is this important? First, because fixating exclusively on the beings to whom you are responding compassionately at that moment may mean you are strengthening your relative compassion in a somewhat limiting way; when we're looking through our personal lenses self-reference is in some way involved. Second, because the altruistic intention is as beneficial as it is vast, always expand your compassionate intent to all beings and sufferings of every kind. And third, because it is so easy for us to ignore our entanglement in materiality, the universe as registered through our sensory experience, we forget that all appearances and phenomena, within and without, lack solidity and inherent existence, including sentient beings and their sufferings.

In the world of appearances, we are now in a time when the manifest sufferings of beings (and not just humans) who are losing sustenance, home, health, habitat, their lives, and even their entire species, are becoming very well known to us. The proximate, visible circumstances appear to be the causes of suffering when you're looking at material reality—war, breaking health system or economy, oppression, illness, disaster, climate change, terrorism, and so on—but these are not the causes: these are the circumstances that bring the causes to fruition. *The 37 Bodhisattva Practices* teaches us that all suffering without exception comes from wishing for one's own happiness, from self-grasping and self-concern, as individuals or as group entities. *This root cause is in the mind.*

To begin to understand this upends our conventional, habitual mind, and we really need to understand it. If we don't, we aren't yet understanding karma, even at a basic level. If we don't understand karma, we don't understand the relationship of virtue and happiness and of nonvirtue and suffering. And if we don't understand that relationship, what does our compassion mean? It is adrift in sentimentality. As bodhisattvas we are not intent to relieve beings only of temporary pain or discomfort, but to liberate ourselves and all beings from the very *causes* of suffering. For this we must understand profoundly. (We will be considering karma further in verse 8.)

Garchen Rinpoche teaches that we will always have some degree of self-grasping as long as we're in a body but that the *mind* can be free. That is why we are studying and practicing Dharma: to free our minds. If we don't free our own minds, how can we hope to benefit others; caught in confusion, how will we bring others to clarity? I vividly remember how in the mid-1990s, going abruptly from extended solitary retreat to undertake peacemaking work in an active civil war in Central Africa, the clarity from months of deep practice at first filled me with open-hearted joy, and then gradually, in the expanding, thickening fog of war, the early openings of communication and relationship began to be occluded by the deep, longstanding, underlying patterns of conflict, and my mind, too, began to stiffen. As my bodhicitta weakened, my usefulness did, too.

Some say that we need to be cleansing our own minds and purifying our own karma before even thinking about liberating others—but we are pointed toward nonduality, so here in relative reality I say do both. Continuously and unremittingly. And don't wait. Bandages are important when you're bleeding, and there's a lot of bleeding going on in samsara, so don't think this-or-that. While we practice for the ultimate purpose let us also bind up the wounds of the world, and while binding the world's wounds know that this is our offering for the liberation of all beings in all worlds.

Your pristine wisdom mind is indivisible from the absolute. The true secluded place is your own true nature, empty, clear, and radiant. To glimpse or to remember this for even one instant is to refresh the mind in its natural integrity, clarity, and limitless love. Resort to this seclusion any time, anywhere. Supplicate the blessings of your teachers and the lineages of truth, practice with confidence, and practice without regard to outcome. This is the mind secluded from error and abandoned to truth.

**Verse 4.** Family and longtime companions will part from each other. Possessions gained with effort will be left behind. Consciousness, a guest, will leave the guesthouse of the body. Let go of all worldly concerns. This is the way of a bodhisattva.

This teaching by Tokme Zangpo can open your mind to a direct understanding of impermanence—if you are patient and willing to contemplate and test it in your own direct observation and experience.

Impermanence and worldly concerns: Nothing we create, work for, rely upon, care about, detest, suffer from, reject, delight in, or cling to will continue forever. What comes together will come apart; what is gathered will disperse. What we have met with we will part from, and even our precious body will fall away like a patch on an old coat at the time of death. We can't even say that our true nature, the true nature of all phenomena, is permanent, for "permanent" seems to apply to something that has material existence. What we could say about our true nature: uncreated, it is undying; uncompounded, it does not disperse; neither coming nor going, it is unchanging. The absolute always already *is*. So we will have to look to phenomenal reality to understand the significance of impermanence for us.

I love impermanence and return again and again to remember and rely on it, usually out of pressing need and always with relief. I came upon a teaching once that makes me laugh out loud because it so reflects my experience, spoken by another lama as, "If you meditate on impermanence, you will become happy for no reason." Ha! Merriment, the champagne of impermanence. And Dilgo Khyentse Rinpoche tells about a master who said, "I will die, you will die. That's all my guru taught me; that's all I practice. Just meditate on that. I promise there is nothing greater."[9]

If you were a non-amphibious fish you'd be hard put to describe water; water is simply the nature of reality for that fish. I think that's how challenging it is for us to approach impermanence: it is simply the nature of phenomena, just the way everything is. And yet see how we hang on, how we push away! We push away that which is going to fall away anyway, like a comment that stings, dissolving as the words are being spoken, and we cling to that which we don't have in our hands even at the moment we're clutching to it, like our reputation, which is held by others, never by ourselves. We're flopping around like our fish, now not in water but on sand, trying to escape coming to terms with impermanence—as if it is something terrible and painful and sad and frightening. Well, dear friends, when you grok impermanence you will find it blissful, so relaxing and calming to the mind. In our conditioned ways, habituated to attachment and aversion, when we think about impermanence we think, "Oh, no, my darling is going to die! Yay, my zit is clearing! Ah, the drought is ending, water's coming! Oh, the glacier

---

9. Dilgo Khyentse, *Heart of Compassion*, 72.

is melting, water's going!" Endlessly caught up in endlessly cycling worldly concerns, we go 'round and 'round, tethered to the peg of our afflictive emotions: get it, lose it; reach for something, push it away; rejoice, weep.

We think of impermanence as an enemy when it's really one of our most precious friends. How wonderful: the sufferings of all beings are temporary! Samsara itself is impermanent! This simple, unadorned understanding is one of the most profound methods for approaching emptiness. Impermanence points inescapably to the illusion-like nature of phenomenal appearances: to the open, clear, empty nature of reality.

When you experience suffering, or even mild discontent, go to impermanence. When you are squirming with grasping or repulsion, remember impermanence. At the time of death, whether sudden or lingering: Ah, consciousness, the guest, is leaving the guesthouse of this body. How shall I leave, then? Clinging to the bag of bones, with all its histories and mysteries? Holding tight to all my sorrows and regrets and pleasures and passions, already dissolved into the past? Or with a cheerful, open mind, recognizing simply that I have been living and now I am dying, and turning to greet the love light of my true nature, relaxing into the liberating embrace of Mother Emptiness?

## Discussion: How do we meditate on impermanence?

Watch. Watch what happens. Watch what happens with what arises in your mind and what comes out of your mouth; watch your moods and emotions and bodily processes; watch what happens with your activities and the activities of others, even a gesture, a word, a glance. Watch what is happening in the world. In nature, watch everything. In the course of the day watch the light, in your sleep watch the dream. Just watch.

Do this for twenty-one days and then inquire within: What have I observed? And then: What sees this?

When you tire of this (which you will, since impermanent curiosity cycles around with impermanent ennui), take up a new contemplation: now consider the concept of *permanence* and your experience of it, its meanings and manifestations in your actual lived experience. After a while, let this open out into contemplating *presence*. What is permanence? What is presence? Are they the same or different? How? And then let the three dance together for a while in your mind: impermanence, permanence, and presence.

Return to this contemplation again and again, mind relaxed, friendly, and receptive. And from time to time: What sees this?

**Verse 5.** In bad company, the three poisons grow stronger. The activities of learning, reflecting, and meditating decline, and love and compassion are lost. Give up such companions. This is the way of a bodhisattva.

Bad company means companions who are unsuited to our purpose and commitments as bodhisattvas. Our core principle and most precious possession is bodhicitta. While absolute bodhicitta can never be extinguished, our relative bodhicitta can gutter like a candle flame, so until we are fully given to bodhicitta we need to guard that holy fire with the greatest of dedication and care, always stoking it higher and brighter. Especially in the early stages of our practice we are wise to support our minds with auspicious conditions for cultivating bodhicitta, and these conditions include the beings with whom we associate.

Companions whose basic motivation is self-interest, who are careless with self and others, cruel, vengeful, manipulative, and so on, or those invested in the eight worldly concerns, are those with whom we are likely to experience an increase in our own mental confusion and afflictive emotions.[10] On the outer level,

---

10. To pursue the "eight worldly concerns" is to hope for happiness and fear suffering, to hope for fame and fear insignificance, to hope for praise and fear blame, and to hope for gain and fear loss. Thus one is ever swinging between hope and fear, and all due to grasping for outcomes based on self-interest rather than on benefit for others.

then, companionship in which our bodhicitta weakens and our confusion and afflictive emotions become stronger is exactly what is to be abandoned. On the inner level, as we have discussed, it is the afflictive emotions and distorting conceptions themselves that we must abandon, and above all their single cause: grasping to the notion of "self" and all the strangulating habits of self-concern that this notion spawns.[11]

Companions who are more than simply unsuitable, who are actually pernicious influences, are those who are disinclined or unable to distinguish virtue from nonvirtue, and in whose company you yourself become less inclined or able to distinguish between these two states of mind and activity. You are in danger among such companions. Though we probably think we already know right from wrong, in fact we often do not. Dharma teaches that virtue is what brings happiness for beings and nonvirtue is what brings suffering. In conventional life, however, where ideas of happiness are most often tied to the material, the immediate, and often the trivial, we are prone to choosing short-term happiness, helping even ourselves and our dear ones in ways that in the longer term actually cause harm, as in teaching young people that material wealth is the most important mark of a successful life or that gain for one justifies usurping or even destroying resources needed by all. Even when considering non-material happiness we tend to think of it in relation to outer circumstances more than to the actual condition of our own minds. In our relationships, for example, are we not more likely to focus on who loves us and who doesn't, and on how they are displaying or withholding that affection, than on the actual quality of our own loving?

For the student and practitioner on the path, when love and compassion and spiritual study and practice begin to waver or decline, we do well to look both around and within. We will certainly see elements of our habitual associations, in companions, activities, and mind, which are contributing to that decline. The

---

11. See Dharmarakshita, *The Wheel of Sharp Weapons*.

remedies are, like the influences, both inner and outer, but always the most important is inner—motivation, intention: the quality of your mind. Taking teachings and reflecting on them in relation to your own life experience refines your understanding of what actually is beneficial or harmful. Examining and evaluating your patterns of thought, emotion, and action will sharpen your ability to distinguish between habit and choice. This is important; we may think we already know the difference between habit and choice, but we are not presently as free as we think we are, so learning to discern when we are at choice and when we are simply following our habitual tendencies strengthens our ability to choose, consciously, what benefits us and others. Finally, meditation in which we observe mind directly is training that hones the clarity that recognizes mind's condition—and this is what places us at choice.

As you become more skillful in discerning your own mind's condition, you might recognize the *mirroring* that often occurs with your so-called bad companions, how their apparent faults are visible in your mindstream as well. Seeing our own afflictions more clearly is probably the greatest gift of interactions with negative companions. A personal example: I was complaining to Good Friend about Annoying Friend, the kind of recitation we all know so well. Good Friend acknowledged the facts of Annoying Friend's behavior and then asked why I was so bent out of shape about it. My mind stopped—and I burst into laughter as I saw: "Her self-importance offends my self-importance!" Annoying Friend was my mirror, showing me my own mind. The self-grasping, not the unsuitable friend, is the evil companion.

On a very practical note: Sometimes we need distinct breaks (even one as brief as the noble bathroom break) from negative conditions or harmful companions. As we focus on cultivating compassion and love for all and inquiring into the very nature of reality, our own gradual shifts and transformations may be enough to make us less appealing to companions who don't share these aspirations. However, with family and other deep, long-lasting connections, it can sometimes be quite challenging. I suggested earlier that we not hesitate to abandon a place or companions where our anger, grasping, and confusion are hardening, but these can also be the very people and circumstances with which we're most entangled, not only by circumstance and responsibilities but also by bonds of true caring. Walking away isn't always possible, nor is it always virtuous. As Garchen Rinpoche often reminds us, we meet other beings due to the force of our karma and are bound to remain associated until that karma has completed—and in challenging circumstances, with many mirrors, we will have abundant opportunities to become aware of our own mental and emotional habits and reactivity. These are, of course, signals that our self-grasping is activated, the self-grasping that is the cause of all our confusion. Recognizing this, and consciously choosing to take the path of bodhicitta, we transform the unsuitable companionship into a true field of practice. However rudimentary or refined our formal practice may be, there is never anything more important than cultivating love and compassion. This is our central practice in any situation, with any companion.

When under the kinds of influences in which aspiration, effort, and accomplishment may seem to be threatened or even degrading, the principal risk is to our minds, to our bodhicitta. When we are honest with ourselves we know whether we are growing in love and compassion or in confusion and emotional reactivity; we know which company elevates and which drags down. Companions who are unsuitable for us are those in whose sphere of influence we more often find ourselves in states of attachment, anger, and jealousy than in the condition of objective compassion and love. Geshe Jampa points out how to respond skillfully in such situations: "Keeping our distance from bad friends does not mean we consider them inherently bad people and lack concern or compassion for them. It simply means we recognize our own weakness and how easily we can be influenced in negative ways and thus decide not to cultivate close friendships with these people."[12]

---

12. Jampa Tegchok, *Transforming the Heart*, 87.

Even with this clarifying counsel we might still be a little uncertain about the abandoning we're talking about, for doesn't the bodhisattva promise never to abandon a sentient being? The distinction that helps us here: abandoning without abandoning. We do our best to bring our practice to mind in every moment— especially the shaky moments—and to create wholesome relationship pathways of body, speech, and mind, as Geshe Jampa is suggesting. Though we may at some point need to leave certain relationships or ways of being with certain others, temporarily or indefinitely, in our intention, in our mind, we never abandon the beings themselves. We always hold them in love and compassion, steadfastly remembering the intrinsic goodness that is the buddha nature in us all. Abandon our own afflictive emotions and there is no need to abandon any being. Strengthen bodhicitta, benefitting all, and the unsuitable companion becomes a companion on the path, whether we ever see that person again in this lifetime or not. This is the abandoning without abandoning.

**Verse 6.** When one follows a true spiritual friend, faults will dissolve and good qualities will grow like a waxing moon. Consider this friend more dear than your own body. This is the way of a bodhisattva.

Kyabje Dudjom Rinpoche showed me that ultimately there is one teacher: truth itself, not other than our true nature, present and perfect from the beginning. It is to seek and realize this that we take up the spiritual quest, while those who know the way understand what we do not: that what we seek is already ours. Their work is ever to point us to this truth while teaching us how to dispel what presently obscures our direct recognition of it.

On the spiritual path we may receive teachings of truth from those who benefit us as sangha companions, instructors, mentors, teachers, or holy gurus, differing in levels of learning and wisdom, scholarship and realization, while alike in giving to the utmost what they have received and understood. True spiritual friends, as

Tokme Zangpo is speaking of them here, are those who give truth, according to the needs and capacities of beings in specific times and places. Just to think of such teachers gives me deep joy. In my holy gurus of this lifetime I behold the embodiment of my highest aspiration and thus know its accomplishment is possible.

Throughout our lifetimes on the path we carry and ripen the qualities our teachers quicken in us. Applying in practice the teachings we receive, we find our ignorance, disordered thoughts, emotional afflictions, and deluded actions diminishing and our excellent potentials increasing like the waxing moon. The teachings "open the eyes of karma in our minds," allowing us to understand cause and consequence, to discern virtue from nonvirtue, and thus to choose the good for all.

As we rely upon speakers of truth and the truth they speak, our conditioned minds begin to relax into their natural order, just as a stringed instrument sounds to the note that attunes the orchestra. Hear the speech of the authentic spiritual friend as authentic Dharma. It is not for us to listen passively, admiring the teacher's eloquence and insight and then returning to our ordinary ways of thinking, or to engage in collecting teachers, teachings, empowerments, and practices. What we need to engage is their essence and what we need to collect is our mind. Gar Rinpoche says to hold the teachings dear and to *apply them within our mindstream*. This means "take the medicine": take the teachings and practices and draw them deep for contemplation and practice. Dedicate yourself to them until they bear fruit in your own understanding and experience. Their purpose is to dispel dualistic delusion. To liberate you.

We don't need Dharma and teacher because we are already free but precisely because we are not, so at the outset we are likely to be approaching the relationship with our habitual perceptual lenses, subjective thinking, and emotion-laden projections more or less intact. Enter the kind spiritual friend, our interrupter, disruptor, and mirror.

It can be dangerous, this relationship—dangerous to our illusions and delusions. Wonderful! Dis-illusioned: free to see things as they are. Our self-grasping and our very identities are called into question by the teachings and practices—and, if we are extremely fortunate, by the kind teacher who interrupts our constant, repetitive process of creating and maintaining identity, which is to say, creating and maintaining illusion. In any given instant, teachings and teacher show us our state, whether of confusion or of clarity. Mirror holds steady as we spar and dance with our own reflections, thinking they are facts and facets of an objective material reality. Our responsibility is to keep looking, to recognize our mental projections as our own unresolved inner conflicts, longings, and potentials. Unrecognized, they fuel our samsaric sufferings; recognized and acknowledged, they fuel our positive transformations, clarifying our subjectivity and freeing us to work directly with our own emotions, thoughts, and confusions. This is how we become responsible for ourselves in any relationship, and in the teacher-student relationship this is how we become capable of actually working *with* our teacher.[13]

In this situation lots of stuff can happen, to put it simply. Considering how challenging it is to release attachment to people and places, to a potato chip, to which sock you pull on first every day, you can imagine the challenge of letting go of attachment to ideas and concepts of self-other, this-that, good-bad, right-wrong, the dualistic building blocks of our so-called realities. The process can be infuriating, excruciating, inspiriting, sad, comical, and on and on, depending in large part on how desperately we are

---

13. Projections are the out-picturing of our own unresolved conflicts and confusions, projected onto beings, circumstances, and events in the outer sphere, as if they have their origins there rather than in our own mind. Eventually, if we are seeking truth, these disowned confusions will come to the fore to be dealt with, for spiritual progress requires taking responsibility for ourselves at ever deeper levels and in ever more precise ways. The teacher shows us our mind; it is up to us to examine our faults and qualities, to recognize both our confusion and our certainty. From a psychological perspective, projections reflect issues of the personality and may call for personality-level work, such as psychological investigation, ethical self-scrutiny, or psychotherapeutic help. Such issues will display in the relationship with the teacher but they are matters of the student's personal inner economy. The teacher mirror may sharpen our recognition of our unresolved personal issues, but the teacher is our spiritual guide, not our psychotherapist.

clutching, how deep-seated and unconscious our resistance is. But karma is trustworthy, aspiration is powerful, and bodhicitta, the highest aspiration, will lead us safely through everything we must face on the path.

Safely through: what does this mean on the bodhisattva way? It means we are liberating ourselves from ignorance so that all beings may rely upon us.

The teacher-student relationship is not for the teacher's benefit or only for yours: it is for the benefit of all. This relationship definitely does not call for slavish adoration, submission, or subservience, nor does it imply that the teacher has attained some kind of perfection at the level of personality. What it does mean is that the true teacher can show you how to ripen the wisdom potential within. If you take up the discipline the teacher gives, you are a disciple—at the outer level a disciple of the teacher, at the inner level a disciple of truth. As is your teacher.

Bodhicitta is the guarantor of a spiritual teacher's purpose and reliability. Garchen Rinpoche told me many years ago, when he asked me to teach and I protested that I was not qualified, "If you have great love and compassion you will benefit others, even if you don't know very much." Ha! This can reassure us all, and I take it dearly to heart. In everyone you rely on, in the spiritual and the conventional spheres alike, look for love and compassion, the good heart—and most crucially in those you are asking to steady and guide you across your own crevasses of ignorance.

At the outset, it is wise to examine yourself and the teacher and to evaluate the fit between you rather than to take a sudden giddy leap. Although sometimes it seems as if the karmic teacher just shows up and the relationship continues through lifetimes, even then, and throughout, we are responsible for our own choices. Is our intention clear and pure in essence, even if our conditioned mind is still all over the place? Good start. As for the teacher we are examining, are words and behavior in some reasonable relationship to each other, or are the words one thing and the actions another? A disjuncture here can be a sign of a teacher's inner freedom or of instability in mind and bodhicitta; either way, if the teacher's behavior and the teachings don't appear to align, it could be difficult for you to set out with clear confidence, because before we have our own direct experience of the teachings and their benefits we may need someone to show us the actual fruits of Dharma practice, not just tell us about them. So it can be helpful to explore a bit at the beginning, to see what disciplines of path and what teachers inspire you and stir your awareness of your own certainty wisdom—because that is the marker for spiritual sovereignty.

Throughout the work of Dharma we are responsible for seeking out and hewing to our own integrity. At each stage of the path we tune motivation to the ever higher aspiration to which bodhicitta continually gives rise, and tune speech and action to impeccability as best we can—impeccability meaning coherence and unity of purpose, motivation, and expression. This is for all of us, new and old, student and teacher, teacher and guru. Waking up and being awake is always in the instant, present moment, in which anyone can glimpse or abide in full awareness or fall into a moment of confusion. Since karmic causes remain in the mindstream until exhausted or purified, and since self-grasping appears to become subtler as practice progresses, anyone can be caught in its snare. As students and as teachers, we need to investigate the condition of our own minds carefully, all the way along, to align ever more finely with our best understanding of the pure teachings and with our own direct experience of truth and love. This is the working method for integrity and the foundation for impeccability.

Relationship with a spiritual teacher is not conventional relationship, and the meaning of devotion in this relationship may not be obvious, perhaps especially for Westerners cherishing beliefs in individualism, egalitarianism, autonomy, and independence. The personalities, the worldly vehicles of both student and teacher, will of course display, but in the case of the true teacher the personality vehicle is in service to the essential purpose of the spiritual enterprise: the liberation of beings. A highly energized inflection point is reached on the bodhisattva way when the disciple, too, recognizes this purpose radiant within. From then on, the *mutual* devotion of teacher and student, fueled by their *shared* devotion to the awakening of all, swiftly dispels clinging and confusion. This lifting of aspiration seems to change the very air one is breathing. Devotion to or for the teacher isn't about the teacher or the student; it is a robust, dynamic expression of their one purpose: the highest.

For the student, the great kindness of the buddha representative who is actually here with us in our lives, to teach and guide us, hand upon shoulder, softens our mind like butter working leather, melting hardness of heart, pride, and arrogance, and dispelling the fearful need to hold separate from the boundless. Longing and gratitude meet deep in the heart, and the spring of loving devotion rises. And for the teacher? When infant cries, mother's milk lets down.

Rare are those with the qualities of the sublime spiritual friend, the true teacher, one with the ultimate and actually here with you in your life. Don't waste the opportunity. Approach such a spiritual friend with respect and gratitude, and in every way cultivate faith and devotion for the teachings and those who bring them to you. To benefit your own mind, reflect on the teacher's qualities that reveal the Dharma and that awaken your understanding and wisdom.

Our teachers are human beings, as we are, who come through family, culture, era, and karma, so it is normal for their peculiarities to be visible to those who rely on them. However, if you are focusing on what you take as imperfections, "counting the teacher's faults," you won't have any time left over for Dharma! For your own sake, recognize that the true spiritual friend is using everything available for your liberation, *including* what may appear as her or his own faults. Our teachers walk with us here in the dust and debris of our ignorance, frailty, and confusion, using their own holy humanity to help us penetrate our confusions and delusions: to reveal our perfection. These feet of clay are most precious, lovable, and worthy of respect and compassion—for teacher even kinder than the Buddha, because here with us in this very lifetime. This display of empowered, empowering humanness I have come to see as one of the greatest of spiritual gifts, inspiring my deep-hearted, transforming devotion and confidence: the artifacts of the teacher's own arduous, altruistic path, giving everything to liberate all. This is the way of the bodhisattva.

Recognizing our teacher as at once both human and spiritual is a significant mirror for our minds that like to externalize and project, categorize and judge—training us in humility and equanimity, without fixation on notions of perfection and imperfection. It also teaches us to *be with* our own apparently limiting humanness as we free our limitless spiritual potential. This is training in pure perception, in recognizing the pristine nature in all mundane appearances, including our own. In teacher as in disciple, perceived imperfection is outward appearance, while essence is primordial perfection. It is important to understand this, even if at first only on an intellectual level, because remembering the nature of the essence is key to working spiritually with all confusing appearances, including those arising in relationships with spiritual teachers and with sanghas.

Over the years I have observed and experienced how certain human issues that can arise in any relationship or group can sometimes seem uniquely challenging to address in what we consider a "spiritual" context, with ourselves, our teachers, and our sanghas. For this reason, I want to touch briefly on some of them here.

*Culture and Buddhadharma.* Students in the West have long been receiving teachers and teachings from Eastern cultures and in translation from other languages, while Eastern teachers coming to the West have been encountering ways and expectations quite new to many of them. The essence is unchanging, but Dharma comes through and can shape culture, and culture can shape how Dharma is communicated and how it looks in a particular time and place. In an exceedingly general way we might say that the broad purposes of culture are to contain, maintain, express, elaborate, and evolve its values and practices, while the purpose of Dharma is to liberate. They are not necessarily at cross purposes, but they are not the same thing. We can learn from, respect, appreciate, and even support and protect the cultures of our kind teachers, their distinctive aesthetics and their rich histories, traditions, and values, without mistaking these cultural forms for the Dharma itself. Many of us, for a time, may take up the dress, ornaments, and mannerisms of our teachers' cultures, to deepen a sense of relationship with them or to identify ourselves as adherents of the adopted tradition. These choices are not faults—unless they increase self-reference, pride, attachment, sectarianism, and so on. Always look innerly, always seek essence, always practice on that. Dharma comes to us through the forms, but it is Dharma that is the medicine.

*Right relationship: power, secrecy, and bodhicitta.* For individuals and sanghas working with spiritual teachers, doubt and confusion can arise over what appear as issues of authority and power. Deep respect and wholesome, well-founded reverence and awe open us to the transmission of Dharma, the blessings of the lineages, and the natural authority of our teachers' compassion, love, and vast understanding. However, when we see in our teachers and Dharma communities selfishness, dominance, and the promotion of servility, fear, and shame, we are seeing a veering off from bodhicitta into personality displays and self-seeking. In such situations we need to pay conscious attention to our own inner compass, our natural ability to recognize true compassion and love in ourselves and others. Tune to true north.

A circumstance with serious potential to disturb the motivation and practice of students and the harmony of the sangha is teacher or student wrongdoing, overt or clandestine, that appears to contradict the teachings and is somehow rendered off-limits for discussion. This can mean that secrecy is being imposed by certain individuals or interest groups, not out of respect for the secret nature of particular teachings or practices but in order to control information and communication that might reveal wrongdoing or upset unbalanced, self-serving power relationships.

Such imbroglios usually seem to involve something in the worn triad of money, sex, and power. Though these troublesome trip-lets seem to be universal in attractions and in risks, there may be cultural overlay in how they are thought of and expressed. For ex-ample, ideas about sex and its meanings in spiritual life, including what is acceptable sexual behavior for women and men and who is permitted to do what with whom, can differ in different cultural traditions, as can convictions and conventions about what ought and ought not to be seen or spoken about openly—and about who gets to decide. While gossip tends to be divisive and harmful, hon-est communication about ethical and moral issues, guided by our Dharma teachings, can cut right through the confusions stirred by injunctions of secrecy.

The notion of transparency in the public sphere is relatively recent, as secrecy has long been imposed by those with power over others. When those who have been silenced begin commu-nicating about their perceptions or experiences of wrongdoing, expectations and conventions can shift, sometimes abruptly and deeply. Some people may be exposed and hurt as once-hidden information surfaces, but if so then it is probably also the case that others have been silenced and hurt all along. This is never an easy moment, for private or public relationships, but it is very often the moment in which fresh possibilities for right relationship open up. The spiritual meaning of power lies not in power over but in power for—not in wielding power over others but in generating power for the good, for all.

*Confusion, doubt, and fear; clarity, compassion, and courage.* At a deep level, since the purpose of the spiritual enterprise is to clarify the primitive confusion in which we all are enthralled, when confusion arises for us we must *see* it. It requires willingness and courage to look directly at our own mind and actions and to acknowledge what is out of alignment with purpose and principle. Authentic aspiration and sturdy spiritual practice depend upon this ongoing commitment and courage, grounded in bodhicitta.

This is true for both student and teacher—and their relationship, in ease and in difficulty, can be for each of them a clear mirror for this inner inquiry.

Those who lack confidence in themselves spiritually, in their own basic goodness and clarity, can be susceptible to manipulation, overt or subtle. Undue, unwholesome influence exerted by those we turn to for compassion and wisdom has the potential to be deeply harmful—undermining our ability to discriminate between virtue and nonvirtue, truth and untruth, in ourselves and in others. This is profound confusion, perilous to our wellbeing and challenging to identify and address. If you find yourself in such a condition, please seek out a trustworthy person with whom you can begin the process of disentangling good threads from bad in the tapestry your karma, potential, and pure aspiration are weaving.

Even in milder circumstances it can be disturbing to recognize that you are experiencing confused mind in relation to your teacher. While it can erode motivation and impede progress if left unexamined, this very confusion can sometimes signal the breaking up of limiting certainties, releasing mind from habitual constructions, and constrictions, of reality. Pay attention to your thoughts: look and listen for fresh information and perspective. And especially pay attention to your clarity, even the slenderest tendrils. What sees your confusion, right in this moment—this *is* the clarity you seek.

Clarity may at first be simply about the fact that you are confused or doubting; it may not immediately yield resolution. When doubting or confusion seems to be resisting all your efforts to resolve it? Turn first to the teachings and to your practice. Rely on what you know to be true, even if it is only that day follows night. Give it some time, always looking innerly—and if the clouds remain thick it may be time to communicate directly with a trusted person, your teacher or someone else—or, most directly and unerringly—with yourself, in the heart of your mind. Deep within, frankly acknowledge that you are caught and ask to be helped.

This is honest and will be fruitful, even if you don't know whom or what you are supplicating. Ignoring your doubt is easier, but then that worm just burrows deeper into the anxious mind.

This naked inner communication, in conjunction with continuous practice, helped me in a time when I felt paralyzed by doubt and fear in relationship with a teacher. Looking and listening within to see my own condition, with compassion and without regard to outcome, allowed me to recognize and acknowledge my painful state—*and* the hidden knowing, the life-filled certainty, that was shaking the frame to which I was clutching. This rendered me available to hear and immediately to act upon what my courageous, compassionate teacher had to tell me.

Sometimes broader communication appears necessary for the wellbeing and integrity of teachers, students, and sangha, as in situations of dangerous, unethical, or abusive conduct by teachers or sangha members. With regard specifically to teachers, His Holiness the Dalai Lama has said that if a teacher has not been able or willing to correct his or her own wrongdoing, then it is proper to communicate openly about it, speaking with positive intent for the benefit of all. The context was the compassionate concern of Western Dharma teachers for their own teachers and sanghas when teacher conduct appeared to diverge from the ethical principles of the Dharma.[14] Still, H. E. Garchen Rinpoche reminds us that even teachers whose faults we ourselves find grievous may be a source of great benefit to someone else, and so it is wise not to pull them down or try to turn people away from them. These two views are not in conflict, for here, as ever, it is motivation that is critical: no pursuit of self-interest, truth telling but no judgement of others, only clarity, respect, love, and compassion for all, with discriminating wisdom and certainty in the Dharma. I have confidence, from experience, that with right motivation skillful means become apparent.

---

14. Tenzin Gyatso, the 14th Dalai Lama, Dharamsala, India, March 1993. See also "Dalai Lama denounces ethical misconduct by Buddhist teachers," by Sam Littlefair. *Lion's Roar*, August 8, 2017.

If, finally, you cannot agree with your teacher, it may be time to go, at least for a while. What good is it to stay, doubting and criticizing? Better not to poison the well for yourself and others. If you can, it is good to communicate about this with your teacher or teachers. In clarity about the fact that you are at an impasse, and with appreciation and respect, ask for their blessings. No right-versus-wrong and no failure here: just see it as it is—and keep practicing. You were on the path before this moment and your path continues for as long as you are walking it. When I once went to tell my teacher I was falling, I asked if I were still on the path. "Do you still aspire to enlightenment?" she asked me. "Yes." "And have you attained it?" "No." "Then you are still on the path." Continue to expand and lift your aspiration and bodhicitta and to hold in pure view, with appreciation and love, all spiritual friends and companions on the path. Including you.

Through the teacher and the lineage, all members of the sangha are connected. Remembering this timeless inner connection helps us see troubles and disturbances of understanding, speech, or conduct as the temporary, insubstantial phenomena they are. While attending as needed to momentary disturbing appearances, seek right relationship guided by the teachings of truth and by the vast love and compassion of bodhicitta.

There is a profound traditional teaching about you and the spiritual friend: If you see the spiritual friend as an ordinary person, you will receive the blessings of an ordinary person; if you see the spiritual friend as a bodhisattva, you will receive the blessings of a bodhisattva; and if you see the spiritual friend as a buddha, you will receive the blessings of a buddha. This is the power of pure view.

The wisdom mind of the true teacher is absolutely reliable because ultimately one with the absolute. This pristine mind is present in all our teachers, as in ourselves, to be realized by each of us through pure aspiration, bodhicitta, and dedication on the path. To hold steady in this knowledge is to cultivate pure view, which sees through ever changing display to primordial essence. It is the appearances that are confusing, because we are reacting to them from the perspective of the "self," with its faulty basis, its karmic predispositions, and its conditioned thoughts and disturbing emotions. But the inner *nature* of these appearances is the absolute: uncaused, unconditioned, unchanging. Rely upon this.

When Garchen Rinpoche first came from Tibet he told us, "Don't make relationship with me as a physical lama. My body is very temporary; it will go and you will be bereft. Instead, make relationship with my mind, which is wisdom itself, and then we are never separate."

**Verse 7.** Who can worldly gods, themselves imprisoned in samsara, protect? Therefore, seek refuge in the Three Jewels, the undeceiving source of refuge. This is the way of a bodhisattva.

In terms familiar to us in this time, we can say that one who seeks refuge is a refugee. Worldly refugees are driven from the known and dear by hunger, violence, disaster, oppression, poverty, hopelessness, terror. The house is on fire: get out *now*.

Though we may not think of ourselves this way, perhaps we should. Are we not caught in the samsaric homeland of delusion and suffering, intent on maintaining it until we can do so no longer? The familiar becomes too painful, or it has fallen apart and we are bewildered, feeling lost and unsafe. In the exhausted mind a door opens for an instant, or we hear a rumor of simple freedom—showing us that we are not free. Not free! A shocking insight into our actual condition. And for some, though not for all, the next moment brings clarity: I must free myself. This is a way for us to understand what it means to seek and take refuge in the Three Jewels: Buddha, Dharma, and Sangha.

Refuge is a formal entryway—a door to pass through and a clearly marked way to follow the teachings of the Buddhadharma. We may study and practice in the Dharma traditions to great benefit without formal refuge, but for those who desire to deepen commitment to this particular path, refuge gives profound support for ongoing study, reflection, and practice, for continuing progress in the Dharma.

At first we may seek and accept refuge because we fear suffering and desire happiness; this early motivation for our own relief is normal and wholesome, and its first step is to abandon harm-doing. As our understanding deepens, we take refuge because we long for liberation from the endless cycle of suffering and its causes, not just for ourselves but for all. This is the altruistic intention, the motivation of the bodhisattva, which opens us to the vast love and compassion of bodhicitta and the commitment, through lifetimes, to bring all beings to freedom. And ultimate refuge is sought by one who is impelled to know reality directly, who practices pure view as both method and result. Practicing the three commitments in one, we cultivate pristine motivation and both particular and universal unconditional love and compassion, held in understanding of the open, empty nature of mind, phenomena, and reality itself.

The Three Jewels help us understand the causes of our confusion, errors, and suffering and give us remedies for those causes. Both the causes and the remedies are in our minds: the causes of suffering, in our misunderstanding of the nature of reality and thus our clinging to the notion of selfness in ourselves, other beings, and phenomena; and the remedies, in bodhicitta and in penetrating insight into true nature.

We speak of outer and inner refuge. Buddha refuge can be understood as historical Buddha Shakyamuni, as every realized buddha, as any true teacher, and as one's own kind teachers, here with us now, giving compassionate, wise instruction and guidance as we learn why and how to walk the path. In the inner meaning, buddha is pristine, primordial wisdom.

Dharma refuge is the body of teachings, methods, and practices. It is not a place; it is the path we walk, where it is bringing us, and how we follow it. The essence of Buddhadharma, boundless expanse radiant with love and compassion, is the inner Dharma refuge.

When we take refuge in the third jewel, Sangha, we join with companions on the way, sources of mutual friendship, support, understanding, and guidance as we walk the path in good company. Sangha essence is love, devotion, and integrity with teachers, teachings, and companions, held in pure view—and more expansive still is the understanding that it includes all beings.

The Prayer of Kuntuzangpo teaches "one ground and two paths, awareness and unawareness."[15] Unawareness is penetrated in an instant by the light of awareness, and in that instant one is awake. Even those with long practice and stable insight can fall into slumber again, a moment or a lifetime of forgetfulness and obscuration, and from that slumber can awaken again, momentarily or fully. As we are not presently qualified to know who is and who is not a buddha or a bodhisattva, and as all beings have buddha nature, every being can be considered sangha, a precious companion on the universal path.

Gar Rinpoche says that all who cultivate the good heart are sangha, so in a general sense sangha is the community of good heart. He emphasizes the importance of actively supporting the indivisibility and harmony of the sangha, just as we maintain the integrity of our prayer mala or rosary. All the beads are strung together with the guru bead, so to let the string break at any point is to let the beads fall away not only from one another but also from the guru, in whom the three refuges are complete.

In this relative reality we are always seeking and taking refuge, but almost always in temporary refuges of limited potency, which often reveal themselves eventually to be snares. In a storm most critters look for shelter; in illness or pain most seek relief. Unfortunately, we humans often compound our ignorance with our choices of refuge: the drug, the heavy or frivolous drama, the repetitive search for distraction and entertainment, the thinking and conduct designed to garner attention, gratification, admiration, security, love, wealth, power, and control.

What our verse refers to as the worldly gods are included here: those holders or symbols of temporal power and might from whom we seek protection, but whose capacity to protect is very limited. Still self-grasping, like us, they are still imprisoned in samsara. How can shackled prisoners free us from our shackles of ignorance? They

---

15. "The Prayer of Kuntuzangpo," Bhaka Tulku and Steven Goodman.

can bestow only what Garchen Rinpoche describes as the temporary happiness behind which is hidden the long-term suffering.

Those who seek ultimate happiness take refuge in truth, the basis of all spiritual refuge, from which we are inseparable. We are never apart from our own nature; we and truth are a union, uncreated and indissoluble. Our motivation to seek and take refuge, arising naturally from this indwelling union, articulates through the conditions of our minds and karmic fruitions as we progress along the path. This we can remember as we work with the circumstances of our lives, as our karma plays out, and as our aspiration for absolute freedom, lifted by bodhicitta, rises ever higher and higher. Whatever may be the particulars of one's path, intrinsic primordial wisdom nature is the supreme refuge from suffering.

It is through our own faith that the compassion of the buddhas, bodhisattvas, our spiritual teachers, and our sangha friends reaches and lifts us, and it is we ourselves who are responsible for generating this faith.[16] It is extremely important to understand this point. Faith may appear at times to rise up in our hearts spontaneously, lifting and vivifying our practice, but it is not sufficient to rely on the occasional upwelling of an emotional experience of faith. The spiritual path is not easy. Faith needs to be the strong staff in our hand, there when we stumble, lose our way, or fear the demons of our minds or the times. Cultivating our faith is like feeding our children—not once or occasionally, in moments of enthusiasm, but repeatedly, continually, as needed.

I am grateful to be able to share with you this perfectly complete teaching from Kyabje Dudjom Rinpoche, whose mind is the sky-like vast expanse, whose compassion is the rainbow arc from beginningless to endless, and whose words are the rainfall of grace and blessings that elucidate our reality:

> When we do not recognize appearance as the pure display of self-arising Dharmakaya awareness,[17] grasping comes about.

---

16. Patrul Rinpoche, *The Words of My Perfect Teacher*, 173.
17. Dharmakaya: primordial purity; open, luminous, pristine, original mind, unborn and undying. The "truth body" of the buddha.

Perception and form manifest, and we cling to them; we also cling to the self who is grasping. Dualistic clinging takes us from our true nature, and we are left wandering in relative reality, exposed in the external world. Like it or not, we are temporarily trapped in samsaric existence. We must accept this and work toward enlightenment within the relative world. Until we realize that self and other are by nature without true existence, we rely on the Buddha, dharma and sangha. These sublime Three Jewels have the exalted means to draw us out of samsara.[18]

## Discussion: Buddhadharma and religion

*I am ready to make a formal commitment to the Buddhist path. From my understanding, taking the refuge vows doesn't mean that I have to see the Buddha as my only teacher and am no longer allowed to be a Christian. I can still consider myself a Christian and a follower of Christ, if I choose, yet at the same time also recognize the Buddha to be my teacher. Am I incorrect in this understanding?*

When I brought to Garchen Rinpoche my dear, old, crusty, conservative, profoundly faithful Roman Catholic priest friend for a blessing, Rinpoche rose instantly from his seat, hands outstretched, exclaiming, "I have great faith and devotion to Jesus Christ!"

Jesus teaches what all buddhas and bodhisattvas teach: the great love, surpassing all bounds and distinctions. Wisdom traditions may differ as to details and method but I think they agree on love. The path of truth is to practice on truth, the path of love is to practice on love—and these two are not two. So I see no conflict between your Christian faith and your faith and practice in the Dharma, if you are practicing the essence of both ways.

Differences between traditions don't have to be conflicts if you

---

18. Sandra Scales, *Sacred Voices of the Nyingma Masters*. Please also read Dilgo Khyentse's precise, profound commentary on refuge in *Heart of Compassion*, 79-87.

are going for essence. If you believe in a creator deity you may find it strange to meet a path that doesn't address the question of "first cause" and that offers a great variety of images of the sublime to mirror back to us our own enlightened qualities.[19] However, both Buddhadharma and Christianity guide beings in using life experience, mind, and love to remove the scales from eyes that search for the ultimate. If you approach the Buddhadharma looking for a belief system, though, you had better look elsewhere, because Dharma is not a system of beliefs about truth but a gathering of methods for realizing truth.

*Can you say something about Buddhism as a religion, or the relationship of Buddhism and religion?*

Buddhadharma is the word I use to denote the body of teachings and practices usually referred to in English as Buddhism. In general speech, Buddhism tends to be spoken of as a religion and religion often seems to imply a system of beliefs—but the Buddhadharma, like its original teacher, does not ask anyone to believe anything but rather to test the teachings and practices for oneself and to take up what brings benefit.

In relation to the universal path from ignorance to wisdom, one meaning of the word dharma is simply truth, or universal spiritual law—so a dharma path would be a path that does not deceive, a path that is true, and that accords with the true nature, potentials, and ultimate purposes of oneself and others. In our time and place, we have the good fortune to arrive at the threshold of the Buddhadharma, a present, living, and unmistaken articulation of the universal inner spiritual path. I think of it as a basket brimming

---

19. "Tibetan Buddhist deities are not creator-beings, like the Judeo-Christian God, nor are they beings to propitiate and pacify. These deities pacify us. And though Dharma doesn't posit a creator as first cause, it definitely addresses cause. Everything that arises within mind is potentially a seed of cause, and everything that arises in phenomenal reality has first arisen in mind. Further, each moment of mind can be seen to arise from the preceding moment of mind. This means that we are the creators of our reality, moment to moment to moment." Du Bois, *Light Years*, 271, n.139.

over with inconceivable blessings and limitless skillful means for attaining the realization attained by Buddha Shakyamuni and all the buddhas of the three times.

Garchen Rinpoche once told me that it is not religion but sectarianism that is problematic, and that sectarianism has no place in the Buddhist view. Rinpoche said, "The essence of Buddhism is not separate from the essence of any other religion. When you understand the Buddhist view truly, your mind becomes vast—and you will have love for all beings without any bias."[20]

20. Garchen Rinpoche, personal communication, 2017.

# CHAPTER THREE

# KARMA, RENUNCIATION, AND BODHICITTA: THE THREE BODHISATTVA TRAININGS (VERSES 8-10)

I have heard Dharma refuge described as "taking safe direction," and I appreciate the two meanings this can have: going in a safe direction, toward liberation, and also taking direction from teachings, teachers, and practice. Both meanings apply to us at this very point, as we turn to Tokme Zangpo's teachings on the three trainings of the bodhisattva, sometimes called the three levels of bodhisattva development. They are developmental levels in the sense that study and practice at each level opens naturally into readiness for the next, but they are not understood and practiced separately from each other. Throughout our progress in the bodhisattva way we are training and maturing in all three.

**Verse 8.** The Buddha taught that all the unbearable suffering of the lower realms is caused by wrongdoing. Therefore, never do wrong, even at the cost of your life. This is the way of a bodhisattva.

"Even if you can't benefit beings, please at least try not to harm them," says Tenzin Gyatso, the 14th Dalai Lama. In fact, we must stop harming beings before we can actually benefit them. The first level of bodhisattva training, then, is restraint of ill action: abandoning actions of mind, speech, and body that cause harm, suffering, for sentient beings. Our understanding of what is and is not harmful, immediately or potentially, matures as we grow and deepen, both personally and spiritually, but our responsibility at every stage and in every moment is very clear: To the degree that you understand your thought, word, or act as harmful to specific beings and to beings in general (and to living things not always considered "sentient," such as the Earth), you have the responsibility to restrain it, to refrain from pursuing it, to the best of your ability.

The impact of causing harm is not just its evident effects on you and others; it is *karmic*—meaning that it sets causes in your mindstream that will eventually ripen into karmic consequences in your life experience.[1] Karma is a natural law; karmic effects are the natural results of positive and negative motivations and actions. Karma has nothing to do with reward or punishment and everything to do with motivation, awareness, and choice—with power and responsibility, in short, for good and for ill.

In the Buddhadharma, perspectives and methods for understanding and working with karma are manifold, for beings at all levels—far-reaching and powerful as information, precise and profound as keys for transformation.[2] Garchen Rinpoche's exquisite, liberating discourses on karma, always a part of his

---

1. Because we are intrinsically attuned to truth, not falsity, the harm intended for the other can also lie on one's heart as a present moral injury. See Robert Jay Lifton's paradigm-shifting study of veterans and the moral injury soldiers bear from their injuries to others: *Home from the War*. This understanding is informing current thought, too, about the moral injuries borne by those who serve in enforcement capacities. See, for example, Francisco Cantú, *The Line Becomes a River*.

2. I am so far from being a scholar that I can barely say this much, so I refer you to those who can elucidate with precision the workings of karma. Particularly helpful to my understanding have been Garchen Rinpoche (oral teachings, transcripts, any published works available), Dilgo Khyentse, Jampa Tegchok, Dharmarakshita, and "The Prayer of Kuntuzangpo." For the operational dynamics of karmic cause and consequence, see also explanations of the Twelve Links of Interdependent Origination—e.g. those of Thrangu Rinpoche and Sonam Rinpoche (see Bibliography).

teachings, explain that the karmic seed of cause is in the mind, as a single thought or emotion, positive or negative, forming and dissolving moment by moment, and most of the time, by habit of unawareness, not consciously recognized. Though our thoughts and emotions may be fleeting, subtle, and at present difficult to discern, in fact we can perceive all that displays in our mind, and we can train to recognize our harmful thoughts and emotions in the very instant of their arising.

Our ordinary mental-emotional-behavioral patterns function as vectors for karmic formation; the most important of these is our conditioned mind. We react to our mind's activity in three principal ways, so habitual as to be almost indiscernible, until we learn to see their action through cultivating the inward attention: mind looking at mind. We have been considering these three habitual patterns already, as the three poisons or three principal afflictive emotions, variously identified as attraction, aversion, confusion; grasping, repulsing, elaborating; passion, aggression, jealousy. Simply put: I want it, I hate it, I'm confused about it so I'll make something up. These three reactions arise from our mental patterns of self-reference and self-concern, as we are reflexively reacting to stimuli in terms of their imagined relationship to the imagined self. *It is in that instant of reaction that karmic cause is set.* This is why it matters that we become able to recognize our mental phenomena—thoughts and emotions—as soon as they arise. In the moment mind recognizes a thought and does not interfere with it, the thought vanishes, leaving no trace. Thought nature and mind nature: same nature. When a thought or emotion arises in our mind, is recognized, and meets with no reaction or involvement at all, it goes as naturally as it came, like a wave in water, coming and going in its own watery nature. No karma is created by a mental arising that simply comes and goes in mind that is both aware and non-reactive.

The three poisons, therefore, naturally point us to their own three antidotes: grasp at nothing, neither push anything away, and no elaboration. If you like it, let it go; if you dislike it, let it go; and if you don't know whether it's desirable or detestable, let it go. "Let it go" means leave it alone, don't engage. This requires that we learn to *tolerate* the instant of recognizing a reaction, simply to *be with* it, without claiming it, rejecting it, or making it into something. We can train, through practice, in this method that liberates seeds of harm-doing from their potential to harm. The person who can abandon the impulse to harm others is the one who can recognize that impulse and disarm it.

It is said that when result appears, necessity ceases. When tree rises up, seed is no more. All karma naturally exhausts itself, so it is what we do with its necessary and temporary appearances now that determines its consequences in the future. When we permit the actions of the three poisons to manifest through our body, speech, or mind, they in turn become causes for our consciousness to manifest the realms of cyclic existence and their sufferings that we have studied in verse 1. We really don't need anyone to tell us that these states of confusion and suffering are directly related to—in fact, arise from—our own mind's impulses and reactions. We can sometimes perceive such dynamics in others, and, facing ourselves directly, we see them in ourselves. But what we are not recognizing in ourselves we tend to see as the motivations and attributes of others, as we have discussed earlier in relation to projection (see also page 64, n.13). This projection, or out-picturing, can shield us temporarily from threatening or undesired knowledge of our own mind's condition, but we actually need that knowledge, both for personality integration and for spiritual integrity. Throughout Padmasambhava's instructions for liberation in the bardo between death and rebirth, which is also a blueprint for awakening in life, at every stage we are instructed to recognize whatever appears as the display of our mind, our own projections.[3]

It is crucial to understand that these transient psycho-emotional states and their projections are themselves insubstantial, coming

---

3. See Padmasambhava, *The Tibetan Book of the Dead.*

and going and changing all the time. But take these individual states with their causes and outflows, gather them together with those of countless other beings, human and otherwise, and we can easily see how a hell-like realm of rage-filled beings, a realm of dull ignorance, or one of ceaseless craving without hope of satisfaction can manifest as material reality. A zone of war is like all of that put together: the outflows of mind-states of aggression, anger-hatred, jealousy, grasping, fear, and ignorance, reflected in each face of suffering, of both perpetrator and victim. Except that ultimately there is no perpetrator and no victim. This drama is a co-creation, rising and falling continuously in our minds, out-pictured, projected, and enacted, and therefore experienced as our lives in the three times.

This is individual and collective karma. Everyone is "all in." Garchen Rinpoche explains that the inner universe of a sentient being arises from individual, personal karma, while the outer universe is created by the habitual imprints and thus the collective karma of all beings. Think of many individuals gathered around a still lake. One takes a pebble and throws it into the water; ripples stir on the lake surface, a circle of ripples, moving outward from the center, eventually touching the shores near and far. Then another stone is tossed, and another and another. The waters fill with movement and turbulence as ripples cross ripples, patterns lapping and overlapping; waves form, first small and then larger, more powerful, swelling and then crashing and thundering onto the shores.

If the wave is breaking on your shore—your body, your mind, your relationships, your life—it is your wave. Even when it is one wave of many, appearing indistinguishable, its origins in your mind will be discernible. Effect and cause do not lose their functional relationship in our mind just because many other beings generate the same effects from the same causes. We can take external reality, in every instant, as a mirror of our own mind. How could I ever have thought that my individual moments of anger were unrelated to the unbearable sufferings of countless beings in the wars of only my own lifetime in only this realm? If there is a field of any kind of suffering anywhere, in any time, I am responsible for my contribution to that. To know this and to take responsibility for one's own seedbed of cause, one's own mind, is to lay claim to our power as creators and co-creators of all that manifests in our realities.

This is the first stage of learning to refrain from harm. In your own mind and emotions, in your relationships, in the world, in nature, study and learn to recognize how the law of cause and effect operates, observing steadily, over time, and in many different circumstances, to gain confidence in karma. The seeds and habits of the afflictive emotions are in your stream of mind—because you have placed them there. Thus, when cause comes together with conducive condition, the outcome is not in doubt: you *will* grasp, erupt in anger, and flounder in ignorance, making up stories to calm your panic of not knowing. This is the wrongdoing our verse is addressing: actions that cause harm, for us and others, this harm both generated by and perpetuating grasping, hatred, and ignorance. These three poisons and their activities arise from clinging to imagined "self" and its imagined interests. Such mind-states and actions, arising not from love and compassion but from deluded self-grasping, harm beings in the relative realms and harm us, karmically, far into the future.

"Never do wrong, even at the cost of your life." This is a little shocking; until now we haven't considered our negative deeds really all that negative, have we? We are basically good-hearted people. How can the wrongdoing we commit be so heinous that we should give up our lives rather than engage in it even one more time? The answer lies in karma, and the answer, too, is shocking. To give up our life rather than commit harm is to lose this one body, while to cause harm rather than give up our life is potentially to lose lifetimes of progress on the path, lifetimes of creating good cause, lifetimes of bodhisattva development. While Buddhadharma teaches that we are not permitted to give away the precious human life before we have realized emptiness and generated bodhicitta (except in an emergency, when compassion takes over and throws us forward in the sublime choicelessness and courage of selfless love), let us nevertheless take just this seriously, in all lifetimes, our relationship with karmic cause and effect.

Many in the West have long been thinking of cause and effect as exactly opposite to the teachings on karma—as in the litigious American legal system: "If I'm suffering it's someone else's fault and they owe me for it." Even as spiritual students we may give easy lip service to karma this, karma that—usually in considering someone else's motivations and behavior rather than our own. I was many years into Dharma study and practice before I undertook sincere study of karma, and only then out of desperate emotional pain and mental anguish. It was when I felt myself driven to probe for the true origins of my own fierce confusion and conflict that I began to look within, directly and without dissembling, at the intimate relationship between my self-concern and the worlds of conflict, pain, disturbance, and wrongdoing I experienced in my life. As I studied and pondered and looked innerly I sensed with increasing certainty that my tangled patterns of mind and behavior were being woven across a loom of lifetimes, and this began to free me from thinking of cause and effect as rooted in this one lifetime or even in material circumstance. Instead, I began gradually to perceive cause in my own mind's condition, both in the long ago and in the present moment. That the seeds of my confusion lay in my own mindstream became incontrovertible. The evidence was everywhere.

The extraordinary thing was the intense *relief* this nascent view and understanding gave me. It was virtually immediate. Even my toddler-level comprehension poured light and clarity into my mind, assuaging obsessive torment. I began to settle into a less defended relationship with my own thoughts and emotions, and with memories, experiences, and imaginings of relationships with other beings and the world. The impulse to project onto others my own distortions and ignorance began to subside, leading quite swiftly to an energetic, vivid urgency to see clearly how *my* thinking, *my* emotions, *my* speech, *my* actions were the seeds of my own suffering—and of my contributions to the sufferings of others. I was beginning to comprehend, through direct observation and experience, something of what Gar Rinpoche means when he says that we will never experience anything for which we have not, ourselves, created the cause. He vividly showed us this in a sangha gathering before a planned trip to Tibet, when he told us that if he returned to Tibet he might be imprisoned again. Oh, the students were weeping and imploring him, "Don't go, don't go! Oh, Rinpoche, don't go! If they're going to put you back in prison, don't go! Stay here!" He just smiled and said, "Well, that shows you don't understand karma." And they called out to him, "But if you have the karma to go back to prison in Tibet, stay here where you're safe!" He said, "That shows you *really* don't understand karma. If I have the karma to be thrown into prison again and I stay in America, they'll throw me into prison in America."

This pith teaching fills me with gratitude and joy: I can trust in karma, I am safe in karma. Nothing is alien to me and I am no victim. Any suffering I experience I have chosen by my own prior activity, and I can now choose how I take it. And if I am in the state of love and compassion I cannot cause further harm to myself or to others. Bodhicitta is the ultimate protection of every being.

We are held in the light play of the Two Truths, absolute and relative. Absolutely, the law of karma is itself empty of any solidity while at the same time it is the law of the land here in all the realms of existence, operating through the subtlest details of the minds and actions of sentient beings. Khyentse Rinpoche: "Relative truth functions inexorably within absolute truth. A thorough realization of the empty nature of all phenomena never led anyone to think that positive actions do not bring happiness, or that negative actions do not bring suffering."[4] Thus Guru Rinpoche's teaching that our view should be as high as the sky and our conduct as fine as barley flour.

Free yourself from suffering by refraining from wrongdoing, thus freeing yourself to create causes of good for yourself and all beings. Take karma personally, very personally. It is your loom,

4. Dilgo Khyentse, *Heart of Compassion*, 90.

your warp and weft, your fibers, and the very fabric you are weaving of mind and life.

## Discussion: Karma

*Do these teachings mean I should not harm someone in order to prevent him from harming me?*

There is a key point to understand about perceived harm from another as it relates to karmic cause and consequence. As Gar Rinpoche has said, you will never experience anything that you haven't set a cause for, so there is no basis for hatred and anger at those seeking to harm you or for the apparent harm inflicted. It is not blame but responsibility that is at issue here. As you cease blaming others you become free to see your own responsibility—and to take it.

This recognition of karmic cause and consequence is vitally important. Not only does it interrupt repeating cycles of wrongdoing based on injury and reaction but it protects your relative bodhicitta, your most precious possession throughout all lifetimes. It is your own anger-hatred that harms your bodhicitta, not someone else's anger-hatred or the fact that you're going to be hurt. This is the point that we need to remember.

In a case of potential violence, for example, it is your karma from past action that is the cause for the person now coming at you with a knife, but it may also be your karma that you have studied martial arts and can swing him harmlessly over your shoulder. Lovely—then you can walk away, or you can help him up (first removing the knife) and then walk away, or you can go have tea together. In a different scenario, you might defend yourself or another by striking with force that hurts an attacker, without ever abandoning your knowledge that your attacker is in essence a buddha and in this reality a confused being, desiring happiness and not knowing how to find it. Just like you. Bodhicitta is not wimp compassion.

I have not seen anything in the Buddhadharma that says you should not protect yourself from somebody trying to hurt you, but there is karmic interplay of intention and action to speak to here, even at the superficial level that my limited understanding can offer. By intending to harm, actually harming, and taking satisfaction in having harmed, a wrongdoer ensures her or his own future suffering. That karmic load is lightened when the intended victim, with great compassion, intentionally chooses to take the injury, giving freely what the assailant intended to take by force. In another instance the skillful action might actually be to harm one in order to prevent that one from harming others. Here, the assailant will reap the karma of the harmful intention, while you, with the motivation of bodhicitta, take on the negative karma of the harmful act itself. It is principally our motivation, the condition of our mind, which makes our action one of virtue or nonvirtue. When you are harmed materially by another, whether your mind is harmed is up to you. These are teachings about not creating negative karma, not causing harm, and freeing the mind. Karmically, what good does it do you to escape material harm if you're generating thoughts of hatred and rage as you're doing it? You're running away from the danger behind you while running straight into the karmic cage of suffering before you.

When presented with harm or its potential it is often what we do with it afterward that is most damaging to us—in our minds holding onto it, repeating it in our thoughts over and over, thinking of all the things we could have done and said, the ways we could have hurt the one who was trying to hurt us, or blaming ourselves for what we said or didn't, did or didn't, wore or didn't, and so on. We elaborate. This is very destructive to us; it is not just acts of body and speech that create karma, it is also, and most significantly, our thoughts. When we walk away from harm we could quite simply, with a mind of clarity and compassion, leave it behind. And if we are not able to escape the assailant and are hurt, even killed, let us protect our bodhicitta. We might go down fighting, but let us not go down hating.

*Does karmic causation happen because of the human experience? Or does it happen because of samsara, and because we are in samsara it will keep happening?*

In relative reality, the realms of existence, we are ruled by karma; karma is not something that "happens" but the actual operating principle of samsaric existence. If a cause is set a consequence will ensue, and when the consequence ripens the cause is no more. Garchen Rinpoche says that a thought of nonvirtue, when recognized in the instant of its arising, is diminished in its karmic impact. Remember this, and practice to clarify mind that recognizes its own condition.

Your karmic seeds of cause already laid down will come to fruition, and as each one ripens it ceases to exist as cause while its appearances play out as your lived experiences. Karmic fruition—appearing as material event, relationship, emotion, confusion, whatever it may be—will arise as appearance at the moment and in the circumstance in which conditions make it possible. What we need to learn is how to work skillfully with these appearances. First, see them just as they are. Add nothing. Second, see your reactions, too, as they are, and allow grasping, aversion, and elaboration to dissolve before speaking or acting. Thus the consequences of your *past* karma arise, display, and dissolve in the *present* moment without becoming seeds of *future* karma rooted in self-referential mental and emotional reactions.

Remember, too, that karmic causes and consequences, like all phenomena, are devoid of intrinsic existence, for nothing that depends upon causes and conditions for its existence can be said to exist inherently. Seed created in mind, falling on fertile ground, ultimately fruiting up as the consequence of the cause: this interplay is a proof of emptiness, the ultimate nature of phenomenal reality.

Finally, let's touch on the relationship of karma and love. Karma simply means action; we also speak of karma as the dynamic of action and effect, of cause and consequence. The cause and the consequence come from and to oneself; we set the cause, and we receive the karmic consequence. Enmeshed in materiality, we tend to think of both causes and consequences as material, but in terms of karma the strongest determinant of effect is at the level of mind, in volition, motivation, mind state. Self-grasping mind tends to generate negative or harmful actions that cause suffering for self and others, while mind of love and compassion, the good heart, generates acts of virtue, of goodness, that bring wellbeing and happiness.

Spiritual teachings and practice stir bodhicitta. As love and compassion increase, self-grasping decreases, and as self-grasping decreases, love and compassion increase. This changes everything. Bodhicitta, deepening and expanding through intention and practice, affects our creation of negative and positive karma: the ratio begins to shift, with love and compassion gradually becoming the greater motive force in our creating of karma. While karma is still kicking us from behind, spiritual aspiration—which is love—now draws us steadily forward. This is the power of bodhicitta, ultimate spiritual aspiration.

From my teachers I have heard, "There is no negativity so great that it cannot be purified by spiritual practice."[5] Karma is of the relative, while the essence nature of spiritual practice is bodhicitta, nondual love-emptiness: truth itself. Nothing is more powerful than truth.

**Verse 9.** Like a dewdrop on a blade of grass, the happiness of the three worlds vanishes in but an instant. Strive for the supreme state of never-changing liberation. This is the way of a bodhisattva.

What is the supreme state of never-changing liberation? Mind abiding in its true nature, the true nature of being, that which neither comes nor goes, and the true nature of existence, that which

---

5. Purification, in Buddhadharma, refers to what reveals the intrinsic purity, the ultimate, void nature of reality. To purify, in this sense, is to dispel the illusions and delusions that obscure one's ability to perceive, to apprehend, the true nature.

is only and always coming and going. To strive for that state is to aspire wholeheartedly to realize it and continuously to practice on it. This is to "take the result as the path."

The second level of bodhisattva training calls for a radical shift of attention and intention: to free our minds from enmeshment in materiality itself, the illusion-like worlds that arise in ignorance. Our challenge is not just that we preoccupy ourselves with the this-and-that of material existence, life in the world; it is that we *identify* with this particular material existence—and with materiality and existence themselves. The terms of our identification with existence require us not to notice that in some indefinable way we are more than it. Or, if we do notice (and we do, frequently, though we may not register it consciously), we must agree not to take this as evidence of anything. Ha! That which we collude not to acknowledge is the very *that* which is our true nature and the true nature of all. It's not as if it is going away; our bodies do, over and over again, while our *thatness* (or *thisness*, if you prefer) neither comes nor goes—and is ever exerting upon us the magnetism of truth.

Geshe Jampa tells us that deeply understanding how existence will always finally fail to satisfy is the essential precondition for generating the altruistic intention.[6] We will have no thought of freeing others from what we ourselves cling to as real and desirable. We've touched on this a bit already and verses still to come will amplify our understanding of it, but we must continually remember that existence is marked by everything changing, good fortune and bad, friends and enemies switching place over and over, karma from the past pushing us from behind, the future just mist in our minds. Nothing here to hold on to. We are the dewdrop on the blade of grass.

There is no efficacy to striving for the supreme state of never changing liberation while clinging to ever changing worldly appearances, so let us understand from the outset that we are not clinging just because we find some aspects of worldly existence

---

6. Jampa Tegchok, *Transforming the Heart*, 151.

pleasing and desirable. No, grasping and clinging function like blinders, or like anesthesia.

To what are we blinding and numbing ourselves? When you note in your mind even a subtle, evanescent tendency of grasping, look further and you will find the thought of self. All grasping is self-grasping. The thought of self is, from the beginning, a misapprehension of reality, a falsity—and, because we are intrinsically one with truth, this falsity, like the fault line in a vessel, means fragility. And thus fear. We must strive constantly to maintain our conviction in solid existence, to protect and reinforce it. And because the thought of self instantly establishes the duality of self-other, we shore up our supposed selfness and react to perceived otherness with all the identity markers we can devise. This is the profound error that underlies xenophobia, misogyny, racism, homophobia, and all forms of "othering," thinking and behavior that solidify and fixate on others as fundamentally, essentially other—as alien. To invalidate beings in this way makes it possible, even desirable and easy, to fear, hate, and harm them. We can do this to ourselves, too, thinking of ourselves as other, somehow wrong or invalid, hating and harming ourselves. All fear is self-grasping, all self-grasping is fear. Without self-grasping, no fear; without fear, no self-grasping. This is the profound teaching of the fearless bodhisattva, Garchen Rinpoche.[7]

All of this is innocently born of error: the erroneous notion of solid, inherently existing selfness in ourselves, in others, in things and phenomena, even in non-material phenomena like thoughts and emotions. This is the error that gives rise to our grasping to worldly appearances and identities.

To loosen our conviction in the world, its pleasures and even its sorrows, which we can see and feel and hear, taste and touch, remember and anticipate, and to turn toward an abstraction called the "supreme state of never changing liberation"—how are we to approach this? You and I, what are we willing to do and not do for

---

7. Garchen Rinpoche, teachings on The Ganges (Mahamudra), July 1, 2018, Garchen Buddhist Institute, Chino Valley, Arizona.

our own release, not even to speak of liberating all? What ransom can we offer, and to whom? I remember a lama recounting how, at a prior lifetime's moment of death, about to attain realization, he was abruptly pulled into another rebirth—"just because of a little attachment thought," he said. Freedom lies on the other side of attachment, whether it be to things, experiences, worldly delights, our dearly cherished miseries, or our own identities, but few want to hear of this and fewer still want to practice it. We can barely tolerate the thought of it. Hear this from Dilgo Khyentse Rinpoche: "If I start teaching about turning away from relatives, possessions, house, land, and other enjoyments of this life, people start to look like donkeys that have been hit on the head with a stick."[8]

Fellow donkeys, let us give away to others what we can and must while reminding ourselves, whenever we forget, that renunciation has meanings far deeper than giving away possessions or abandoning home and family. Gar Rinpoche reminds us always that what is to be renounced are the *causes* of suffering: ignorance of the actual nature of reality, the delusion of selfness, and the afflictive emotions to which these give rise. In the realms of existence, the pleasure and the pain are one coin with two faces, ever flashing back and forth. Clinging to anything, material or experiential, is like grasping at a wave.

Renunciation doesn't mean don't live your life. While the few may abandon worldly life for mountain solitudes, for most of us this present life context is the very best condition in which to practice the essence of renunciation. What we need to become certain of is how we are *using* our human life. Our minds begin to turn toward renunciation when we truly understand our dilemma; caught in the net of our own self-clinging, we desire freedom from this entrapment and its repetitive cycles of suffering. At an even deeper level, though, it is not just escape or relief we are seeking. We receive teachings on the futility of samsara, we recognize exemplars of joy and freedom in our teachers, but there is more. Eventually we are impelled to renunciation by an

8. Dilgo Khyentse, *Heart of Compassion*, 96.

intimation of indwelling truth, sounding the note of ultimate freedom within. Liberation is *the* word that points us to the nature of our endeavors.

Even the most positive ideations are obstacles to liberation when we cling to them. A system of beliefs, for example, can be useful as a stepping stone to direct knowing beyond beliefs, but it can also be a straitjacket. If you have beliefs, let yourself know that they are vehicles, or places of rest in the long journey, or ideals and images that inspire and lead us forward. This is quite different from thinking, "My belief is to be protected and valued at all costs, even at the cost of your life if you disagree with me." To hate or kill someone because she or he believes something you don't is to kill over an opinion. Think how often your cherished opinions waver, shift, and change over time—they are like bubbles! Perhaps if we were to speak more of faith and less of belief there would be fewer wars. People seem willing to die and kill for beliefs, but faith is actually a form of devotion, which in essence is love. True faith doesn't close the heart and mind: it opens them.

What liberates is not the abandoning of things or people or places but of our deluded notions, our untruths and dissimulations, our fears, hatreds, conflicts, and panics—the three and five mindstream poisons: grasping, aggression, ignorance, the basic three, plus pride and jealousy. These conditions of mind are suffering, and freedom from them is not just happiness but liberation from the prison of self, because their root is our clinging to that false notion. Samsara is what we create and re-create this way. But it is like a weaving: cut many of the peripheral threads and you have a smaller weaving with ragged edges; cut the one thread that holds the whole fabric together and it falls apart entirely. That one thread is self-grasping. And what is the sharp knife that will cut that thread? It is bodhicitta. Love for others, for all, spontaneous effulgence of the wisdom understanding the open, empty nature of created appearances.

Cultivate actively and wholeheartedly the altruistic mind, bodhicitta. Think of the loving mother, grasping at worldly happiness for her children. *Her* children. But introduce the thought, "My child represents all children, the cherished children of all beings: may they all have happiness!"—and mind instantly, effortlessly expands beyond self-clinging, abides in love, if only for that instant. Repeat the thought with each instant of grasping and it becomes the mind-path of love.

Self and other are like illusions. Placing illusion-like other before illusion-like self dispels the illusion. Strive for the supreme state of never-changing liberation.

## Discussion: The inner abandonings; renunciation

*I hear and read about the great beings who have abandoned place and possessions in order to pursue spiritual development. Is that really necessary? Should I be trying to do that?*

The great ones abandon people, places, and things because they understand emptiness *and* they understand the seductive, miasmic power of habit, the mind's inertial tendency. They brave the *inner* abandonings: abandoning the afflictive emotions themselves, and most especially abandoning their causes. What are those, again? Our ignorance and confusion about the nature of reality, our grasping to the false notion of inherent existence in self or anything else, and therefore our enmeshment in and obsessive preoccupation with material existence.

*A confusion about grasping. The last time I saw you, you said to me, "Your job right now is to stay alive as long as possible and to be happy." My husband is a better bodhisattva than anyone I know; we are having to do some pretty extreme things to keep me alive.*

Grasping, yes, is the seed for future suffering. On the other hand, you can simply be doing your best to fulfill your commitment, not clutching and grasping but simply recognizing, "Could die tomorrow, could die today, doing my best to stay alive as long as possible and be happy." The difference is like holding a little wild bird with a clutching hand or an open hand. You've already had a lot of practice in holding your life openly: coming to the edge, stepping back; hoping, releasing hope; fearing, releasing fear. You know how to do this. You may not be able to do it in every moment, because as long as you have a body—and I am happy you are still in it—there will be some self-grasping; the body is a compelling point of reference that we keep coming back to. Perhaps your practice now is simply to be completely open-minded about how long this life lasts and in what condition.

*What I'm finding is that as I'm going along in this little dance I'm getting scared, and when I get scared I grasp harder. It kind of fluctuates: back and forth, back and forth [moving hand back and forth].*

Yes. Then I invite you to practice this, just as you are doing: moving your hand back and forth, back and forth. When fear and grasping come, if you can still move your hand, do that. A very good reminder: fear comes and goes, goes and comes, while mind sees both the coming and the going. Then you are your own teacher, because mind recognizing fear is in that instant free of fear. So as your mind recognizes fear and grasping, lean into that awareness. Let your body help you with it: recognize the fear, recognize the grasping, open the hands, and rest in an instant of freedom of mind, like the open space the hands inscribe.

*Some hours of the day I think, "Wow! How did I luck into this?" And other hours of the day, "Okay, I'll do anything to get out of this."*

I'm sure you remember Garchen Rinpoche's instruction: be grateful for every sign that your karmic predispositions are being purified, and so be especially grateful for every experience of physical illness.

*That's the "how did I luck into this?" And then comes the "okay, I'm done, let me out."*

Yes, well, some day you will be done and you will be out; that is certain. But out of what? Out of this body, with its mental and physical suffering, or out of the karma that has brought this wave to your shore? Let your mind relax into its natural awareness. When you're thinking "Wonderful! I must be really purifying because this suffering is intense," mind recognizing that thought is wisdom mind; when you're thinking "I can't stand this another day, I want out, this suffering is beyond me," mind recognizing that thought is also wisdom mind. Rest there. You have nothing to prove, nothing you have to accomplish.

*Could you say more about renunciation and attachment?*

Yes. Free your mind.

Renunciation isn't about our things, it is about our clinging. You can give away all your possessions and weep with chagrin, or you can keep all your possessions and free yourself of attachment to them. Freedom of the mind is freedom of the *mind*. No matter what worldly circumstance you're confronted with, you don't have to be caught in it mentally. Living in the world, we live in the framework of karma, so you have to deal with the results of your past karma and you have to take responsibility for the karma you're creating now. But you don't have to allow your mind to be controlled by mundane circumstance, the columns of figures, the harsh speech, your childhood sorrows, the political issues of the day. Remember your bodhisattva aspiration and let the mind rest there, even for an instant. Glance into the sky and recall your true nature, open and empty like space. You can be reciting mantra, praying that your work will help beings, contemplating a teaching you've heard, resting in the stillness between thoughts or words. The mind can be free—as it is, intrinsically, from the beginning.

We're all confused by materiality. We all have worldly ideas, preoccupations, and attachments, and most of us are going to be in worldly circumstances for most of our lives—so we need to establish ourselves in the certainty that we don't have to leave the world in order to free our minds. But we do have to change our way of being with our minds. This is why we are constantly learning, reflecting, and meditating "in order to free ourselves and others from the ocean of cyclic existence."

You can be a hundred percent practicing Dharma while living in the world, and you can live in the world at one with the essence of Dharma. Gar Rinpoche gave me insight into the meaning of renunciation when he told me, "Don't think in terms of bringing Dharma into your life. Lift your life into the Dharma."

**Verse 10.** When mothers who have loved you since beginningless time are suffering, what good is your own happiness? Therefore, give rise to bodhicitta in order to liberate infinite sentient beings. This is the way of a bodhisattva.

Now we come to the critical point: generating the aspiration to free all beings from ignorance, the cause of suffering, to establish all in the supreme state. To this aspiration and path we now commit ourselves, in this and all moments and lifetimes to come, until we attain the heart of enlightenment. This is bodhicitta. To realize ultimate bodhicitta, our practice on the bodhisattva path is relative bodhicitta, in its two aspects: aspiring and actualizing. Aspiring bodhicitta points us toward the result; actualizing bodhicitta brings us there.

Those who have realized this path sing the praises of bodhicitta. As I follow the path I, too, sing the praises of bodhicitta: wish-fulfilling jewel, universal medicine, mother of buddhas; enlightenment seed; ground, path, and fruit of all spiritual longing and aspiration; wisdom's mirror, light of the heart, warmth of the mind. There is nothing more precious to me than bodhicitta. Not even the lama? Shining like the sun, melting the ice-blocks of our minds, cherishing every being absolutely, unwavering in aspiration for us, unstoppable in acts of courage and kindness for beings and our world, always pointing to the open, expansive nature of all phenomena and all being, the lama *is* bodhicitta: love-emptiness unbounded and potent, timeless and vivid, right here, right now. I aspire to be like my lama, a liberator of beings. The way of bodhicitta is the path I follow in the lama's footsteps. I know it will bring me to the ultimate freedom—and that in one being's realization all beings leap free.

The unrepayable kindness of the lama calls us to extend to all beings the same love, compassion, wisdom, patience, and insistence that the lama extends to us: ultimately to attain buddhahood for their sake. The unrepayable kindness of our parents—of all our life companions—has given us life, care, kindness, challenges, tolerance, laughter, tender ministration to our hurts, strong encouragement when we falter and fear, firm correction when we err. Not all parents and relations are all of this all the time; like us, they have been limited in their love and kindness by their own ignorance and fallibility. But over and over again, throughout our transmigrations through time, space, and form, countless parents have given us countless lives, bodies to wear, so it is said that all beings have been our mother, our kind parents, who have loved us "since beginningless time." I think of all those from whom I have received bodies and care, as a dung beetle, a wolf, a person; if they are suffering, do I not want to relieve them, to establish them in happiness?

Generating bodhicitta is the third foundation level of our training. There is little possibility of generating the intention to love and liberate others while still seeking primarily our own satisfactions, or to think of the happiness of others except in the limited terms in which we think of ours, so let us liberate ourselves that we may eventually help to free others. It's really that simple—but the commitment involved is absolute.

Buddhist traditions offer a formal bodhisattva vow, taken after one takes refuge in the Three Jewels; thus for Buddhists it is a Buddhist vow. But you don't have to be a Buddhist, or even a human being, to love, to care about suffering beings, to generate bodhicitta, to realize wisdom, to be a bodhisattva. A bodhisattva can take any form in order to help beings. Many who come to the Buddhadharma and other wisdom traditions, and many who simply walk an unnamed path of goodness, are already bodhisattvas, whether they know this consciously or not—in every lifetime seeking to benefit beings.

There are many skillful means to help us generate the relative bodhicitta that we recognize as love and compassion. In verse II we will study two powerful practices, equanimity and tonglen (exchanging self for others), in some detail. Here I want to mention three simple, profound practices of mind that clear and nourish the inner terrain in which the seed of relative bodhicitta grows:

- Practicing gratitude. Giving thanks for literally everything we encounter and experience, whether we see it as positive or negative. This trains the mind to recognize interdependence and to see what is, simply and directly, without elaboration.

- Noticing and contemplating examples of the love and compassion of beings great and small, human and non-human, present and past. This shows us both the simplicity and the grandeur of the altruistic mind and its expressions, inspiring and encouraging us, strengthening our gratitude, and turning our mind to the potentials—the always already present and potent seeds—of love and compassion in ourselves.

- Contemplating the sufferings of ourselves and others. This reveals to us what suffering actually is, reduces our grasping and repulsion in relation to particular experiences or examples of suffering, and heats up our determination to liberate ourselves and others.

There is a crucial point about motivation to remember here: relative bodhicitta is the *reflection and expression* of absolute bodhicitta. Our human experiences of relative love and compassion spring from and reflect their essence nature, while still being limited by our identification with materiality. Thus we need to develop a very clear understanding of the importance of motivation and aspiration, as Tokme's teachings make clear. Truth is everywhere, all-pervading and universal, and those who seek truth with their whole hearts and minds will find truth, whole. As practitioners of the bodhisattva way, we will eventually realize absolute love and compassion—*if* that is our wholehearted aspiration and commitment.

## Discussion: Aspiration and desire; the notion of spiritual failure

*Please say more about aspiration.*

There are many exoteric paths (outer paths, formal paths) that we may take in different lifetimes, as we move in and through relative reality, but I think the one universal esoteric or inner path is the path to ultimate realization, to truth. If a being does not in some way understand this as the highest potential of life, then the goals and activities of that life will be constrained—as if a canopy hovers above and we are content to remain beneath it. The altruistic aspiration pierces that canopy. If you hold the highest purpose, you are moving in some degree of alignment with that regardless of how your activities appear. You might be a religious scholar, somber of mien, or a ditch digger, mind one with love-emptiness. You might be a lawyer or politician, outwardly contending, inwardly always seeking ways to foster harmony and right relationship, or a warrior, cultivating unconditional love for the beings called enemies, even those trying to kill you, even those you kill.

We step onto the path because we are seeking, and we must always know and remember that we are seeking not in response to lack or absence but in resonance with *presence*. If this were not the case there would be no spiritual longing; we do not long for what we do not know, have never known or even heard of. Longing is a form of knowing. Gar Rinpoche has said, "The transcendent knowledge *inherent within this mind* must be awakened." Longing thus gives rise to aspiration—to awaken that which is always already complete and alight within. We practice the outer, in the dimension of forms, to recall and stir the indwelling essence. Don't allow yourself to fixate on forms. Go for essence. Be true to that.

*What is the difference between aspiration and desire?*

Altruistic aspiration lifts us; it is for others, thus essentially of love. Desire based in self-concern furthers self-concern, deepening the confusion. Desire can also be for others' wellbeing but will tend to have material points of reference still rooted in self-interest. Personality-based desire is related to attraction, grasping, avidity, and to worldly concerns; altruistic desire can open the door to limitless aspiration. Wishing can also be altruistically oriented, but it's a rather flabby intention. We might wish that all sentient beings could be relieved of suffering, but how much energy is there in that? How much dedication is driving that wish until we take the step of commitment? "I will do whatever I can for the happiness of all." The wish might even arise in a moment of poignant recognition of beings' suffering, but without the energy of commitment it doesn't *fuel* us. Aspiration throws your heart over the fence. Really: your heart. And where your heart goes you will follow. Aspiration is altruistic love and dedicated intention, lifting you out of self-concern into the illumined space of selfless love.

*What about desire in the sense of "clutching desire"?*

Clutching desire is clutching. Even when it looks like "spiritual" desire. For a while we may grasp for and cling to teachers, teachings, empowerments, practices, retreats, ideas of liberation and realization, but ultimately we will give up grasping for these high-minded things as well, because the afflictive emotions, even when expressed in spiritual context and modes, are still afflictive emotions. However, for the time being I think it's better for me to long for your awakening and mine than to long for a potato chip! If you have desires, entertain those that move you in the direction to which you aspire for the benefit of all. Ultimately, we will give up the afflictive emotions themselves—slowly by slowly, as a dear lama used to put it. Slowly by slowly, we move toward the point where we reach an astonishing realization: that we actually desire to be free of our limitations, our emotional afflictions, our compulsive, disordered thinking. We may not consciously cling to the emotions of hatred and anger, but we turn to them instantly when provoked, stoking self-righteousness and pride, and for a long time we cling to the emotions of desire and clinging, actually savoring their poignant, heartbreaking sweetness. As for our ignorance, our elaborations, our concepts and theories and explanations and justifications, we think they represent our own excellent grasp on reality.

*What about acceptance, contentment? Is that important for a spiritual practitioner?*

Yes, it's good to be content with and grateful for the circumstances and conditions in which we find ourselves, even when they are difficult, even when we know we need to change them or leave them. If not, we are not fully present, we're saying no to present reality, and we're in a hopeless situation if we're saying no to reality, to what simply is. The situation as it is—this is always and only the point from which change or happiness becomes possible. When you're unhappy with your circumstances, the first thing to do is just what your mother told you: literally, count the blessings in your life, relationships, heart, and mind—and turn to lift someone else from difficulty. If it is necessary or beneficial to change your circumstances, then you can try to do so. With no attachment to outcome.

*I have read that there are forty-seven ways a bodhisattva can fail and I've done forty-eight of them, but the one thing I can hang onto is that I have not given up on myself yet.*

There is really only one way a bodhisattva can fail, and that is to give up on a sentient being, to abandon a sentient being. The intention to liberate every being is a commitment of mind, the central commitment of the bodhisattva, and that commitment includes never abandoning oneself. Never to abandon a sentient being means never to abandon love and compassion, never to abandon your understanding of the true nature of reality, and thus never to abandon certainty that every being is of that nature.

*Is it that you're living with that as your intention?*

Yes. I think of it sometimes as never letting go of the thread that from lifetime to lifetime draws us through—and that thread is our commitment to truth, indissolubly one with love. We're born, we die, and in between we're all going to have suffering and confusion and ecstasy and all the rest of it. Through all of life's experiences, from the beginning to the end, hold to the thread of this clear intention and knowing.

I should also note that in a given lifetime a being's purpose—yours, too—might not look like whatever you imagine a spiritual purpose ought to look like. I once knew a woman who appeared to be quite materialistic. She had the shoes, the latest electronics, and in her retail career she dedicated herself to selling lots of stuff to lots of people for lots of money. But she had no confusion about the purpose of a human life and the quality of mind that we call love. I eventually came to understand that in this life she was learning to master materiality. Very instructive to me, sitting on my cushion, reciting my prayers, hoping and striving to "transcend" material existence. Clearly, I did not understand the Two Truths—and their nondual union.

Find within yourself the source of your dissatisfaction with existence; find within yourself the source of your longing. That is divine dissatisfaction, wellspring of spiritual aspiration. Once you find your aspiration, I urgently implore you to give yourself to it one-hundred percent. Don't hold back—because true aspiration will lead you to its accomplishment. If you don't have the aspiration, you won't be seeking to accomplish it; if you do have the aspiration, you will be following it. Even if you only have a simple practice and very little time to give to it, you can make tremendous progress toward fulfilling your aspiration in the Dharma—because it is what you do with your mind that is the essence of practice, and your mind is with you twenty-four hours a day. But your spiritual aspiration has to *rule* you. You have to be given over entirely to it. Then every worldly circumstance you encounter becomes a practice vehicle for you.

# CHAPTER FOUR

# BODHICITTA, RELATIVE AND ABSOLUTE (VERSES 11-24)

## Exchanging self for others: Equanimity, tonglen, and the great love

**Verse 11.** All suffering without exception comes from seeking your own happiness. The perfect buddhas are born from the altruistic mind. Therefore, truly exchange your own happiness for the suffering of others. This is the way of a bodhisattva.

This teaching is the heart of the bodhisattva path. Of all the profound and perfect pith instructions given in *The 37 Bodhisattva Practices*, verse 11 is the essence, the key to understanding and mastering them all. We will do well to take the teaching in this verse simply and literally, just as it is, apply it within our minds, give voice to its meaning in our speech, and let it inform all our actions.

All suffering has but one cause: grasping to "self." Each and every instance of self-grasping is a cause of suffering and each and every experience of suffering arises from that single cause. To liberate ourselves from suffering, then, means to abandon our compulsive clinging to self, both the illusion of its true existence and our ongoing subjective experience of selfness. With each degree of freedom from self-fixation comes a corresponding degree of amplitude in our inclination and capacity to notice, consider, and care about others—which, wonderfully, further undercuts the self-seeking conviction and tendency. This is the relative experience of altruistic mind, gradually evolving and maturing.

No self-fixation means also no other-fixation. Construe no "self" and no "other" arises. Thus crumbles the only basis for the afflictive emotional reactions that lay down karmic causes of suffering; for othering, with its made-up fears and hatreds; and for the wars of minds, relationships, clans, and nations—because their root cause is no more. When we come to the point of tolerating the idea of the empty, open, clear, luminous nature of reality, and then eventually have direct experience of this, it is as if one blink of an eye opens to our view the entire universe. When duality collapses, the nondual is revealed as infinite openness and clarity, spontaneously effulgent with compassionate love, selfless and otherless. In the nondual there is not even the name of self or other. This is the ultimate altruistic mind, birth chamber of the perfect buddhas.

Exchanging your own happiness for the suffering of others? The meaning is inherent in what we have already seen. We give up fixating on our own happiness *in order to* cultivate love and compassion for others—a muscular, vibrant love and compassion, knowing others' suffering as our own, longing for their freedom with and even before our own. Now we begin examining—closely, personally, intimately—how to practice, how to live and grow bodhicitta here in our present conditions and circumstances, here in the realms of existence. This is the profound bodhisattva training offered by our teacher, Tokme Zangpo, who has surely lived these lessons just as we are to do, in order to accomplish what he accomplished.

Simply to give rise to the bodhisattva aspiration is immense in significance and power. Though we may be meeting the word bodhicitta and its meaning for the very first time, we can in fact generate that highest altruistic intention right this minute, and instantly it can take root in our mindstream. It seems that even hearing of bodhicitta begins to melt the heart-mind hardened and occluded in self-grasping. To imagine that we could love every being as much as we love those most dear to us, that we could care about even one, and then all, even more than we care about ourselves—in that moment we are astonished and illumined, subtly and deeply changed. This is so even for one who rejects outright the very idea of others-before-self. Just that shocking thought, now in the mind's continuum, will continue to exert its subtle, profound, magnetizing influence—because this is truth, and truth is at all times and in all ways more potent than non-truth.

The aspiring bodhisattva commits to generating the altruistic intention; the actualizing bodhisattva acts to accomplish that intention. Having planted the aspiration in our mindstream, we now turn our minds and activities to bringing it forth. The gardener hauls rocks and prepares the soil, removes what impedes or rots the tender seedling, adds what nourishes, and in working the garden walks pathways among the growing plants. In like manner, we cultivate bodhicitta in the garden of our mind by engaging in the activities in which bodhisattvas engage—and the stepping stones of the path coalesce beneath our feet as we walk.

Though actualizing is gradual, we are now at the pivotal moment: turning altruistic aspiration and intention to committed action. It is at this very point that we are affirming: "I will take up and follow the practices of the bodhisattva, in order to awaken fully the potential within."

What is in the way of our actualizing the bodhisattva aspiration? Only our illusion-based self-grasping, our self-concern. Not our wholesome self-respect and not our love and compassion for ourselves as one among all beings, but the self motive and its dualistic fixation. In its external manifestations it can be easy to recognize, but it is also very subtle and both powerful and obdurate. It is this point of essential identification with our perceived existence, and with existence itself, that motivates all our deluded, unskillful, and harmful actions of body, speech, and mind. But this deep, pervasive mental grasping at illusory selfness is itself insubstantial. Grasper, grasped, and grasping have no inherent existence. Empty of self-ness, we and all phenomena, including all our apparent ignorance and confusion, are intrinsically free.

Let us not think in terms of annihilating or destroying the illusion-like self, the so-called ego. That is a murderous impulse. Have compassion for your "ego"; it is a deluded friend, born of innocent misapprehension and ignorance.[1] Gar Rinpoche once told me that even after penetrating the illusion of solidity, as long as there is a body there is some clinging to the idea of self, because the body is a point of reference to which the mind habitually returns. He also frequently reminds us that cultivating mind seeking to benefit others is the path of all buddhas, past, present, and future—because that mind's essence is love, which invisibly, gradually dissolves the dualistic delusion, together with its cause.

Actualizing the bodhisattva aspiration relies on both inner and outer skillful means. Both are based on the desired result. For example, we may think about and practice with the intellectual concepts of universal love and compassion long before we are aware of their activity within. Mind thus prepared becomes, little by little, like a finely tuned instrument, resonating to higher and more subtle frequencies. In the same way, reciting the mantra of Tara or another deity figure is first an activity dedicated to realizing compassion, with a visualized form and so on, while eventually the practice reveals mantra and deity within, compassion spontaneous and all-pervading. Both outer and inner methods rely on the always already present truth we are seeking to realize, so they are really more remembrance than method. Nothing new happening, just recalling what is. Over and over, as recalling subtly becomes resonating, which subtly becomes realizing.

●

---

1. The terms ego and self are insufficiently nuanced in English; they can have slightly different connotations in spiritual, psychological, and general parlance. In all three domains, though, both concepts refer to ideations of inherently existing entities and their characteristics.

In the Buddhadharma, gradual, purposeful training in relative bodhicitta characterizes the traditional path of the bodhisattva. Here, we will now take up the practices of equanimity and tonglen. With equanimity practice we create a clear basis for actualizing bodhicitta: recognizing the existence and the equal worth of all beings. At the outset, you are simply trying and training to see everyone as at least being worthy of your attention, while at the next level beings do have your attention: you are wanting them to be happy and free of suffering. You are beginning to develop altruism in your view, and this makes possible the profound compassion practice of tonglen: giving and receiving, exchanging one's own happiness for the suffering of others. The third level is the great love, empty and luminous radiance of mind's true nature.

## Equanimity: Basis for entraining selfless love

All beings have buddha nature, the unchanging, indestructible essence of all phenomena. On the basis of ignorance, however, we consider ourselves more important than others, and then, among those we hold dear, we hold some more and some less dear, while also disliking these more than those, and so on. Self-reference creates preference: we are constantly categorizing and ranking according to what makes us feel good about ourselves—or bad about ourselves, if that is our habit or our default stance in life. Making subjective distinctions reinforces our constructed identity and our belief in its solidity, and thus the habit of distinctions based on self-reference ripens, in repeating patterns of like-dislike, attraction-aversion, love-hate, unfolding dramas of confusion in one fictive narrative after another.

As we parade under our banners of partiality, compassion is most likely to arise for those on "our side." Such compassion, real enough as we experience it, is in fact highly relative to circumstance, preference, and change, as our minds flip from like to dislike, back and forth, back and forth, like loose shutters in the wind. Moment to moment and lifetime to lifetime, due to emptiness, ignorance, and karma, friends and enemies are constantly changing places. Therefore, recognizing the *essential equality* of those we see as friends or enemies is critical to generating compassion and love for all beings—compassion and love that are objective, reflecting the actual nature of beings, rather than subjective and emotional, reflecting partiality and limitation based on the illusion of inherent selfness and otherness. In Dharma usage, this is equanimity: mind stable in clear knowing of the essential equality of all beings and phenomena. One essence, one taste: the primordially pure.

Mind of equanimity comprehends all beings as worthy. In this mind bodhicitta naturally arises and we find ourselves friendly, affectionate, and welcoming to all. Until we stabilize and gain confidence in this view, we intentionally, actively train in equanimity, making beings equal in our conscious thinking, our speech, and our actions. This will open us to actually recognizing each and every being as a dear relative.

The practice goes like this: In your mind, place, visualize, or imagine three beings directly in front of you: Person A, Person B, and Person C. For Person A you already have high positive regard, respect, appreciation, affection, love; think here of the one you love most in this life, so important and precious to you. Person B is someone whom you don't know or know only slightly, toward whom you are neutral, feeling neither attraction nor aversion. This is not ambivalence but rather a kind of suspension or balance, not leaning toward either positive or negative. This might be someone you have just heard of or seen in passing, for example. And finally, Person C, whom you actively and intensely dislike, disdain, resent, or even hate.[2]

Now you are going to practice sequentially.

- With Person A, for whom you already have strong, positive, warm, cherishing feelings, intentionally call forth and consciously experience these feelings. Embrace this person

---

2. In our equanimity practice, the entities we're focusing on as A, B, and C don't have to be human beings or any other kinds of beings; they could be relationships, situations, images, sounds, experiences, and so on—but as our interactions with humans often seem to be the most challenging to our equanimity, good to focus here at the outset.

in your mind, recalling all A's goodness and affection for you and the joys of this loving connection. Allow your appreciative, grateful emotions to well up in warmth and deep love for this being, and rest in this happy state for a while. In each session reaffirm, generate, and enjoy for Person A all the gratitude, warmth, and love you are capable of in that moment.

- Now turn to Person B, whom you neither like nor dislike, and intentionally cultivate for B the same positive, warm, loving, appreciative regard you have for A, until you recognize B also as close and important to you, until you hold B as dear in your mind and heart as Person A. In each session, generate for B as much gratitude, warmth, appreciation, compassion, kindness, and love as you can.

- Finally, do the same with Person C, the object of your active dislike, jealousy, or hatred. Recognize that the other face of the hateful mind-state is its opposite potential: the same affection, loving kindness, and consideration that you hold for Person A and that you are becoming able to hold for Person B. Consider further how Person C is actually helping you to see your own negativity and thus be able to purify it: what kindness! Generate the desire and intention to repay C's kindness with your own kind thoughts and acts, and practice on this in each session, humbly, sincerely, and gratefully, until you are bringing to Person C the same warmth of caring and love you feel for A and B, like a basket overflowing with goodness and delight, with gratitude and deep appreciation.

- Practice over and over, until Persons C, B, and A are genuinely equal in your mind and feelings.

Although it might initially seem impossible to practice this way with someone you actively dislike or even hate, it can actually be easier than with someone you don't know or toward whom you have only a neutral attitude. If you have intense negative feelings about someone, you are already in an intimate relationship. Preoccupied with that person, you wonder what he thinks about you. Am I going to see her walking down the street? What am I going to say, what is he going to say? You're obsessed; it's like a love affair, but it's a hate affair. In the same way that love can turn abruptly to hate, so can hate, an afflictive emotion, suddenly clear to reveal love, the natural state.

You will sometimes feel some success or progress in your practice and sometimes not. Just keep practicing. When you see your actual thoughts, feelings, reactions, and behavior showing signs of change, the practice is working for you. When you find yourself truly desiring and acting to reciprocate Person A's many kindnesses to you, your practice is stirring your heart and moving your limbs. When you respond with genuine warm-heartedness upon thinking about Persons B and C, you will know your practice is taking root. When, upon seeing Person B or C—and especially when Person C presents you with the same challenges as before—you actually feel delight, joy, appreciation, you will know you are developing equanimity. Continue to practice, day to day, on and off the cushion, with whatever persons A, B, and C come across your path or mind. Then expand your practice to include not just humans but other kinds of beings, as well as situations, circumstances, experiences, memories, and so on.

Equanimity practice seems simple, and it is; as if it could require only ten minutes of your time, and it could. But I urge you to practice on equanimity over and over again until you sweat, until tears well up and flow, until your mind genuinely holds all beings in the vast, irresistible embrace of unconditional love. Deeper than your ordinary awareness the warmth of bodhicitta is melting your partiality and preference, based on self-grasping and self-other thinking. You will gradually begin to experience, not just in your mind but also in your daily life, not only the peace of true equanimity but indeed a genuine sense of intimacy and friendship with all you meet.

## Tonglen[3]

Completely exchanging one's own happiness for the suffering of others—tonglen, in Tibetan—is also known as giving and taking: giving your wellbeing and happiness and taking the suffering of others. In beginning tonglen practice, there is conscious intention involved. Aware of another's suffering, you want to take that suffering away; that is compassion. Aware of another's unhappiness, you desire that they enjoy happiness; that is love. We are familiar with these caring, generous mind states in ourselves, the motivation to relieve suffering and give happiness. We have probably also, at some time in our lives, experienced this compassion so powerfully that we would willingly have given all our possessions, our own wellbeing, and even our lives, for the benefit of another, and when we have heard of others doing so we have been stirred and inspired. Over time, as you engage sincere, continuous practice on relative bodhicitta, your capacity to love will deepen and expand, and in great love the exchange of self for other is as natural and effortless as breathing.

The practice of tonglen, motivated by love and compassion, is a pristine, powerful skillful means to deepen and lift our bodhicitta and to relieve the sufferings of beings. Garchen Rinpoche has often said to me, when I have been caught in any degree of confusion or suffering, "Practice tonglen." Don't focus on your own suffering but instead *use* your suffering—to liberate the suffering of all. Rinpoche also assures us that the benefits of tonglen are actual, not metaphorical: that the suffering of beings comes naturally to those who are profoundly cultivating bodhicitta, and in bodhicitta that suffering is purified. This is tonglen.

Remember that tonglen and all practices of relative bodhicitta rely upon the seed of absolute bodhicitta always already within; if this were not so, there would be nothing from which relative bodhicitta could grow. We don't somehow acquire sublime

---

3. A tonglen teaching from H. E. Garchen Rinpoche, given to him in prison by his root lama, Khenpo Munsel, is included in Appendix A.

qualities from outside. Spiritual friends, teachers, teachings, and practice are helping us to sweep away our obscurations, revealing absolute bodhicitta, the ultimate state, radiant and all-pervading.

When offering tonglen, you can think of specific beings or situations of trouble or suffering, and in your mind's eye place them directly in front of you. Arouse in yourself intense compassion and love, stirring a fervent desire and intention to take away their suffering and to give them your own wellbeing and happiness. Imagine or sense bodhicitta in your spiritual heart-mind as warmth, a flame, a transforming radiance. As you breathe in, draw into the warmth and light of ultimate bodhicitta within you all the suffering, nonvirtue, difficulty, unhappiness, need, or pain of the being with whom you are practicing. Instantly, spontaneously, effortlessly, when the suffering touches bodhicitta it is transformed, becoming entirely one with absolute bodhicitta in your heart-mind, from which now radiate all goodness, benefit, and love, in whatever ways or forms those beings need.

Remember that there is no intrinsic, solid selfness to you or your activity, to those for whom you practice, or to their suffering. Specifically, there is no "you" who is "doing" anything whatsoever. To think otherwise is a form of self-clinging, of course, and as you practice to benefit another, your own confused attachment to selfness is also being naturally purified. This is the subtle, inconceivable power of bodhicitta.

It can be very helpful, especially when beginning tonglen practice, to sense or imagine yourself not as your present body but as insubstantial, rainbow-like: no solidity, just radiant openness, pure love, into which the ignorance and suffering of another is effortlessly drawn. Effortlessly, effortlessly. You don't have to think anything about it or do anything with it. When obscuration meets bodhicitta it is instantly one with bodhicitta, and bodhicitta is what returns to those for whom you are offering tonglen.

Tonglen "rides astride the breath." On the inbreath we take the suffering of another, it dissolves in bodhicitta, and on the outbreath flows all that is needed. So tonglen is as natural as your breathing: nothing fancy, just in and out, the way you usually breathe. Any time, any place, in and out, in and out—effortless, profoundly efficacious, and always available. On every inbreath you could be taking the suffering of entire worlds or that of a single insect. As long as we are alive we are breathing, so as long as we are alive—*and* with our very last breath—we have the means to offer this great generosity practice of love for the liberation of beings.

Now, for a moment, picture our motherly planet—experiencing war, disease, famine, earthquakes, volcanoes, tsunamis. Allow yourself to be consciously aware of all this great mother provides, and then be aware of the difficulties she herself experiences, even in our own era, even right in this present moment. You might imagine her sufferings as a gray light or smoky substance, or form no image at all. Just take it all in. Nice, easy, ordinary breath, and the suffering flows into and becomes one with bodhicitta in your spiritual heart. Breathe out and the entire planet is illumined in perfect love and compassion, within and without. What could be easier than this, or more powerful?

Exchanging self for others kindles relative bodhicitta, altruistic love, burning away the afflictions of dualistic fixation, that deep confusion about self and other. Deluded clinging to notions of your own solid existence and any confused ideas you may have about the nature of reality transmute in bodhicitta, leaving only what is always already here: love-wisdom, pristine, radiant openness. If from now until the time you attain the heart of enlightenment you practice in this way, you will be undeluded in your intention, undeluded in your practice, and undeluded in your accomplishment.

Gar Rinpoche says, "What is natural comes easily." Tonglen, exchanging self for others, is easy. It is ease itself, really. What may not be easy is remembering to do it, because we're so caught up in ourselves. One moment we have the highest intention and the firm, happy resolve to offer tonglen over and over, and a few hours later we realize we completely forgot about it! So we practice "on the cushion," meaning a formal practice not commingled with other activities, to develop our tonglen mind, reflexes, and muscles. And we also practice while walking down the street, doing the dishes, at the airport, in the office, in the body parts section of the grocery store. Bring tonglen anywhere and everywhere, any time and all the time. Whenever you are reminded of suffering, confusion, need—of anything that isn't perfect clarity and wellbeing—at that very moment, just with one breath in, one breath out, offer the exchange. Then continue with your regular activities. Reminded again, again breathe in and out, taking the suffering, returning love and compassion. You don't "make" something of it: you're just breathing. You don't think or say to someone, "Now I'm practicing tonglen for you, so please sit there and be grateful while I purify your suffering." That would be absurd: you're not purifying anyone's suffering, you're just breathing. It is bodhicitta that is purifying the suffering, theirs and yours, in the open, empty nature of being.

An especially powerful point of tonglen practice: In your own moments of illness, fear, despair—and the more intense your suffering the better, for this practice—offer tonglen, taking all the suffering of all beings who are experiencing what is so painful for you and returning to all the great freedom, the great love. I sometimes offer the exchange with hands together at the heart, then opening to form a tray on which I place all my suffering and its causes, as I speak these words: "May mine be sufficient. May my suffering be sufficient to liberate all."

How is this possible? The suffering is like an illusion, as are we: never solid to begin with. When illusory practitioner vows to liberate illusory beings from illusion of suffering, absolute love pervades space-like emptiness, expressing as illusory bodhisattva performing illusion of practice for illusory condition of suffering. In the purity of the three spheres the illusion, never having arisen, dissolves in an instant. The great secret of tonglen practice is just this: the great love, bodhicitta, reveals no self, no other, no suffering.

This, then, is the core practice of bodhisattvas: the practice of tonglen, formal or secret. Core, because exchanging self for others is the natural expression of love, and love is the core, the very heart of the path.

# The great love

*Let compassion mount the mighty steed of love—*
*and turn them loose!*
*Manes streaming, churning flanks gleaming,*
*eyes fierce with freedom,*
*the whole lost feral herd will follow them home.*

Love: this is the essence of Dharma. Caring concern and compassion, these are bodhicitta, committed to liberating beings from suffering. Mounted on the mighty steed of love, bodhicitta is fully charged: compelling, irresistible, wholly and irreversibly given, pouring forth with no let or hindrance. Unstoppable. This is passion not as afflictive emotion but passion as entirety: the entirety of body, speech, and mind given for freedom, for truth, from now to the heart of enlightenment.

Absolute love is uncreated and undying, changeless, non-referential, and omnipotent. It pervades all and contains all. It is this with which we are breathing in and out, all the time. It is the basis, the method, and the completion of all our longings, all our aspirations.

In a worldly sense we would like to love and be loved, and to have a life filled with meaningful, loving relationships. That is precious—and it pales in the brilliance of even one moment dedicated to loving all beings without distinction or regard to outcome. Our purpose is not to be loved: our purpose is to love.

As our bodhicitta rises ever higher and higher we will increasingly understand that while we live in relative reality our aspirations reach to the infinite. What matters is that we know reality as it is, and that we love each and all with neither reference nor condition, neither expectation nor limitation, vastly and profoundly, in bodhicitta. This is impersonal love, the great love—the natural expression of emptiness. Impersonal doesn't mean you don't love the one, but that you love the one in the many and the many in the one: the one as one face of the infinite. Impersonal love is love without clinging. How will you love all while clinging to one, or even to many? To abandon the clinging is to *free* the loving—to expand into love for all.

We can practice this intention in our relationships or not. If we don't, no matter how sublime our behavior appears, we are still practicing delusion and affliction. If we do, we will not inhabit with conventional mind even the relationships in which we appear most "normal."

For a bodhisattva to have easy, peaceful relationships is very nice, but it doesn't necessarily come with the territory, or at least not right away. In fact, your relationships may sometimes seem to become rockier, both because you will be purifying karma through spiritual practice and because you are no longer thinking and acting conventionally. In bodhicitta, with some understanding of emptiness and karma, we seek to bring beings to true happiness, not just to the ever changing smorgasbord of conventional pleasures. Some adjustments will be called for in the way those practicing to abandon attachment live and work with those practicing attachment. I think that with goodwill and mutual respect pathways of right relationship will reveal themselves.

The bodhisattva is not withdrawing from but coming always closer to the world, illusions of separation pierced by suffering and love. At the time of the devastating Asian tsunami of 2005, a dear yogi friend wrote from there, asking in despair, "What do I do about this suffering and anguish, my own and that of others? How do we cope with the great anguish that we feel because of the anguish of others?" This is a profound question for us. As we develop in bodhicitta, we become more caring, more compassionate, more loving; the heart and mind become more tender and open—and we feel ever more keenly the anguish of beings, in this time, this world, and throughout time and worlds. That is our heart-mind opening to its inseparability from the hearts and minds of all beings and all existence. Our commitment and our practice open us to the cries of the world so we can know we are in no way separate. That is the wellspring of bodhicitta. Unbearable compassion—that's what we're *supposed* to be in. We mustn't get stuck in mourning or despair, or even in philosophizing. Feel the pain, let the heart break open, and love bigger.

We have spoken extensively about self-grasping as the only obstacle to realizing great love and compassion. Alone in my little prayer place one evening, I began to weep, sharply assailed by recognizing the gap between my aspiration and my present state. From my heart I cried out aloud to Garchen Rinpoche, "How will I ever dissolve this egregious ego?" Those were my exact words. Instantly came back his exact words: "Your ego will dissolve in your love for others."

## Discussion: Suffering and compassion; attachment and love; equanimity and tonglen

*Seems as if I was a better practitioner some years ago, but of course that's false: I'm just noticing my self-grasping more clearly. It's a bit painful.*

It's true that when we turn the light on we see more clearly what's been festering there in the back of the closet, but if you don't see it, you won't do anything about it.

*So I should be grateful for that.*

Yes, and there is also this: While there are many practices to generate compassion, and it is wise and beneficial to do those practices that are especially meaningful to you, one of the most important practices for generating compassion is to recognize your own fault-ridden, deluded, grasping, confused, suffering self—and to recognize all this simply as suffering. When you see your own condition clearly, compassion naturally arises for others: "Oh, they're just as deluded as I am! And it is just as painful for them." It's a great shock. We don't realize how crazy we are, and we don't realize that everybody else is just as crazy for the same crazy reasons: because we're all clinging to this idea that we are a self that has to be protected and elaborated at all costs and in all situations. And really, it doesn't exist, so we are all deluded, flailing and thrashing about.

When we recognize our actual condition of confusion and travail *simply as suffering*, easily we have compassion for both others and ourselves. When you see directly that you yourself are caught in anger and that anger is suffering, it's so much easier from then on to have compassion for others who are angry—because their anger, too, is just suffering, and you know what that is like. While you have the self-righteous view that your anger is not deluded but that those who annoy you are just annoying people, how can you have compassion for others who are poisoned by their anger? Until you recognize that you yourself are drinking that poison, you think it is fine wine. Until you recognize that your lust and avarice, your strangulating attachments, are actually a source of suffering for you now and in the future, you don't have much compassion for other people's attachment. In fact, you want to feed it; you think it's going to make them happy, because that's how we think about the things we're grasping for.

Thus compassion arises from that painful place of recognizing how deluded we ourselves are, that we ourselves are in the state of suffering. I don't know that it can arise authentically from any other place. As long as we don't actually know suffering and its true causes, personally, directly, experientially, I don't know if our compassion is really reliable, rather than tinged with commiseration or pity, highly relative to circumstance and therefore conditional and wavering. What I do know about myself is that it is my willingness to see clearly my own delusion, my own suffering, my own confusion, my own aversion, my own grasping, that allows me to know authentic compassion for those same delusions in others. So please don't turn your face away from your own suffering. Look right at it. Look right at it—and don't blink first.

Examining the circumstances of your life for the causes of your confusion and suffering is likely to deepen fixation on illusions of materiality. Material circumstances and conditions, such as relationship, history, or biology, may explain relative influences, but conditions are conditioning, not causation. The true causes of our suffering are the seeds of confusion in our mindstream, laid down by our own actions of body, speech, and mind. Dharma teachings tell us, very clearly, that confusion and suffering arise from nonvirtue and happiness and good fortune arise from virtue. This is the fundamental principle of karma we must understand or we have no reliable basis for discerning good cause from bad. It doesn't require a belief system; it requires careful investigation and observation. The work of the spiritual practitioner is always to refine our own mind, like the rough stone in the tumbler, ever finer and finer, to reveal the jewel.

*You have talked a number of times about distinguishing between attachment and genuine, selfless love. It seems as if that might be a pitfall in starting with these practices.*

Actually, it's not a pitfall at all. We start exactly where we are in every moment: there is no other place from which to start. It is unlikely that at this moment our love for most of the people in our lives is unconditional and without any attachment whatsoever, not to mention our regard for people we hate or don't even know. But this is simply where we're starting: with attachment, aversion, and ignorance. They are the grist for our bodhicitta mill.

*What is the difference between neutrality and indifference? In equanimity practice, wouldn't Person B, the neutral one, be the more ideal one to be practicing on?*

I don't think so. Love is the absolute, so we can say that neutrality contains some degree of obscuration. Neutral is neither positive nor negative, not caring particularly for either one or another; that is like tepid water. Indifference, not caring at all? That is like ice, closer to hate. And always remember: our very human love, mixed with attachment and aversion, is a reflection of ultimate, unconditional, limitless, unwavering altruistic love. They are not separate.

*Is it possible to do tonglen practice for yourself, if you're really in a bad place?*

Yes, of course, because we, too, are among "all sentient beings," and when we practice tonglen or any other good-hearted activity we embed our practice in the aspiration to benefit all. When practicing specifically for yourself, you might imagine all sentient beings there with you, filling space, and sense, imagine, or visualize yourself as a sublime being offering tonglen for all, including yourself. Imagine or visualize your ordinary body sitting in front of you—and as the sublime being who is offering the practice you are insubstantial, a body of light. This helps you not become confused by thinking "I" am doing a practice for "me"; there is no "I," either giving or taking. So just slip into something more comfortable: your radiant, transparent, insubstantial body of light.

*I love the idea of tonglen but I am a bit frightened at the thought of actually doing it. Won't I make myself vulnerable to becoming sick if I practice for someone who's sick or depressed or whatever?*

Good question, one that many ask and others are embarrassed to ask. Most important here: all phenomena, all our experiences, are created, not self-existing. Suffering, too, arises based on cause and consequence, rooted in simple ignorance of the true nature of reality and proliferating through self-grasping. The appearance of suffering, therefore, is empty in essence while vividly, dynamically displaying in our experience. Bodhicitta is also without solidity or substance, while in the absolute power of primordial purity it is purifying illusions of suffering. When we practice to relieve the suffering of others, we practice in this knowledge. There is no thought of "I."

And karma ain't catchin'—remember that you will never experience anything for which you yourself have not created cause.

*When someone is sick or in pain, it seems to me that the most important aspect of that is how they are responding to the physical suffering. In tonglen, I'm not trying to feel that pain or become sick myself; I'm trying to take in and transform their mental response to the pain.*

Take the whole thing. But take it without concept, without "trying," without a thought of "doing," without a thought of "I." Fearlessly practice taking the being's whole suffering, drawing it into the stream of absolute bodhicitta within you, bringing illusion into truth. As the suffering effortlessly enters, it effortlessly transforms.

You say you are trying to take in and transform the other person's mental response to the suffering—but this is our conventional way of thinking, based on concepts we reify and cling to: concepts of self and other, of the apparent solidity of physical reality, and even of mental and emotional experience. There is no "I" here who is trying to "do something," and certainly we are not able to transform the mind of another being; like novice fly casters, we can barely catch and release a thought in our own mind.

Tonglen is our teacher. Effortlessly, no thought of I or other, no trying, no ownership, no rejection, no attachment to outcome, in compassion and love we recognize and welcome the suffering of another. With clear intention and no action on our part, other than our natural inbreath, the suffering dissolves into pure bodhicitta, and whatever that being needs flows effortlessly on the outbreath. It is not just the other being's suffering that is transformed: it is also our own self-reference and self-grasping.

Garchen Rinpoche reminds us that tonglen is actual exchange, that it actually benefits, that the suffering actually comes to you. This is compassion: suffering *with*. This is what my yogi friend was writing about. There is no "self" giving and receiving. It is to bodhicitta within that the suffering comes and in which it is transmuted, and it is bodhicitta that flows out on the return breath. Just breathing in and breathing out in a normal way, on the inbreath you draw in the suffering of an individual being or, say, the suffering of everybody involved in the Holocaust, victims, perpetrators, witnesses, bystanders, relatives, historians. As you breathe naturally in and out, in the ceaseless stream of absolute bodhicitta all suffering dissolves. It is effortless. You're breathing anyway: why not save the world?

The effortlessness of tonglen practice is a very important point. Anything effortful involves some degree of self-concern. "I am cultivating bodhicitta, I am striving to attain enlightenment, I am practicing tonglen, I, I, I . . ." Really, you're just breathing in and breathing out, with compassionate heart. I don't know whether you've noticed, in the years you've lived on this planet, that you don't actually have to breathe; your body takes care of this for you, unless your respiratory function is somehow compromised. So as you're going through life, breathing in and breathing out, you're really not doing anything at all—but on every inbreath ignorance can be drawn into light, and on every outbreath light can illumine darkness.

Often people find it helpful to practice tonglen sensing or visualizing light. You might visualize a smoky, dark light dissolving in bodhicitta, on the outbreath flowing as clear light. However, you can also take in homelessness and send out houses. You can offer tonglen in your vernacular, in the way that is vivid and meaningful for you in that specific moment or circumstance.

Don't be afraid of making mistakes in your inner practice or in your outer activities to benefit others. Bodhisattvas make mistakes and are willing to make mistakes. We cultivate the highest and truest motivation, compassion and love for all, and then do the best we can. If we're not making mistakes, we're probably not risking enough of ourselves. Remember that your motivation, the condition of your own mind, is what determines ultimate outcome. According to your abilities, hazard yourself for the benefit of all. We are human beings walking step by step on the bodhisattva way, brave, generous, and undefended.

## Bringing suffering onto the path (verses 12-21)

This, dear friends, is where the sandal meets the dust. When we are not living in accord with our true nature and purpose we are living inauthentically, and the inauthentic life is fundamentally disturbed, mind and conduct mired in delusion. Bodhicitta transforms the deluded relationship to reality.

We have begun to actualize bodhicitta now. Practicing on equanimity and tonglen, we have now placed ourselves directly *within* the field of suffering—as a vehicle for its transformation. This is the essence of the bodhisattva way, expressed as the intention and the beauteous offering of tonglen, exchanging self for others. And this is the courage of the spiritual warrior: taking our own mind's display, our own field of karmic purification, as the crucible of transformation for all.

Now, with the teachings in this section of our text, we turn to a careful accounting of our own confusions and misfortunes, those circumstances that are most challenging for us to endure and also most powerful as mirrors of both our confusion and our capacity to reveal its intrinsic clarity. Here, for the liberation of all, we learn how to bring suffering onto the path.

Have you ever been caught in emotional and mental disturbance so acute, so intractable, that you determined this time truly to take the lessons from it rather than continue to numb or suppress it, because you knew this suffering was not just your own but experienced by many? That is an example of bringing suffering onto the path. For the benefit of others we become courageous and strong, facing ourselves in order to see clearly and abandon the delusions that clinging to "self" throws up in our way.

We are now committing to actualize bodhicitta in this very lifetime, in this very body, without attachment to outcome. Our aspiration is the highest; our repeated, regular articulation of it in daily life is intimate, gritty, and demanding, as we learn how to transform our most personal of obscurations into stepping stones—or trampolines, springboards to freedom.

Any moment of confusion, misery, or turmoil holds transformational potential if we understand it as our opportunity to see things just as they are, and thus to take responsibility for the causes and consequences we create. In your life up to now I have no doubt that you have already experienced this, so I think you already have a basis for understanding what it means to bring suffering onto the path. It means using our own difficulties, even our own ignorance, to benefit others. This could be as simple as cautioning another about the place where we ourselves have tripped and fallen, physically or morally. More deeply, it means mining our own mountains of delusion for their hidden ores of wisdom—using ours to free others from theirs. First, though: it means using our experiences, inner and outer, to see directly, nakedly, *how* we create suffering. Conditions are our mirrors, showing us the causes in our own mind, speech, and action. We meet the present condition, then, with the intention of seeing in our mind and behavior the seeds of cause, the thoughts, emotions, speech, and actions that are deluded and harmful. Practicing and learning like this is foundational: we are using our own most trying circumstances to transform their very causes.

Our bodhisattva training provides the actual methods to accomplish this. They are profound, completely accessible and practical, and they require courage and humility; a robust, self-aware sense of humor is also very helpful. Gar Rinpoche has taught me that courage comes from compassion and that great courage comes from love. In compassion and love, then, we step forward, vigorously, to take responsibility for the actions that will make real our bodhisattva aspiration.

We will consider verses 12-21 together as a group, each one confronting us with radical perspectives on our karmic challenges of life and mind. We will see how mind, the sower of cause, can transform its own view and intention and thus also the ways we work with result. Remember our teachings on karma as we go through these verses, especially the reminder that we will never meet with anything in life for which we ourselves have not at some moment created cause. Enjoyable and painful circumstances are seeds coming to fruition, for release. As we encounter obstacles and difficulties, especially when they weigh heavily upon us, we derive strength and courage from remembering that we are now, in this very moment, in the precise conditions that ripen and exhaust their causes.

Experiences of ripening negative karma will come to us all, throughout our lives and our lifetimes, so we train not just to tolerate and endure them but actually to rely upon them. When consequence manifests, its cause is no more. *Rely on your suffering to liberate you from its causes.*

For these reverses of fortune, practice the reverse of self-concern. Hold closely in mind now the core teachings on tonglen, exchanging self for others; the instructions we are about to receive vividly show us how to fulfil its great promise.

**Verse 12.** Even if someone driven by great desire steals all your wealth or lets others steal it, dedicate to them your body, possessions, and all virtue of the three times. This is the way of a bodhisattva.

The focus in this teaching, on material loss, loss of wealth, we easily understand as misfortune, and sometimes disaster, of which all of us have some experience in this and every lifetime, human or not. Mindful of how wealth and resources arouse possessiveness and clinging in us, and possibly jealousy and resentment in others, recall our earlier discussions about attachment and impermanence. Nothing lasts; everything comes and goes, revealing that what we imagine to be in our possession is like water in the hand, impossible to hold onto and never ours to begin with. The attachment *tendency*, however, if not released, will remain with us, as a karmic imprint, assuring that we will continue to experience having and losing, enjoying and suffering. The exchange of self for others here—in mind and perhaps also in action—is freely to give everything to those who would steal something.

This pith instruction applies far beyond the narrow bounds of material possession and loss. Think of loss of face, theft of mind's ease, age or illness stealing away health and vitality, the beloved life taken too young—the numberless kinds of non-material wealth that can never be kept, whose loss penetrates our every delusion of possession and permanence.

Let us take up this teaching in some detail, with an edited excerpt from an actual teaching session, exploring how our inner inquiry can turn appearances inside out—to reveal the lesson that liberates. This can serve as a method for working with all the teachings in this section and with the many occasions in our lives in which we can bring suffering onto the path. Here is the session excerpt:

**Barbara:** For those who have had our homes broken into or vandalized, our cars and other possessions taken, is this how we responded—dedicating to our thief everything we have and are? Anger, fear, desiring revenge are more common reactions. The real problem for us when something we value is taken from us, material or not, is actually our self-grasping afflictions of mind and emotion. Our reactions to our wealth being stolen are compounded by our fixation on self, as we identify what's taken as an extension of ourselves. A sense of violation then arouses more fear, anger, vengefulness. For just a moment now, remember or imagine yourself in a situation in which something you valued was taken from you, or someone broke into your home, your family—or even your very body. Let yourself feel the emotions and bodily manifestations. [Pause as friends reflect] Now again imagine being in that moment, seeing the disarray and the material loss, feeling the violation, but without the anger, without the fear. [Pause]

*I almost got there when someone stole our firewood. My first response was all the things we normally do. Then I thought, "That person needs the firewood to keep warm." So I was able to balance that first response a little bit.*

*I had a house burglary many years ago and reacted with great anger—and now I can't remember anything that was taken!*

*In a break-in I experienced, when reimagining it just now I wasn't able to be there without the fear. What had been really hard was seeing the intruder's knife. What was taken made no difference: it was life that was important. Everybody was fine, but I can't change what I feel about that knife.*

What do you feel about it?

*[Weeping] When I saw the knife I realized just how close we came to violence, to real danger. That's hard to change.*[4]

What would it take for you to release that? What would you have to do, in your own mind, to come to the place where you could think instead, "I'm glad nobody was hurt, neither our family nor the intruder." In other words, to embrace the situation with *all* the beings in it. What would it take you to get there?

*A lot of compassion.*

Yes. Can you do that? Because there's no reason to continue carrying this around with you, and every reason to see the skillful pathway that takes you from "I and my family might have been hurt!" to "He could be my own son, I'm so relieved he didn't cause harm." When the love is vast, you don't want anyone hurt—and the greatest harm comes to those who cause harm.

*I saw his face, because I was woken up and he was over me. I thought it was someone I knew and remember wondering, "Why is my friend here?" I went back to sleep and then woke up realizing it wasn't my friend.*

Yet it *was* your friend: your old karmic friend was there—to help you purify karma and generate love and compassion.

---

4. We may tend to return again and again, in our minds, to extremely disturbing or traumatic experiences, clinging to and elaborating on them, identifying with the events, emotions, potentials. Thus we maintain an ongoing relationship to the experience, keeping it in the present, continuing to invest in it. This becomes a powerful narrative process. Because what occurred is already in the past, gone, we can only keep it alive in our minds by rehearsing it again and again. This can be a way of seeking mastery over memories of helplessness and harm, actual or potential, but in fact it keeps us enthralled by it—in thrall to it. Mastery is to see and be with what is, in the present moment, awake and aware, letting it come and letting it go, in the flow of time and consciousness. See also "Self, Trauma, and Being: Reflections on Psychology and Ontology," in Du Bois, *Light Years*, 264, n.135.

This is what I mean by radical: going to the root. It is radical to think not only, "Maybe I won't have to be angry anymore," but also, "For the one who caused or threatened grave harm, I will practice great love and compassion. My friend came not to take but to give—an opportunity for me to cultivate the quality that is the priceless jewel: bodhicitta." There is no greater gift than that. So the friend who keeps coming in the night, again and again as the years go by, bringing the opportunity to generate bodhicitta on the basis of that moment of great fear and danger, that is a spiritual friend. Our thief steals away a self-clinging being, with its fearful, anxious ways, and leaves behind a generous, grateful, compassionate one.

One of the powerful gifts of Tokme Zangpo's essence teachings is that they clearly, even dramatically, point the way to freedom *through* our confusion about phenomenal existence. Enmeshed in materiality, we think of cause and consequence, good and bad, virtuous and nonvirtuous, beneficial and harmful, in terms of what has palpable, visible, identifiable appearance and effect. We look for cause in what is actually not causative but circumstantial. In these teachings on bringing suffering onto the path we see the radical invitation to the spiritual view: the view that penetrates confusion and illusion, showing us how to use material reality and our present enmeshment in it not as a prison but as a window— and not just to see through but to leap through.

We give the thief everything, far beyond what he desired to take from us: our "body, possessions, and all virtue of the three times." Even that vast generosity has its reflection in the compassion, loving kindness, and selfless concern that we are already capable of. It is important to recognize this. While it may be beyond our present capacities to respond this way in every circumstance, it is not beyond our capacity in some moments to do so, or at least to imagine doing so. Now our friend who told us what happened in her home one night will practice on this teaching in fresh relationship to her "friend in the night." In *this* moment she can work with her mind until she has generated vast aspiration and love for *this* friend. On that basis we extend the clear intention to other circumstances and beings, in past, present, or future. If you start with what's hardest then what's easiest is easy, and if you start with what's easy, when the hard challenge comes along you've already practiced for it. The message in this is to start with what's facing you—and what's facing us is always what's in our face. So work it. Use these challenging teachings to challenge yourself; use them assiduously to change your own mind.

The bodhisattva ideal is sometimes likened to the mind that sees all beings as one's own beloved child: you don't want that child to create unhappiness for itself. I think we can all see some reflection of that in our own experience, and being able to see in our own experience an insight or quality somehow akin to the bodhisattva mind is exquisitely significant—because it shows us directly how the great bodhisattva qualities articulate potentials already within us. The qualities that we speak of as bodhisattva qualities are not foreign to us.

When your mind is well established in bodhicitta, nothing will harm you. It is the perfect armor. Because it is love. When you have unwavering, vast love, your concern and care are always for the other, not for the self, and if you're thinking with love of the other and not thinking of self, it's as if self doesn't exist—so then what can be harmed? In the moment of great danger or suffering, thinking of others, murmuring silently, "I dedicate to them my body, possessions, all my virtues," or sounding the heartfelt compassionate cry of the mother, "Oh, my darling!"—in that instant your mind and intention are one with the mind and intention of all bodhisattvas. Maybe in the next moment you think, "But damn, he stole my watch!" Then you remember, "Oh! But I already gave him my body, possessions, and all my virtues, so my watch was already his! He stole his own watch!" Not only that, but in the view of karma you acknowledge that in the past you have stolen from your thief—so now, the circle complete, your current loss becomes the seed of your generosity. The past is redeemed and the future freer because of your thief's visit. And your thief is benefitted by your generosity, for if he intends to steal from you, does so, and takes satisfaction in it, he incurs the full negative karma of intention, action, and completion, while if you willingly give him everything he bears only the karma of his original intention to steal. So now in turn you are the kind thief, stealing from him some of his potential negative karma! A veritable cascade of blessings flows on the endless bodhicitta stream.

Do you see, now, how you have something to work with? Sometimes, in nature, by the water or in the woods, you pick up a stone that has a particular feel in your hand, a particular quality for your mind, and carry it in your pocket: a touchstone. You can use each of these verses as touchstones, to remind you of the bodhisattva capacity that is actually yours, not yet fully flowered but now in the process of flowering. The touchstone reminds you, "Oh, this is who I really am." Instead of identifying with what has been habitual, conventional, limiting, we take the open, expansive perspective of love and compassion. This changes everything, now and into the future. It even changes the past, because now you look back in love and compassion, even on your own sufferings and regrets.

*I'm thinking about this capacity for compassion as something that can continually be developed. A stranger taking something from me would probably be an easier place for me to practice than if someone I loved and trusted deceived me. But it sounds as if you are very hopeful that if we keep on with this practice we could eventually come to a place of compassion.*

Actually, I have no hope whatsoever.

*Really?*

I have certainty. Why? First, I am certain that I have met some human beings in this lifetime who have fully accomplished this path. One is Garchen Rinpoche, and he has assured me that he really had to practice to get there, even before those twenty years in the Chinese prison. The Dalai Lama, too, has said that as a boy he was quick to anger, that he still has a tendency to anger, and that if he doesn't practice he's going to become angry. I also have certainty because I've been on the path for a few days myself, and I see change. I am not an accomplished or realized practitioner, but I see change. I'm definitely here to testify to the power of self-grasping—so I'm here also to testify to the power of aspiration, clear intention, and love to transform self-grasping. Every iota of our self-grasping that is released is a degree of freedom in our minds that benefits us and everyone we touch. About that, too, I am certain.

An artist friend of mine once said that, in the making of an artist, talent isn't the principal requirement: "The difference between a person who paints and a person who doesn't paint is that the person who paints paints."[5] Same with buddhas: it is said that the difference between a buddha and a non-buddha is that the person who realized buddhahood made the effort. Our aspirations have great power when we bring them into action. That is why I began our meeting tonight with "this is where the sandal meets the dust." This is where our effort truly begins to take hold, where we generate traction to move forward.

*When I first started reading this group of verses I couldn't tell the difference between the attitude and behavior they describe and what I would call excessive meekness. Now I think the main difference is that remaining a doormat doesn't change the afflictive emotions, it just suppresses them, which causes even greater suffering. Practicing in this way, to release those emotions and replace them with compassion, doesn't involve suffering.*

Well, it involves suffering, but the suffering is used as fuel for its own transformation. We need to directly experience and to face our afflictive emotions, our intense anger and fear, our desire for self-preservation, to plumb them, to *be with* them, to know them, intimately—and thus to recognize their raw power as life, as creative energy. Freed of delusion, our emotions can be a powerful motive force and fuel for

---

5. Cynthia Price, personal communication.

right speech, right action. We want to harness that power for good. We don't want to diminish the power of life force or the vitality of our emotional life, and we don't want to pacify ourselves in a vapid way. We want to deeply, vitally *desire* the good of all beings. All that energy with which we protect what we consider us and ours—we want to *free* that energy, to protect and free all.

Wimp compassion is shrinking from the moment, shrinking from drawing forth that huge power and using it to benefit all. When you see reality as it is and act from great compassion, you are a spiritual warrior: a bodhisattva.

This unique, unrepeatable life, this precious human life: you have to make it count for what you know to be the most important thing—so you must know, firmly and steadfastly, what *is* the most important thing. Some of us aspire to awaken completely for the benefit of all; others might aspire to become kinder. The two aspirations are on a continuum. If I'm aspiring to complete awakening in this lifetime and I don't accomplish that, what are the chances that I'll become kinder in the course of my efforts? And if I aspire to become kinder, is it not likely that my increasing kindness will gradually expand into an even more potent altruism? So whatever aspiration you hold that inspires you to throw your heart over the fence, do that, do that.

*I think these practices can be very easily co-opted by our confusion, in that we might thoroughly believe we're following these rules but the motivation can be co-opted by gaming it, to escape one's own fear. So I wonder if a person needs to practice on self-awareness before beginning tonglen or the thirty-seven bodhisattva practices.*

You are suggesting that our high motivation could be co-opted by our low habituation? No doubt! This is why we practice, and practice some more, and then practice still more—to lift our low habituation into our high motivation.

I think where one starts depends on the individual, but really, we all need to engage all the levels of practice all the time. Tokme

Zangpo's teachings are the fast track to knowing one's own mind, its entrapment *and* its potential for freedom. And it is important to have teachers. Your teacher can help you see that which you're doing your best not to see. If you are co-opting the Dharma in service of your self-grasping and afflictive emotions you're not going to make progress, and that will be visible—to you if you're willing to look, and certainly to those who live closely with you, and to your teachers and sangha.

It is very helpful to have sangha, a community of practitioners. To do this inner work and let it unfold in our actual daily lives, we need to be strong and open-hearted. Caught up in our self-concern, we feel it is risky to let our confusion and affliction show; people might see, "Oh, she has *stuff*." As if you're the only one. When we're practicing regularly we come to recognize stuff simply as stuff. We can recognize it in others because we've got it, too, and we can recognize it in ourselves because experiences and other beings are our mirrors. If you have the good Dharma-karma that brings you to authentic teachings and practices, you have the path to walk right through any and all stuff—and if you also have sangha, you have companions on that path.

Now, the sangha is not just those who sit in teachings together in this way: the sangha is also your own mind. Cultivating the inward attention is going to show you when you're fabricating and posing, taking up the forms of practice but skimming the surface rather than mining the meaning. The Dharma is for progress. Until we reach the point where we realize that nothing having the name of progress was ever needed in the first place, we study and practice, and sangha can be very helpful: challenging, mirroring, understanding, encouraging, inspiring, supporting.

And, briefly, an observation about fear. The bodhisattva, the spiritual warrior, is often described as fearless. Understanding karma, she acknowledges its ripening results with gratitude and courage, and understanding that all phenomena are empty of inherent existence, she has nothing to fear. Mind, true nature, buddha nature, is indestructible.

So, dear friends, did you get a taste of the sandal meeting the dust tonight?

**Verse 13.** Even if someone cuts off your head when you haven't done anything wrong, take all their negative deeds upon yourself through the power of compassion. This is the way of a bodhisattva.

This is bringing the tonglen principle into action in the very face of apparent aggression, danger, and destruction. The one who endangers us is more endangered than we are; we stand to lose one head and one life, while our assailant stands to throw away lifetimes of virtue and opportunity. We can also see the cutting off of our head as a blow to our great pride, our fixation on self, our self-concern and self-interest in all circumstances, our arrogance and aloofness, our stiff neck that resists bending.

We are not harmed in our true nature by anything that happens to us, and at the relative level we are benefitted by what appear to be harms, which are the signs that our own negative karma is being purified. That is a very high view to take in a moment of danger, but in moments of relative safety we can recall not only this view but also the ever accessible practices of great compassion and patient endurance without generating anger (to be considered further in verse 27). It is our afflictive emotions that lead to our suffering, and they are in our own consciousness. Even in the midst of terror and agony, even when we are physically harmed or killed, our mind is not harmed if we meet aggression not with anger but with compassion and love for the harm-doer, who is under the power of great affliction. We do this by counting to ten, yes, and especially by restraining the negative impulse with the power of the positive intention. Because love is of the absolute it is of the nature of truth, while hatred and anger are delusional states arising from the ever changing afflictions of thought and emotion; based in falsity, they have no ground of their own. Truth is always, in every circumstance and every condition, more powerful than untruth.

The Dalai Lama, Tenzin Gyatso, once asked a lama recently released from a Chinese prison about dangers he had met during his time there. The lama said he had faced one terrible danger: on several occasions he had almost lost his bodhicitta.[6] Your head can be cut away from you and your pride can be impaled. Protect your bodhicitta with the armor of love and compassion.

**Verse 14.** Even if others slander you throughout a billion worlds, in return, speak with a loving mind of their good qualities. This is the way of a bodhisattva.

If someone speaks ill of you, either those words are based on truth or they are not. True or false, while they may disturb or even harm you in your worldly circumstances, they can at the same time free your mind.

If your accuser's words are true, look within to investigate your own thoughts, actions, and speech, and bring your faults to correction. Take responsibility for what you are responsible for—and thus disarm your anger and desire to retaliate, seeing that in fact you yourself are the author of that negative report. If the report is false, it can still affront your pride and damage your reputation; the first is your own creation and the second is beyond your control, since it resides in the minds of others. Dispensing with rancor, use all the impact and fallout of negative speech about you to shake your clinging attachment to your good name and fame. And as to pride: it is dense self-grasping, swollen and resistant to insight, committed to the mistaken narrative of self—so your accuser is giving you an opportunity to examine and relax your grip on your deepest confusion.

Don't kill the messenger! Praise that person's positive qualities and actions. Even searching for and privately acknowledging them as positive will benefit your own mind, while publicly holding them up to others as excellent qualities and actions will benefit your

---

6. The bodhisattva lama Palden Gyatso; see his *The Autobiography of a Tibetan Monk.*

mind greatly. Allow kindness and gratitude to arise in your mind by remembering buddha nature, always within, only momentarily obscured by our ignorance. And recognize the fault in finding fault with others; when it is done to you, be very sure it is not also then done by you. Keep clearing the karmic slate, your mind. For the good of all beings, inscribe there only what you know is true.

**Verse 15.** Even if someone exposes your hidden faults and insults you in front of others, view that person as a teacher and bow with respect. This is the way of a bodhisattva.

Ah yes, public humiliation. Shaming exposure, the searing flush: where to look, how to hide? How to defend myself, discredit the speaker? Paralyzing confusion. Fame and infamy are one of the Eight Worldly Dharmas' pairs of opposites, along with gain and loss, pleasure and pain, and praise and blame. The desired and the dreaded, dancing together. As always with hope and fear, what I hope will happen I fear will not, and what I fear might happen I hope will not. Little grace in that dance.

Secret faults are corrosive and deadly. Let them be seen and spoken of; in fact, be the first to expose them, if not to others then at least to yourself, in confessing, resolving, and acting to correct them. And be grateful and respectful to the one who helps this happen, no matter how painful the moment of unwilled exposure. You don't have to become best buddies with someone who strips you bare in public, but in your mind you can stand naked and at ease, unburdened. Dilgo Khyentse Rinpoche's elegant advice: "Your reputation is an alluring mirage that can easily lead you astray. Discard it without a second thought, like the snot you blow from your nose."[7]

The true spiritual friend is at it again: looking like an enemy, revealed as the friend. And your bodhisattva intention is at it again: transforming apparent adversity into spiritual benefit for all.

---

7. Dilgo Khyentse, *Heart of Compassion*, 123.

**Verse 16.** Even if someone you have cared for as dearly as your own child regards you as an enemy, love that person even more, as a mother would her ailing child. This is the way of a bodhisattva.

This verse is a bit painful to read, isn't it—being blamed and resented by one we have cherished? Have we not all had experiences of this kind, wounding our hearts and disturbing our minds day and night, tormented by betrayal and shame? Have we ourselves not been at one moment the caring, attached parent, friend, or teacher and at another the ungrateful, rejecting one? We can therefore understand viscerally how the teaching here is at the heart of the bodhisattva's commitment. As all beings have been our mothers, so are we mothers to all beings. No matter the circumstance, the provocation, the insult, injury, or disgrace, our aspiration, intention, and practice are to hold every being in compassion and love, to desire and act for their wellbeing and ultimate liberation.

It is our own attachment, resentment, or indifference that make someone appear to us an enemy or an ingrate, not their actual words or actions, as our afflictive emotions create adversity out of arising appearances. When someone hurts you, remember karma and the true nature we all share—and simply, if not easily, love more.

**Verse 17.** Even if someone of equal or lower status, driven by pride, treats you with disdain, respectfully place them on your crown as your teacher. This is the way of a bodhisattva.

Counterintuitive, upending, turning our minds inside out—that is what these teachings are, that is what they are doing for us. Wonderful! And now this pointed, shocking instruction: The precious, infinitely kind guru, object of our gratitude, love, and devotion, teacher of the knowable mystery, whom we place upon our crown, always higher than ourselves, from whom we receive gracious blessings—*this* is how we are to regard someone no better than we, someone possibly even worse than we, who treats us with disdain? If we have not been caught by the previous verses, here we are caught. Our self-concern and self-importance are outraged, repulsed; we are riveted in refusal, appalled and thrown into disarray. Happy, happy! We are exposed! Now we have a chance!

If you haven't yet encountered the Tibetan Buddhist text called *The Wheel of Sharp Weapons*, right now run to the bookstore, order it, or borrow it, because right now, this very instant, your mind is like an open mouth, hungry for the hard-to-hear and finally satisfying teachings about self-concern:

> (3) We spend our whole life in the search for enjoyment, / Yet tremble with fear at the mere thought of pain . . . / But the brave Bodhisattvas accept suffering gladly / And gain from their courage a true lasting joy . . . . (47) All of the sufferings that we have endured / In the lives we have led in the three lower states, / As well as our pains of the present and future, / Are the same as the case of the forger of arrows / Who later was killed by an arrow he had made. / Our suffering is the wheel of sharp weapons returning / Full circle upon us from wrongs we have done. . . . (53) Batter him, batter him, rip out the heart / Of our grasping for ego, our love for ourselves! / Trample him, trample him, dance on the head / Of this treacherous concept of selfish concern! / Tear out the heart of this self-centered butcher / Who slaughters our chance to gain final release![8]

*The Wheel of Sharp Weapons*, a brilliant sword flashing and cutting away illusion, dramatically, incisively reiterates what Tokme has told us in verse ii: "All suffering without exception comes from seeking your own happiness. The perfect buddhas are born from the altruistic mind." And now here again our teacher gives us the exchange of self for others to dissolve our clinging to the illusion of "I": elevate the one who debases you.

---

8. Dharmarakshita, *Wheel of Sharp Weapons*, passim.

•

In these verses about bringing suffering onto the path Tokme is teaching us *how* to place others before self, *how* to exchange our own happiness for the suffering of others—and indeed we need all this instruction, because this is surely the opposite of what we normally do.

If you have developed some degree of the inward attention you can perceive quite clearly the thoughts in your mind, and you can see that in the early stages of study and practice, your thoughts, one after another, in one way or another, are mostly about you. Perhaps a bit further on, with some stirring of altruistic motivation, even those thoughts that are about helping others are about you helping others, and how wonderful that is, how unselfish you are. One day on my cushion, stirred by bodhicitta, suddenly I recognized that I was in fact being moved to tears by perceptions of my own self-lessness! Ha! It's a very tricky mind we've elaborated based on the simple, profound misapprehension of selfness. So the discipline of even thinking of placing others before self is shocking to the system. As when you begin to abstain from a desired substance craving takes over your mind, so the intention and commitment to place others before self may be followed immediately by what seems like an upsurge of selfishness. Don't be alarmed. When we enunciate the aspiration actually to give up attachment and grasping to self, to generate the great love for others, and to know the emptiness of phenomena, all that is in the way of our seeing truly and loving vastly will become more visible to us. Don't lose courage. Just keep on practicing. This is a very important point. We are now in the actual training in bringing suffering and misfortune onto the path.

Though we may find immediately clarifying and instructive these Dharma teachings on how to correct our confused thinking, the fact is that very few actually practice these instructions literally. You may remember, though, that this is precisely what Garchen Rinpoche said to me when he handed me *The 37 Bodhisattva Practices*: "Take them literally. Practice them. This is how I became who I am." These are the teachings about how to recognize and actually use the experiences that are most difficult for our self-clinging to tolerate—to use them as the raw, rich energy that transforms them on the spot. These are the methods for bringing negativity onto the path, and so of course when we begin to consider and practice them we will find our negativities flying up in our face, like hornets from the nest we're whacking. Don't stop! Whack, whack!

Difficulty and suffering are in the world, in life, in samsara, where beings exist. We are not to turn away from the suffering but from its causes, in our own mindstreams and actions. If you turn away from suffering you're going to turn away from suffering beings, including yourself, while the deep vow of the bodhisattva is never to abandon a sentient being, including yourself. Bringing difficult experiences of life, mind, emotion, and relationship onto the path is the method by which we take responsibility for our own confusion—and release our deluded view into clarity and power.

**Verse 18.** Though you may be impoverished, always disparaged, gripped by disease, and tormented by spirits, never lose courage but take on all the pain and misdeeds of all beings. This is the way of a bodhisattva.

**Verse 19.** Though you may be famous and admired by many who bow to you, and as rich as the Wealth God himself, having seen that worldly fortune is without essence, do not be proud. This is the way of a bodhisattva.

Insisting on the primacy of spiritual over conventional view and action, these two excellent instructions reverse the order of importance we accord to appearances of good and bad fortune. The dreaded and the desired, the feared and the craved, the repulsive and the enchanting—we can be ruled by our reactions to them. Our freedom is in the reversal, the exchange. In degradation, abandon despair. Bear with what is unbearable for you, and with the courage of vast compassion take to yourself what is unbearable for others. In wealth of repute and worldly resources, recognize their vapidity and vacuity; understand the profound confusion that holds material value as a sign of one's own, and give generously to the needy. Abandon arrogance; see all with equanimity and cultivate love and compassion. Understand the emptiness of all created appearances. With the clear light of insight dispel the miasmic trances of worldly sufferings and enrichments.

In the face of your own suffering and clinging, remember bodhicitta, love for all beings. In that very instant your suffering is lightened. It becomes so easy to bear! Don't believe me; see for yourself. Today, tomorrow, or the next day some variant of pain or of enchanted entanglement will come your way, trivial or immense. The instant you note your mental-emotional reaction beginning to arise, take this dreadful or desirable experience and offer it for the release of others, that all who are experiencing this or any form of ignorance, suffering, or mental entanglement may be freed from it. Instantaneously your affliction becomes like a jewel, an adornment for you—because you have taken it as the extraordinary moment in which you generate bodhicitta.

There is no teaching or practice more radical than this. Exchange self for other and self releases into its essential nature. No self, no other: no suffering.

## Discussion: To do and not to do, this is the question

*I have heard people, especially humanitarians and social activists, talk about Buddhists as fatalistic and passive in relation to the suffering of real people in the real world, saying, "It's just their karma."*

I haven't met any Dharma teachings that say we should not try to dispel appearances and conditions of suffering. We want to relieve the suffering of others in every way we can, with bandages for bleeding and wisdom for ignorance. It is my karma that I am lost, it is yours that you see me and hold out your hand, and it is ours that we meet in this way in this moment.

*I have recently seen how nothing is about my external circumstances, about people, places, or things. It's all about my inner experience. So much of what I do is really trying to manipulate and control that inner experience—feelings or beliefs I have attachment or aversion to. Somehow, when I see one of those and just don't do anything about it, it shifts on its own. There is a kind of relief, a release, when this happens, when I realize, "Oh, I don't need to do anything."*

That's it, exactly. We can recognize what arises, see it arise, see it abide momentarily, and see it dissolve. Because it is empty of any nature of its own, it will vanish if you don't do something with it. What remains is mind itself. You are then seeing your own nature, the nature of all phenomena. The awake mind, the enlightened mind, is not somewhere else. It is right here, right now.

**Verse 20.** If the enemy—your own anger—is not tamed, subduing outer enemies will only make them increase. Therefore, subdue your own mind with the army of love and compassion. This is the way of a bodhisattva.

This is one of the most important teachings in the Buddhadharma, which consistently reminds us that of all the afflictions or confusions in our mindstream the most dangerous is anger. When we think of enemies we usually think of someone or something outside us, which threatens to harm us or those we care about—while the real harm-doer is within, in the afflictive emotions and conflictual thoughts that lead us to harm ourselves and others. Anger is foremost among those.

The basket of anger-hatred contains everything from mild annoyance or irritation to the raging inferno of murderous, annihilating rage, just as the basket of attachment contains everything from mild interest to the slavering maw. Attachment is sometimes said to be the most difficult to recognize because it can be so subtle, but anger, too, is sometimes so subtle as to appear to be its actual opposite. Virtue and nonvirtue: more frequently than we imagine we mistake the one for the other, in actions of body, speech, and mind. This is perhaps particularly the case with our anger, which so often cloaks itself in self-righteous projections that justify our holding others (even things and events, in past, present, and future) as somehow the causes or validations of our anger. Our capacity to recognize and withdraw our projections shows us that the aversive reaction is not based on the being or object but is arising in one's own mind. While this sounds obvious it can easily be missed in the supercharged atmosphere of accusing, angry, disgusted emotions, and in the self-righteousness that is so often involved in anger.

A uniquely dangerous form of aversion-repulsion is self-hatred. Taken to its end it is suicide, which Garchen Rinpoche has called the extreme of self-grasping. And it is so mistaken, so deluded: we can harbor such negativity towards ourselves when in fact our true nature is untouchable, impeccable, indestructible. Millions of moments of not seeing this are swept away by one instant of seeing it directly. As a longtime practitioner friend said, despite all our practice and our great love "sometimes we really do blow it," erupting in huge rage, for example, or turning away from one in need. But don't do self-hatred or hatred of others or things or events. Don't even generate hatred or aversion for the afflictive emotion itself; however stubborn that affliction may appear to be, each instance of it is a temporary arising, lacking any inherent existence.

When the negative karma is purifying and suffering is rolling right over you, don't reject the suffering: acknowledge it and accept it as your own creation and now the gift of karmic completion. If you want to and can, also address the circumstance; if someone wrongs you, you can try to right the wrong. But don't say no to experiencing it. Don't push away that which is hard for you. Don't be afraid to suffer. The suffering *is* the purification—and the opportunity to offer it for the release of all.

The wisdom nature of anger is clarity, as in the pellucid clarity that sees what is, directly, nakedly, and the dynamic, fierce clarity of compassionate wrath, the protector. When strong anger arises for you, look right at it without engaging. Let it be what it is: the pristine clarity of your mind.

## Discussion: Anger and outrage, bodhicitta, love

*Anger is like acid . . . my anger controls me . . . anger is powerful . . . I'm really interested in my anger . . . there's a weird pleasure that I get from being angry.*

Anger sometimes seems to carry us away, pick us up and throw us around, sweeping away all self-awareness. In an instant it can take over both mind and behavior. And anger seems to seek an object—which means a target, because the basic trajectory of anger is toward destruction. So there is often apt to be a dramatic production involved, an arresting little theater of mind and especially of speech, or speeches: orations and declamations, aloud or in our mind, about how one's anger is not only justified but moral, curative, beneficial. Writer, producer, director, star, and arts critic: self, of course. It is the element of self-interest in self-righteous anger that unmasks it. Moral outrage leans more toward altruism.

*I've noticed that I'm terrified of getting angry now. After taking refuge with Garchen Rinpoche I don't want to break this chain, I want to keep this bodhicitta. Previously, when strong anger has come up, afterwards I have felt as if I've lost something and I really have to work to get it back.*

Yes, anger can have a negative impact on our relative bodhicitta; in a fit of anger your mind is momentarily parting from caring and compassion. The altruistic intention does require cultivation and diligence of mind to maintain. As our minds at present are unstable and wavering, thoughts coming and going like leaves on the wind, the excellent intention can waver, too; it can literally slip our mind in a moment of inattention, however wholeheartedly and sincerely we have taken it up. But bodhicitta is of our true nature and anger is based in falsehood, so that damage can quite easily be repaired. The altruistic intention is in the mind, and the causes of damage to it and the remedies are also in the mind. You don't have to go into the wilderness in a hair shirt and beat yourself with a chain for twenty years. Mentally refreshing and revivifying the bodhisattva intention, rededicating your activities and your life to the liberation of all, swiftly restores your confidence and enthusiasm. There is also a profound, powerful, and highly accessible practice that can be offered at any time to purify and restore, when you feel the lapse has been injurious for your mind: the Four Opponent Powers (Appendix B).

*A few times during the day I've sensed that in the night I had dreamed of hatred coming toward me, usurping my energy, and I woke up feeling as if I'd been attacked.*

The remedy is love. When you wake up and realize you've been zapped with hatred—wonderful; that is your moment to generate great love and compassion. Love recognizes that the source of hatred is always suffering of some sort; any hatred directed toward you is generated by a being in a state of confusion. If there is actual or potential harm you may want to and be able to protect yourself or others. However, if you take an action or establish an energetic or mental protection or boundary, be sure it is not of a nature to deflect hatred back to the being from whom it is coming; the intent of that would be to harm the other. Rather than creating an oppositional energy, we create the safety zone of love. Safe for all. Anger can quickly increase danger for all, while holding the intention of love steadies self, others, and the situation. Whatever action must be taken can be taken without anger, even a forceful action to protect others; altruistic love is, by definition, right action. Again, the worse it gets the better it is. In the moment when you are being attacked by hatred you are giving birth to love.

Our true nature cannot ever, in any way, be harmed. Even when the relative reality being, the one we each call "I," appears to be harmed, its true nature cannot be. Emptiness cannot harm emptiness. Hatred is not solid, possessed of inherent existence, nor is the being who is sending it your way, and nor are you. Truth is more powerful than any of those illusions—and will dissolve them. You don't have to personalize it in any way. The more vast your motivation the more beneficial it is. So if someone or some force is attacking you with hatred and you are generating great love and compassion for that being, generate it at the same time for all beings, that all may be freed from hatred.

Most important is your own mind, free of ignorance, attachment, and aversion. This applies to everything we are studying and practicing on the bodhisattva path. Hatred is the residue of anger, Gar Rinpoche has said, so to be free of hatred, liberate the anger. Weed the garden right now! Desiring to benefit those who are causing you harm—that is how a bodhisattva thinks, that is how a bodhisattva acts. This is so important that in the Drikung Kagyu lineage of Buddhadharma the first prayer recited in the order of practice is for those we call harm-doers, enemies: "All mother sentient beings, especially those enemies who hate me, obstructers who harm me, and those who create obstacles on my path to liberation and omniscience, may they experience happiness, be separated from suffering, and swiftly will I establish them in the state of unsurpassed, perfect, complete, and precious buddhahood." Even if we're halting in it, not yet very accomplished, in response to any harm we generate love and make prayers of aspiration that all harm-doers be freed. This is how we become true bodhisattvas, by developing that motivation and acting on it at every possible opportunity. Thus our worst enemy, the one who arouses our greatest anger and hatred, is actually our greatest benefactor: in practicing for that one's happiness and liberation we secure our own.

The absolute antidote to anger is absolute love. The motive to destroy is destroyed by love. The great love means love for everything, attachment and aversion for nothing. We don't have to manufacture this vast love—we only need to keep sweeping away what presently obscures it from our sight.

**Verse 21.** Sensory pleasures are like salt water: the more you drink, the greater your thirst. Abandon at once all things that bring forth clinging attachment. This is the way of a bodhisattva.

Here we bring onto the path craving, attachment, desire.

When the good stuff of life is rolling over us it is very easy to develop clinging attachment, one of our most controlling afflictive emotions, some say the major one. Garchen Rinpoche often gives this example when he's talking about attachment: he picks up his tea, takes a sip, and murmurs "Mmm, yum." No translation required: he is clearly showing how easily attachment to pleasure increases, as does seeking your own satisfaction, having what you want rather than what you don't want. Such moments occur a hundred times a day. Whether the attachment is to beings or things, it is quite simple: if you're not attached to it and it's not harmful, you don't have to give it up. Giving up an object of attachment can help to dislodge a specific habit, but the work is really in the mind. It is desirous attachment itself that we must and will abandon— with varying degrees of difficulty in our present condition but with increasing willingness and ease as we come to understand love-emptiness.

We can want and cling to what we have tasted in the past, what we are tasting in this very moment, and what we yearn to taste in the future. As my beloved university professor once said of himself, "I have a whim of iron." Excellent description of how the momentary wisp of attraction can become the despotic ruler of the three times. And as with any afflictive emotion or disturbing thought, recognizing clinging attachment arising at any moment is the exact, precise, and precisely exact moment at which to abandon it. Weed the garden right now.

Practicing at the material level, we can certainly abandon what we are desiring, and that can be helpful, as we've discussed. However, don't bother to do this if you're going to regret it. Your purpose in putting away the things you like is to free your mind of its habit to crave and cling. If you then regret giving up the object, want it back, or feel annoyed at having let it go, not only are you still following after attraction and desire but now you are also cultivating aversion. This is a boomerang effect for apparently positive action taken with divided mind. If you are going to give up the object of attachment, truly give it up and don't take it back, not even in your fantasies—instead, take advantage of all your desirous fantasies to give up attachment over and over again. This, again, is a spur to cultivating awareness and discernment, learning to see clearly the actual condition of one's mind and motivations right here, right now. And of course, as we have seen, the object of desirous clinging that we really must give away over and over and over again is the mind of desirous clinging.

How do we know when we have subdued or abandoned clinging attachment? Fine with what comes our way, fine with what does not. This equanimity reveals that our happiness comes not from without but from within, relying not on conditions and circumstances but on our own mind, empty of selfness.

## Discussion: Training; altruism and anxiety; the process of habituation

*"Don't give something away and then keep clinging to it with your mind"—is that related to the teaching that we should practice at the level we are capable of, rather than forcing ourselves to do something beyond our abilities and building resentment about it?*

Yes, the instruction is given to "train gently" in the bodhisattva practices—not to spare us difficulty but to support our bodhicitta, our great treasure. Presently our love and compassion wax and wane relative to the changing condition of our mind; this is why we call it relative bodhicitta. Training violently or extravagantly in the bodhisattva's practices can temporarily affect our relative bodhicitta and our motivation and efforts to cultivate it in the same way that over-doing physical training can impede its goal, as exceeding capacity can temporarily limit or diminish both enthusiasm and capacity. So we train gradually. And because we are talking about training the mind, to train *gradually* means to train *continuously*, from now until full realization—to refine present awareness of the condition of our mind, our motivation in the moment, and to grow our love and compassion.

There are times when we must and will exceed our capacity, as when we take compassionate action in an emergency; such moments are most often spontaneous, without self-motive, and therefore not usually followed by regret that we tried to help. It's not that one shouldn't engage in acts of goodness until fully and at all times in altruistic mind; it is that regret for such actions reflects motivation that is not clear and wholehearted but rather compounded with self-interest. The purpose of love and compassion is that they be given away—freely, without pride, attachment, or regard for outcome. When you give away and then regret doing so, you are undercutting and thus weakening the altruistic intention. The direct and unencumbered way: aware of your mind's condition and your motivation in the present moment, clarify and focus your intention to benefit beings and exercise your full capacity, in that moment, to do so. This strengthens you in every way, especially in generating sincere, authentic compassion and love: bodhicitta. This is the reason for training gently in the bodhisattva practices.

*As we are considering over and over the virtue of making others more important than ourselves, I'm wondering about the emotional affliction that some people call codependency. Part of the affliction is to carry out appeasing behavior in order to elicit positive regard from others. This can be very insidious; we can be carrying it out and have no awareness of it. Could you address this in relation to our practice?*

The term codependency is clinical language; for us it might be clarifying to call it compulsive caretaking, because the compulsive aspect is the clue to its purpose. Compulsive behavior is always intended to relieve one's own anxiety, so compulsive caretaking is really about oneself, not about another. There may be compassion involved, but as the underlying motive is to protect the sense of self it may be more self-concerned compulsion than it is altruistic caretaking. That is not to say that a person caught in the dynamics of compulsive caretaking cannot at the same time be motivated by caring concern and compassion, or even practicing to generate bodhisattva aspiration—for we practice on the basis of intention, knowing that perfection is inherent but not yet fully manifest. That is why we practice, after all.

The key is to see whether or not your motivation is authentically about the other or about you. You can see your motivation just by looking within. You may not always perceive the deepest, subtlest, most powerful motivation right away, but as you cultivate the inward attention you will increasingly be able to discern your motivation at any given moment. In situations when it is possible, try this experiment: The moment you see that your motivation has even a grain of self-interest, stop right there—stop in your tracks, stop in the middle of a sentence if you have to, just for an instant. Clarify your intention and then proceed. It can be quite startling to interact with someone who is practicing in that way, who actually stops in the middle of a sentence: "Oops, I need to check my motivation. I see there's some self-interest here so I'm going to step away and come back after I've clarified things a bit more." But what a gift to give to those who are interacting with you. And to yourself. This is not relevant to emergency situations, of course, in which you take the necessary or available action and later replay it in your mind with conscious, clear motivation, to lay down a clear pathway in the brain.

*In compulsive caretaking, would you say that the basic error involved is grasping for a particular outcome?*

The compulsive aspect of the behavior signals that it is principally to manage your own anxiety. It may be anxiety about perceived or dreaded loss of control, or, more deeply, about one's worth or the pervading sense of oneself as being not good enough. Deeper still lies existential dread: threatened loss of identity, a perceived threat to the intactness of the constructed and socially validated "self" we strive so vigilantly to maintain. Anxiety is a form of fear. It can be extremely frightening to sense that one's self-intactness is threatened, from without or from within. Even recognizing one's own intense anxiety can be frightening, as it may seem to confirm the perceived or imagined danger to the "self." That is why the behavior can be so compulsive and why it can be so difficult to acknowledge, as we strive to prevent this anxiety even from coming to consciousness.

As practitioners, we cultivate the inward attention that allows us to see this and other afflictive emotions in the "three moments": as they arise, while they momentarily abide, and as they dissolve. We will become increasingly able to see even the beginnings of anxiety arising, along with our immediate impulse to deny, suppress, manage, and control it—and every time we can see and tolerate that, without going into our automatic program, whatever it may be, the anxiety habit has less hold over us. (Please be aware that I am speaking here about spiritual practice. For people suffering with the condition called anxiety disorder or the invasive anxiety we call panic disorder or panic attack, specific meditative disciplines may or may not be helpful or even safe; that judgement should be taken with guidance from those who have mental health expertise and also familiarity with meditative and awareness practices.)

Cultivating the inward attention is a powerful practice that we engage over and over again, because the afflictive emotions are deeply habituated patterns of perceiving, thinking, and reacting, which operate as if they are continuous. They are not, actually; they are arising moment to moment. This means that each time we can see the affliction arising and refrain from our habituated reaction to it, refrain from imposing the program to which we normally resort, it weakens the habituation and frees the mind a bit. If you practice this on a regular basis you will quite soon start to notice a difference, perceptible enough that you'll be able to see the efficacy of the method—sweeping away that which prevents you from seeing your own clear mind, always already present.

Like, dislike; want, reject. We're like the dog in the experimental lab: stimulus and response, same each time, over and over again. The tiny seed of grasping or repulsion in the mind seems so innocent. Mmm, yum. Ugh, yuck. And each time we gloss over or otherwise act on our afflictive emotions and thoughts we are tightening the ropes that bind us, creating habits so ingrained that they become invisible to us. They become just the way we *be* in the world. But our habits are not who we are; they are just our habits, strengthened with each repetition. Being comfortable with our likes and dislikes and never questioning our identification with them, our sense that they are who we are: this is the state we all are in—until we understand the actual relationship of our mind's productions to the conditions they manifest.

Our minds tend to reify that which has no inherent existence, and then to generate attachment, aversion, or confusion in relation to it, each time reinforcing our conviction in its solidity and our own. It is this mental habituation that we must and will abandon on the bodhisattva way. But remember that the habituation, too, is nothing solid, however binding it may seem; it is a learned, acquired, practiced, and yet empty tendency of mind and behavior, and can change.

To change ingrained habituations of mind and their expressions in our speech and action we must be able to recognize and acknowledge them. *The 37 Bodhisattva Practices* sharpen our attention to our habits by identifying them and their causes so clearly, and by showing us how to correct them on a daily basis. We must also refine our ability to recognize the ways in which the process of habituation actually occurs. Learning to see the conditions and the machinations of our consciousness will definitely show us the moments in which mind reifies thoughts and emotions and then reacts to them as ornaments of the self or threats to the self. *This is what we need to see: the points at which, over and over, we do this with our minds.* Seeing this, we are at choice—because the moment when we see ourselves about to choose yet again the action of body, speech, or mind that is an afflictive habit is the very moment in which we are free: free to refrain from that habitual choice. Instead, simply stop, for an instant, and allow the habitual reaction to dissolve. In that instant we are free. Habituate that.

Consider the lifespan of a thought or any mental arising as a bell curve charting the three moments: inception, abiding, and cessation. To recognize a thought, tendency, or impulse at any point on this curve is to be, in that instant, free of habituation or coercion. It is the regular practice of inward attention and awareness that allows us to see this, and this is a principal reason we meditate. When we see the mind clearly we have power over it, and not just power to restrain it but power to use it for good. This is what it means to tame oneself: to take complete responsibility for one's own mind's process and contents. It is a very advanced level when we talk about complete responsibility, but it's a practice that begins just like this. Nothing daunting about it; we sit in a room, we laugh at ourselves, alone or with others, we support one another in understanding and resolve, we practice alone, moment by moment—and slowly, gradually, over time, a new habituation develops: the habit of seeing clearly and choosing wisely, in wisdom awareness.

## Absolute bodhicitta: Transcending duality, attachment, and suffering

Suffering and confusion fully pervade the realms of existence because their origin, the self-notion and all that stems from it, is the actual *mode of existence* of sentient beings. Upon this fulcrum turn the dynamics of cause and consequence and thus the wheel of samsara. Therefore bodhicitta also must fully pervade manifest reality—and for this must transcend it. Our relative bodhicitta rising ever higher and higher, our minds are now opening to the ultimate.

Ultimate bodhicitta is our true nature, empty and radiant, expressing in our conventional reality as the love and compassion we call relative bodhicitta. The butter is naturally in the milk.

**Verse 22.** The way things appear is your own mind. Mind itself primordially transcends fabricated extremes. Knowing just this, do not create concepts of subject and object. This is the way of a bodhisattva.

Let this pith teaching from Tokme Zangpo roll around in your mind like a luminous marble, turning and turning, mysterious and magnetic, an irresistible invitation to profound awareness. Insight may seem to come and go, glimpsed or sensed for a moment, then dissolving. As a dear student memorably put it, half laughing in consternation and irony, "I just can't grasp the insubstantiality!" We are poised at the crux, about to comprehend something immensely, urgently significant, for here we begin, consciously and intentionally, to deepen our understanding of the actual nature of mind, beings, and phenomena, and thus of suffering and its liberation. Here we taste truth, the nondual union of appearance and emptiness, of familiar and vast: the intimate infinite.

In our conventional ways of thinking we find it very strange to hear that appearances are our own mind. Does this mean that the table actually is my mind, or that it was created by my mind, or that it is a reflection of my mind? Garchen Rinpoche advises us to take these teachings literally, but it seems we often interpret literal to mean material. For the moment, then, just try to suspend the notion that the appearances we call phenomenal reality manifest by jumping out of your head.

At the relative, conventional level, we can say that appearances are our own mind in this sense: Because our minds are *conditioned*— by experience, thinking, habits, karma—our minds are also always *conditioning* whatever we encounter. Our present consciousness is influenced and shaped by innumerable factors—such as age, sex, gender, culture, economies, health, language, ethnicity, genes, relationships, education, religion, nationality, history—and by all the thoughts, emotions, and experiences we have lived up until this moment and in this very moment. Thus, as I see, feel, hear, taste, smell, touch, or sense with my physical senses or my awareness any phenomenon, whether appearing externally or internally, that experience is registering in a mind that is anything but a tabula rasa, a blank slate. My consciousness in every moment seems to be adding to, revising, or in some way recalibrating every prior registration of experience, and thus conditioning every succeeding one. When I see my sister, for example, though I think she is familiar, even think I know her, I am actually perceiving her in terms of how I've seen her before, the kinds of things she has said to me, our shared history, the years apart. And more: I see her through filters of my own self-concept, subtle beliefs about family, webs of hope and fear, thoughts and emotions waving and weaving beneath the surface activity of consciousness. So my sister has little space even to exist in my mind; there is hardly any sister there, in my system of registrations and elaborations. This is the chain of delusion, continuously fabricating our experienced realities while obscuring our direct perception of phenomena simply as they are.

Khyentse Rinpoche explains: "The endless succession of past, present, and future thoughts leads us to believe that there is something inherently and consistently present, and we call it 'mind.' But actually, . . . past thoughts are as dead as a corpse. Future thoughts have not yet arisen. So how could these two, which do not exist, be part of an entity that inherently exists?" He goes on to say, "[If] you examine [your] thoughts more closely, you will see that none of them truly exist. To formulate the existence of something that has no existence at all is called delusion. It is only your lack of awareness and your grasping that make thoughts seem to have some kind of reality. If thoughts had any inherent existence in the absolute nature of mind, they should at least have a form, or be located somewhere. But there is nothing."

There is nothing. Yet this nothing is not just a blank but rather an all-perceiving clarity-emptiness: "Clarity and emptiness are inseparably united in the true nature of mind, which is beyond all concepts of existence and nonexistence."[9] Khyentse Rinpoche is pointing to our natural state, always already present and complete,

9. Dilgo Khyentse, *Heart of Compassion,* 141-143.

available to view when the mind's engagement in subject-object duality is, even for an instant, suspended.

Understand the empty nature of one thought or one thing and you understand the empty nature of all thoughts and all things. Appearances lose their power over your mind. One instant's direct experience of this is the heart of all your practice from then on, as you familiarize yourself with and stabilize this penetrating insight into the true nature of reality, relative and absolute.

Nothing is more important to understand. This may be the only thing we truly do need to understand, yet many of us find it challenging, if not frankly dismaying, to make an approach to this teaching. Enmeshed in and fully identifying with material reality, we can swoon with a kind of mental vertigo and recoil when introduced to the insubstantiality, the essential emptiness, of the appearances and experiences that we take as the very fundaments of our reality. A word of reassurance from an old acrophobe: there is no edge, no precipice to fall from, and no one to fall.

Ha! Reassured now?

To help us approach this teaching—and to solve all our problems forever—here are seven points for contemplation:[10]

1. Mind—open, empty, clear, and luminous, like space.
2. This is the primordial perfection, ground of all.
3. All phenomena, within and without, are of this same nature.
4. Thus mind and appearance: one taste.
5. Thus all objects of grasping and repulsing—including the notion of self—are of this same space-like nature.
6. Thus all causes of suffering collapse, dissolving in the open, empty, clear, luminous expanse.
7. Thus samsara collapses, one with the absolute expanse.

---

10. Please bear in mind that this is being offered not by a scholar or meditation master but by an ordinary practitioner, using concepts to point to that which is beyond concept. Wordy. Please take what is useful to you and check your understanding and any questions or doubts with your teachers and other sources in which you have confidence.

*Mind—open, empty, clear, and luminous, like space.* For some, real-ization of the open, empty nature of mind and phenomena comes as direct insight, while for many the approach is gradual, calling on both analytic and contemplative reflection and on meditative practice. Our intelligence is our good companion on the way, an obstacle only if we cling to it—and then, of course, it is the cling-ing, not the intelligence, that is the obstacle.

We can look for this open, luminous mind: What color is it? How big? Where are its edges and center? Does it even have a center and edges? Can you taste it, touch it? Does it come and go, appear and disappear? No matter where or how we look for mind, it seems we can't put our hands on it, can't define it, qualify it, say what it's made of, where it comes from. However, of our own familiar, functioning, working minds there are some things we can observe directly. We know that our mind can place us anywhere, in any period of time, any state of thought or emotion. You can in an instant imagine being on a far planet in a vast universe, within your own thighbone, or on the guillotine stage with Mary, Queen of Scots, her little dog hiding in her skirts. You can place yourself in a setting of beauty and peace, sweetly at ease, or in a scene of violence and fear, sweating, panicky, heart racing, stomach knot-ting—and in an instant such imaginations dissolve, one with their empty nature. Of our thoughts, emotions, plans, triumphs, and regrets we can observe the same.

We can say, then, that mind's nature seems to be open, unbound-ed, unfettered, unimpeded, all-pervading—and creative. Analogies to sky and space note that everything that exists is abiding in and pervaded by space, so we sometimes say "the space-like nature of mind." We can also discern or sense a present, awake quality in our mind, which recognizes phenomena, inner and outer, including its own condition and nature. This recognizing quality is often referred to as clarity, luminosity, or awareness.

*This is the primordial perfection, ground of all. All phenomena, within and without, are of this same nature,* this inseparable union of clarity-emptiness, with neither beginning nor end. *Thus mind and appearance: one taste.* Thus, as Tokme says, "The way things appear is your own mind."

*Thus all objects of grasping and repulsing—including the notion of self—are of this same nature: open, empty, clear, and luminous, like space.* Absolute and relative: same nature. Appearance and emptiness: nondual. All phenomena, within and without—all that you can see, touch, hear, smell, taste, experience, remember, imagine, think, or feel—are of this same nature, vividly appearing without inherently existing: void of selfness. You are of this same nature. You yourself are the indivisible union of relative and absolute, of appearance and emptiness.

*Thus all causes of suffering collapse and dissolve in the open, luminous expanse.* Of one nature with the mind in which they arise and dissolve, self-grasping and the afflictive emotions naturally collapse, like waves in the boundless sea. The very notion of self, source of all suffering, is not other than the open, empty, clear expanse, the space-like nature of mind. Thus are "liberated" in their own nature all causes of suffering and the basis of samsara itself. *Thus samsara collapses, one with the absolute expanse.* Samsara, field of karmic causation and consequence in which we think we are trapped, is like an illusion, having neither basis nor trajectory nor power, neither past nor present nor future. Samsara is our creation, having no existence apart from its creator, mind, which brings it forth moment by moment. When emptiness dissolves into emptiness, what remains?

This, then, is the once-terrifying emptiness. It is simply how we *be.* Simplicity itself: beingness, isness. Geshe Jampa says that "empty of inherent existence is the ultimate or deepest way in which all phenomena exist . . . [Persons and phenomena are conventional truths that] appear to our mind on a day-to-day basis, while ultimate truths are their deeper mode of existence."[11] There is nothing to fear: this is the end of all our fears.

To realize emptiness is liberation. Even to hear of emptiness diminishes self-grasping, though at first we may seem to tighten

11. Jampa Tegchok, *Transforming* the Heart, 223-225.

our grip in alarm or incomprehension. To rest in and practice on emptiness over and over again is to liberate ourselves moment to moment. We rely on this, returning again and again to this knowledge, and when doubt and uncertainty arise we remember the teachings on reality's true nature, our true nature. In these ways we gain intellectual understanding and familiarity, increasing our tolerance for the concept of emptiness. Over time, with continuing practice, we observe, reflect, and resolve for ourselves, through our own direct experience, that all objects of attachment and aversion, and attachment and aversion themselves, are empty of inherent existence: insubstantial, impermanent, and interdependent, one with and recognized *by, in,* and *as* that which neither comes nor goes. Nothing to grasp for or push away, all afflictive emotions and conflictual thoughts resolve in the vast expanse.

Sometimes your thoughts seem to be flowing in an unbroken, uninterrupted stream; at other times it seems as if a single, particular thought is persisting, dogging your mind without a break, on and on, for hours or days. But in either case, as Dilgo Khyentse Rinpoche has shown us, it's actually just this thought right here, right now—this one, which has no nature of its own, only the same nature as all your other thoughts, the same primordial, empty nature as awareness itself. All appearances are of the same nature as mind. All appearances and one's own mind, then, are not one and the other but simply, essentially, one.

Tokme also says, "Mind itself primordially transcends fabricated extremes"—on the one hand, the conviction that things exist in and of themselves or, on the other, that nothing exists at all. These are the "two extremes" or the "two errors": eternalism and nihilism. An eternalist takes substanceless appearance for substantial reality; a nihilist takes emptiness for nothingness. Well, here and now I am sitting in a chair, talking with you; experientially, something certainly exists. Equally clearly, as we well know from our experience of living in a body, in a world, with other beings, nothing in phenomenal reality, including us, exists unchanging and forever, which means that apparent existence, though vividly displaying, is not intrinsic, inherent. Thus the "two refutations": phenomena cannot be said to exist and cannot be said not to exist.

Phenomena, including beings, exist *conventionally* while not being possessed of *intrinsic* existence. This is the nature of all phenomena. Ultimate reality is not a phenomenon, it is beingness itself: unborn, having neither beginning nor end, cause nor condition, characteristic nor definition.

"Knowing just this," Tokme instructs, "do not create concepts of subject and object." But as soon as "I" is identified, instantly and necessarily there is seen to be "other." Not understanding correctly the nature of reality, imputing selfness to experiencer, experienced, and experiencing,[12] dualistic delusion gives rise to all the realms of confusion and chaos that we call samsaric existence. This dualism is profoundly mistaken, so to live by it is profoundly deluded. In this state, engaged in constructing our identity and our perceived reality as solid and self-existent, structuring them with our thoughts based in I-me-mine, and investing them with the full coloration of impressions and experiences arising from self-reference, we are actually unable to perceive objects, beings, appearances, or mind itself in their original state. We perceive everything, everything, through the filter of this-that, self-other. That is engaging in subject-object duality.

The bodhisattva practices on reality *as it is*. How?

It's as if we're each a little train running on our own little track, *click, click, click,* around and around. Train momentarily jumps the track: great opportunity. Life's tiny upsets and catastrophes, its shocking joys and radical rendings, can shatter the appearances of solidity and continuity we work so hard to sustain. Such moments can be tremendously potent for us. For an instant we are without script, without repertoire or strategy. In a gap. Can we allow that, simply *be with* it? Practice supports us here, especially practice that disciplines and relaxes our minds to tolerate and eventually to rest in bare attention: no fabrication, no elaboration.

---

12. To realize these three in their emptiness nature is to realize the "purity of the three spheres" of agent, action, and object.

One of the quiet powers of meditation and contemplation is to give us moments and sequences of moments in which we are simply without program. Of course, we can be sitting in just the right posture, looking very like meditators, and still be on the track—*click, click, click.* Listen carefully: Every time you see that, you're beyond it, even if just for that instant. What recognizes confusion is clarity itself, luminous natural mind. In every instant that you recognize your mind's arisings, for just that instant you are not *in* those arisings: you are free. Free! Undivided, non-dual. Whole. Recognition and liberation are simultaneous.[13]

To familiarize yourself with this is practice. We can know moment after moment of such instants, each a brief glimpse of natural mind, and recognized as such. That brilliant, penetrating insight can quickly give way again to the confused habitual state—*click, click, click*—but the radical insight has not been destroyed and the true nature did not go anywhere: only your recognition did. And only temporarily.

Don't try to repeat the experience of insight by fabricating or recreating it. Instead, practice faithfully on what the experience has shown you. Expectation, craving, and doubt are obstacles to recognizing what is, so keep practicing, without regard to outcome. Have confidence in your direct experience.

I have to rely on this information all the time. My conditioned mind wants to react to appearances as true, to cling to my thoughts and experiences as having continuity and significance, to retain or repeat any experience of direct insight. Material reality and our sense experiences are seductive; our habitual notions and behaviors are convincing and compelling to us. This is the dynamic we call karmic predisposition; its inertial vector is that we will tend to do that which we've tended to do. Practice to interrupt the deadening habits of conventional mind and behavior. Take every opportunity to see things as they are. Wake up, for the sake of all.

---

13. Padmasambhava, *The Tibetan Book of the Dead*, passim, particularly in the Bardo of the Wrathful Deities.

Tokme Zangpo's profound pith teachings in this verse are what we call pointing out instructions on the nature of mind. It is for us to follow where they point, through study, contemplation, and meditation. It's not enough for our teachers to tell us these things; we need to test the teachings and instructions to find out if and how they work for us. And what does it mean if they do? It means we are becoming free. That is why we call it the liberating Dharma.

To help others escape the bonds of confusion and suffering we must help them untie themselves—and first, of course, we must untie ourselves. I'm untying; sometimes it's difficult, painful, sometimes it's easy and joyful, and I'm sure it's the same for you. There are moments on the path when you're confronted with yourself, your mind, your behavior, your habits, and you think, "This is hopeless, I'll never become the luminous being I am told I truly am." However, it is not a matter of becoming but of recognizing: your actual empty, clear, present nature.

Even in suffering, confusion, or doubt you may register a subtle, evanescent pulse of recognition, of knowing—an intimation of certainty. If it were not so, when you heard the news that it was possible to step out of your suffering, why did you pay attention?

Some years ago a group of miners in Chile became trapped deep below ground, in the tunnels of the collapsed mine.[14] They were there for sixty-nine days, people on the surface praying, technicians searching out means to rescue them. The world seemed to hold its breath. When their headlamps gave out the miners' darkness was impenetrable. They knew they might, right then, be in their tomb. They didn't forget there was sky above, but even when their rescuers reached them the miners needed to draw on faith and courage to abandon the tomb, to trust the little rescue capsule to draw them up again through the massive, imploded rock and earth. And on emerging they were at first stunned, blinded by the light, like newborn critters. How like us this is, trapped in the dark tunnels of our minds, needing faith and courage to choose rescue, and then

---

14. This recollection is from 2010, when the event occurred and was widely reported on in the media.

momentarily bewildered, blinded by the longed-for, overpowering light. We can rise from dark confusion into vast, luminous reality just as it is, ourselves able to throw the light-hook of compassion to those still lost. It takes courage to do so. It takes courage to be a practitioner, to be a bodhisattva, and this courageous constancy is rooted in radical love—the activity of the ultimate, its expressive radiance and warmth—pouring forth spontaneously in the instant that we realize the true nature of mind, of all beings and phenomena, of reality itself.

> *When the thick hide of appearances*
> *is pierced by the arrow of emptiness,*
> *the milk of love pours forth.*

**Verse 23.** When you come across things that attract you, like beautiful rainbows in summertime, do not regard them as real and abandon clinging attachment. This is the way of a bodhisattva.

**Verse 24.** All suffering is like the death of your child in a dream. How exhausting it is to hold illusory appearances as real! Therefore, when you meet with difficult circumstances, see them as illusory. This is the way of a bodhisattva.

These two verses will now show us, simply and directly, how understanding emptiness pulls the thread binding together the entire fabric of illusion-like appearances.

Having seen that all appearances, inner and outer, are of the same open, empty nature as mind itself, what do we now know about encountering what we find pleasing and displeasing, attractive and repugnant? The rainbow in summertime: an image so tender, lovely, and evanescent, so like the beautiful things of life that we long for and cling to—and utterly insubstantial, as are the senses that enjoy them. The death of your child in a dream: you wake up anguished in the night and in the morning weeping, unutterably sad. The whole day takes on the hue and weight of sorrow—and yet no one died. You are borne down by grief for something that didn't happen. We reach for and turn from, cling to and push away: how can we not become weary?

Dudjom Rinpoche likens the moment of directly seeing true nature to taking a cloth off your head: relief![15] This is the relief of liberation, and as Dilgo Khyentse Rinpoche says, "Once you have been able to recognize the empty nature of mind, attachment and desire will not arise when your mind sees something beautiful, and hatred and repulsion will not develop whenever it comes across anything horrible or unpleasant. Since these negative emotions no longer arise, the mind is no longer deceived or deluded, karma is not accumulated, and the stream of suffering is cut."[16]

End of story.

The deepest, innermost meanings of these teachings are self-secret: they will bloom in your mind when you are able to understand them. The only harm they can do is for you to misuse them—to tell yourself or others, "Oh well, everything is empty, nothing is real, so I can do whatever I please." Actually, it is the opposite. Geshe Jampa: The "outstanding person is one who knows that phenomena are empty of true existence and who is also able to posit karma and its results, seeing that although nothing exists truly, cause and effect are viable."[17] Because mind and phenomena are intrinsically empty, it definitely, definitively matters what we do with our minds, with our speech, and with our actions. What exists in our mind and activity is there only because we put it there. We are completely responsible.

The truths of emptiness, interdependence, karma, and love are the most profound ethics. When you understand that emptiness is the womb of creation and the very proof of existence, and that the ceaseless creation and dissolution of conventional appearances are the very proof of emptiness, you recognize your own specific,

---

15. Dudjom Rinpoche, *Extracting the Quintessence of Accomplishment*, 12.
16. Dilgo Khyentse, *Heart of Compassion*, 144.
17. Jampa Tegchok, *Transforming the Heart*, 261.

immediate, necessary responsibility and power. And when you recognize and take up your responsibility, your holy power for the good of all, you are truly actualizing bodhicitta.

## Discussion: Responsibility, power, the Two Truths

*The thought that nothing matters breeds apathy, and that's the worst thing for me.*

Apathy is a form of withdrawal, avoidance. To think that everything is empty, thus nothing matters—this is a deep confusion about the nature of reality and the responsibility and power of beings, especially of humans, because we have free will. Karma means cause and consequence. We are creating karma all the time except when we're resting in true nature, and when we are creating the cause, be it positive or negative, we are also choosing the consequence. This understanding is power. We are endlessly creative, and all that power of vision and expression is the worldly source of worldly wonders that endure through centuries. People are still marveling at cave paintings made by our ancients: lyrical, expressive symbols and narratives of life. The same power of creativity is also the source of evils beyond speech. We choose. The more awake, the greater the responsibility.

The Buddhadharma offers teachings for beings—not just humans—of every condition and at every level, every kind of intelligence, every kind of mind. We need to think about the teachings and to test them in our own lives, to see for ourselves if they are clarifying our condition, benefitting our mind. The surest indicator to look for is the state of your bodhicitta, your compassion and love. If your bodhicitta is not rising, or is even sinking, please seek additional teachings and guidance, both inner and outer. Keep studying, contemplating, and practicing on what you have understood and have confidence in and your certainty in the Dharma will grow. Remember that truth *is*; you are never separate from that.

*When I hear these teachings about the absolute, what is very helpful for me is remembering their relation to the relative. I think the danger lies in grasping on to one or the other point of view. Seeing things from the point of view of the relative, where our afflictions arise, is awfully small and cramped, but grasping too much to the point of view of the absolute and wanting somehow to live there doesn't allow us to really manifest the high view in our day-to-day life.*

Yes. Absolute and relative both are. This is the truth of the Two Truths. Form is emptiness, emptiness form: relative and absolute, existence and being, primordially one and inseparable, from the beginningless.

# CHAPTER FIVE

# THE SIX PERFECTIONS (VERSES 25-30)

We may think of great spiritual masters as being actually different from us in nature: able to realize because already realized. But the seed of enlightenment, *tathagatagarbha*, is within all. Are you admiring the master's great wisdom and love while thinking that realization is beyond you? Why do you think so many buddha and bodhisattva images depict them gracefully pointing out the path ahead? Our teachers revere their teachers, who show the way; they profoundly honor the teacher's feet by standing up on their own, to walk the path the teacher shows.

Effort is the antidote to spiritual laziness and self-doubt. Not anxious striving, but sincere commitment to the bodhisattva way, motivated by compassionate concern and love for beings. Anxious striving is more apt to be a continuation, now in the spiritual domain, of our habits of personality—especially the habit of self-doubt and the thought that there is something wrong with us, that we're not good enough. Not good enough for what? To be? Something wrong with us because we are confused, because we suffer, because we have not yet recognized the wisdom to which our teachers point? Our confusion is a speck in the eye. Truth is. If I don't see it, it is only—*only*—because I am clinging to what is false. That is basically what anxious striving is: deluded clinging and grasping, which is precisely what obscures from our view the longed-for natural state.

I, too, used to be an anxious, striving practitioner with a painful burden of something-wrong-with-me, but even my small experience in the Dharma has allowed me to relax, at least a bit, as I observe how the blessings of teachers, teachings, and practice clear away what temporarily obscures the jewel ever present within. Many years ago, frustrated and rebellious, I complained one day to a friend, "I'm taking teachings, I'm studying, I'm practicing, but is all this activity really going to bring me to enlightenment?" My wise friend replied, "Let me put it to you this way: If, like Orpheus, you sit on a hillside to sing up the sun, will your song really bring up the sun? Probably not—but you'll be awake to see the sun when it rises."[1] It is in this spirit that we turn now to deepen our bodhisattva training, sweeping away laziness and anxious striving, generating good heart for the path.

Foundational to the bodhisattva trainings are the *paramitas* or the Six Perfections (Transcendental Virtues, Far-reaching Attitudes): generosity, ethics, patience, effort, meditative concentration, and wisdom. The paramitas are specific practices and ways of living in the world: mindsets, attitudes, and intentions that mature our relative bodhicitta. I have heard the Sanskrit word *paramita* explained as "gone to the other shore"—transcending dualistic delusion. One of my first teachers, the profound and humble Khenchen Palden Sherab, spoke of the paramitas as the natural radiance of bodhicitta.[2] Whatever level you have reached in your bodhicitta, your great, empty love, the Six Perfections will express that naturally.

We will consider the paramitas in a specific order, which can be seen as a developmental framework, although they aren't necessarily practiced only in this order or separately from each other. We already know these far-reaching attitudes in our ordinary lives, for just as relative bodhicitta reflects ultimate bodhicitta, so conventional generosity, for example, reflects transcendent generosity.

---

1. Priscilla Mueller, personal communication, 1986.
2. See his teachings on Prajnaparamita and the Six Perfections in Ven. Khenpo Palden Sherab Rinpoche, *Prajnaparamita: The Six Perfections*.

The perfection practices are said to develop in the mind like this: *Generosity*, abundantly giving to benefit others, is a caring mind toward beings that leads one naturally to refrain from harming them, giving rise to a pure morality and *ethics*. Moral ethics require and also create the basis for *patience*, antidote to anger, and patience makes possible joyful *effort*, diligence, perseverance in the face of time, obstacles, and discouragement. This enables us to engage fruitfully with the disciplines for developing *meditative concentration*, which clarifies and stabilizes mind, allowing us to recognize and rest in the natural *wisdom* state.

Seen as medicine for the disordered, painful mind, I think of the paramitas also as six elixirs: *generosity* for greed, miserliness, grasping, and the impoverished mind; *ethics* for the wild mind of self-seeking and thus the arrogance of wrongdoing; *patience* for hatred, anger, and the intolerance that shutters the good heart; *joyful effort* for indolence, laziness, discouragement, loss of heart, as a restorative for confidence and a bellows to fire up faith; *meditative concentration* for mental clarity and stability and thus for relaxing and recognizing the natural wisdom state. Finally, *transcendent wisdom* is not "for" something, it simply is: ultimate wisdom, the true nature, primordial perfection. The elixir of truth is truth.

**Verse 25.** When even one's body must be given up when aspiring for enlightenment, what need is there to mention material things? Therefore, practice generosity, without hope of reward or karmic results. This is the way of a bodhisattva.

Are we not, in every instant, breathing in and breathing out with all of existence—cosmos, natural world, critters like and unlike ourselves—giving and receiving in a ceaseless, co-creating cycle of reciprocity and interdependence? We might think of generosity as just the giving part, but that is only half the story, for inbreath and outbreath are a circle of interbeing.[3] We can understand this

---

3. See Thich Nhat Hanh, *Interbeing: Fourteen Guidelines for Engaged Buddhism*. Also, The Order of Interbeing: orderofinterbeing.org.

naturally occurring cycle of generativity and receptivity as the dynamic matrix for life, a continuous, living exchange with those who conceive, birth, and raise us; the cells, plants, and animals who give their momentary lives for our momentary lives; the subtle energy of the stars and the great power of the elements. Our growth and development as humans depend on the gifts and challenges of everyone and everything we interact with, which all, in this cycle, are in some way our progenitors. Even our most positive qualities mature not just through enjoyable conditions but also through the "slings and arrows of outrageous fortune," frequently dealt us by other beings. All whose friendship and all whose enmity shape who we become, in every lifetime, in every form, on all these we rely, and they on us. This abundant, generative exchange is, in a word, generosity. Simply by existing, we are participants in its sacred cycle. As bodhisattvas, we participate intentionally.

It is taught that we live countless lives in myriads of forms as we transmigrate through the realms of existence, and thus a bodhisattva, human and non-human, will give away countless bodies on the path to enlightenment, just by living and dying, and in particular lifetimes by acts of great compassion and courage, such as during war and catastrophe, to save others. If I am willing to give my bodies for you, why would I not be willing to give you anything and everything else, "without hope of reward or karmic results"?

Buddhadharma addresses three particular meanings of generosity: material giving, giving freedom from fear, and giving Dharma. The first, material generosity, is giving something tangible to benefit others. The intention isn't limited to material benefit; it could be to relieve beings' difficulties or to secure their happiness, but as giving material things is relatively easy for many this is a natural starting point in developing the practice of generosity. When even material giving affronts one's selfish clinging, a practice to help the generosity-challenged is just to pass a penny back and forth between your two hands, one giving, one receiving.

It is the transcendent nature of the perfection practices that takes them beyond the qualities we are familiar with in conventional life.

Let's use material generosity to help us understand this. I am going to give a candy to my friend. There are two people involved, whom we perceive as solid and real, as we perceive also the candy and the action taking place. I pass the candy to my friend, who receives it in his hand. The action is intended, it occurs, it is completed, and . . . we think something happened, don't we? However, all these apparently existing elements are impermanent, insubstantial, composite, and so on. Neither my friend nor I, nor the candy, is solid and inherently existing—so how could the action that we perceive as real have truly occurred? Real, yet not true: real, in relative terms; untrue, ultimately. Appearing in dependence upon causes and conditions, giver, action, and receiver lack inherent existence. Intention to benefit, with no reification of giver, receiver, or action, is pure motivation, transcendent generosity—the "purity of the three spheres" (agent, action, object). Appearance arises and dissolves, leaving no karmic trace in the mind from elaboration or fixation, because there is none. Emptiness-clarity pervades.

You don't even need a functioning body to practice generosity. One of my spiritual friends is gradually losing the capabilities of her body due to degenerative disease. Any person in that condition might think, "I'm trapped in my wheelchair and bed, can't get up to go to the bathroom, can't use my hands, my mind isn't always clear: obviously I can't do spiritual practice." But she knows better. She desires that beings be happy and free from suffering. That desire in itself is generosity practice. Generate this intention of great love while recalling the empty nature of all appearances and you are practicing generosity paramita.

Your mind is free to cultivate transcendent generosity or any of the transcendent attitudes at any time, in any place, in any condition. I could heap a fortune upon you, intending it for your sole benefit, and though the fortune might be great the benefit would be limited—because vast benefit comes from vast aspiration. Always remember the profound meaning in Tokme's verse 36: "In brief, wherever you are and whatever you are doing, always examine the state of your mind." We look into the condition of our mind to ascertain that we are in fact intending benefit by our actions, without investment in self, appearances, or outcomes. Motivation is everything. If your motivation is love and compassion, even though you may not in this lifetime see a beneficial outcome, that good seed will at some point, in some manner, produce good result.

The second generosity is to give beings freedom from fear. It could be as simple as lifting from a puddle an insect who is going to drown or as broadly impactful as encouraging your town or country's beneficial reception of refugees. You are protecting living beings from danger and fear. Simple words and acts of understanding and caring concern also lift away fear, which so often compounds the anguish of loss, illness, loneliness, poverty, and conflict.

The third and highest generosity is referred to as giving Dharma. The word Dharma means Buddhadharma, but it also means truth, spiritual law—and whether we are scholars, yogis, or beginning students, whether we follow the Buddhadharma or another path, we all have some truth, some Dharma to give. For example, your friend's child has died and he is deeply grieving. What you understand is that all beings die, sorrow is normal, and this bereaved parent's grief is the continuing expression of his love even as it is also mixed with attachment—so you witness with him in his immense loss, the relative reality, and you join him in remembering and dwelling in the love, which reflects absolute, transcendent reality. No words of relative and absolute need be spoken: only grief and love. That is an example of giving Dharma.

When you give Dharma you are giving wisdom that dispels ignorance, the cause of all suffering; this is liberating the mind, in some degree, however limited or momentary. We can always find a way to communicate to another what we ourselves are learning from spiritual study and practice, and from life, whether we have received one teaching or have completed years of contemplation in mountain solitudes. Here, as in all our activities, we dedicate both intention and merit to the benefit of all while offering what we can for those we touch here and now.

I think of Garchen Rinpoche as Buddha Bodhicitta. In giving Dharma and in living his life he shows us, simply and directly, the essence of the bodhisattva's good heart. One of the characteristics of his teachings is that he gives us "how it works," explaining patiently and clearly how we can lift our lives into the Dharma, transforming the ordinary field of suffering into a vast field of merit. Rinpoche frequently conveys a startling teaching that demonstrates how every moment of conventional life can be paramita practice. For example, he has suggested that when you go shopping for a particular item, instead of poking around in the store to find the least expensive one, consider the manufacturer, the shop owners, their families and employees, and buy the slightly more expensive item, consciously and generously contributing to the profits and wellbeing of everyone involved. And think, says Rinpoche, of the taxes you pay to town, state, and nation, giving us roads, hospitals, schools, security services, and so on. I have often heard him say that when we pay the government we are giving to every single individual in the country. Taxes: a great generosity practice! Who thinks like this? A great bodhisattva. You, if you choose.

Giving freely and wisely, with love and compassion for all, without attachment to outcome and recalling emptiness and inter-being, is the perfection of generosity.

**Verse 26.** If you lack moral discipline, you cannot accomplish even your own purpose, so wanting to achieve the purpose of others is truly absurd. Therefore, protect your discipline without concern for worldly existence. This is the way of a bodhisattva.

All ethics and morality rely on some degree of basic consideration and respect for others and thus some willingness to adjust our behavior to avoid causing harm. Without that willingness we really have little to offer others even in the limited conventional sense, and no possibility at all of accomplishing their ultimate purpose or our own.

Ethical discipline can be described as refraining from negative actions, practicing positive actions, and fulfilling the ultimate purpose of beings. In general, the framework of ethical discipline in the Buddhadharma is given in the ten negative actions to be abandoned and the ten positive actions to be cultivated (for each, three of body, four of speech, and three of mind). I include them here in some detail because every time I review them I find my mind benefitted by their clarity and precision. They are an excellent mind sifter.

## The Ten Nonvirtuous

### Body

1. Taking life, especially knowingly and with intent, motivated by self-interest and afflictive emotions; just being alive means we are constantly killing beings, but to kill on purpose with selfish motive is a heavy nonvirtue.

2. Stealing: taking what is not given, especially what is not given freely and intentionally, and not only material things but also such intangibles as stealing another's good name by false report.

3. Sexual misconduct: causing harm through sexual behavior, especially that which damages the relationship commitments and bonds of oneself or others.

### Speech

1. Lying: by omission or commission, communicating what one knows is untrue, especially for personal advantage (Gar Rinpoche sometimes speaks of the "virtuous lie" that brings harmony to situations of conflict or that protects endangered beings).

2. Divisive speech: sowing discord and division among people, considered a heavy negative action, sometimes called "creating schism in the sangha"; includes libel, slander, and calumny.

3. Harsh speech: painful, disturbing, unkind words that stir waves of reaction in the minds of others and create obstacles to harmonious, happy relationships.

4. Worthless chatter: idle talk, unmindful and without benefit, distracting from clear intention and purposeful, beneficial activity. (Here, too, Gar Rinpoche has said that even idle chatter can be virtuous when it brings harmony and happiness to others. Always he is reminding us of intent: love and compassion can transform any word or action to good.)

*Mind*

1. Covetousness: desiring what is not yours, envying those who have what you want, which also means you are forgetting or ignoring karmic cause and consequence.

2. Wishing harm on others, arising from anger (itself often fed by covetousness, envy, jealousy).

3. Wrong views arising from ignorance of the nature of reality, especially in relation to karma.

## The Ten Virtuous (in general, the opposites of the Ten Nonvirtuous)

*Body*
1. Respecting and protecting life and physical integrity, for oneself and others, including Earth and the basic elements of life.

2. Respecting and protecting what belongs to others and to all: public goods and the public good, and not just the good of human beings; integrity in relation to others: not pulling others down.

3. Respecting the gifts, purposes, and responsibilities of sexuality and protecting the bonds of intimacy, love, and commitment in one's own and others' relationships.

*Speech*
1. Utterances of truth in speech, writing, and other means of communication, including visual images, music, theater, media, and so on.

2. Using communication to foster and protect good relationships and harmony among beings.

3. Using communications of kindness, respect, encouragement, and positive intentions to promote wellbeing and confidence.

4. Communication that brings benefits (benefits of clarity, goodness, happiness, harmony, and so on).

*Mind*

1. Generosity.

2. Altruistic love and patience.

3. Recognizing and acting in the light of karma, interdependence, and love.

To protect one's ethical discipline "without concern for worldly existence" means clear discernment regarding motivation in the present moment. We are not engaging in ethical conduct in order to secure good repute, more money, or self-satisfaction; those would be aspirations for worldly existence.

There are circumstances in which caring about the worldly implications of our ethics can be important, such as when our ethical mind and conduct allow others to rely on us with confidence as trustworthy friends, parents, teachers, leaders, and so on. This is especially significant for spiritual teachers, whose acts and words are beneficial principally because they arise in pure motivation, in bodhicitta—so those who teach, train, and guide others on the path must commit to impeccability. Since we are all works in progress, to be impeccable as a human being means to do your best to know your mind's condition at every moment and thus be capable of recognizing motivation, refraining from harmful action, and building intention and capacity to act for the benefit of all. Taking responsibility for one's own derelictions and shortcomings is essential to impeccability. For people in positions of respect and power as well as for those in humble positions, this sometimes includes openly acknowledging one's errors, being willing to hear how they affect others, and committing to sincerely consider and address one's faults.

Integrity is of the essence in ethics and morality, and understanding karma is a sound basis for developing integrity. The student of karma learns that karmic cause and consequence are our own affair, arising in our own mind's conditions and motivations, no one else's. This is a sharp spur to cultivating the kind of integrity and impeccability that characterize sound moral ethics.

In everything Gar Rinpoche says and does he demonstrates the high moral ethics of love-emptiness, and both he and Jetsun Milarepa teach that the essence of ethics is to abandon deceiving others. Authentic ethics are like a well-cast bell, ringing true, while pretense or performance, however convincing, eventually reveal their fault line: self-grasping. As our self-grasping diminishes in caring concern for others and with insight into emptiness, our steadily increasing bodhicitta expresses naturally in moral discipline and ethical conduct.

**Verse 27.** For bodhisattvas who desire a wealth of virtue, all harm is like a precious treasure. Therefore, without hostility, be patient with everyone. This is the way of a bodhisattva.

Our positive qualities develop in being exercised, like muscles, and some of the best exercises for cultivating virtue are those called forth in confronting our nonvirtue, especially our afflicted reactions to the nonvirtuous actions of others—which of course often mirror our own. It is relatively easy to be patient in one's carefully arranged little world, treated with respect and consideration, surrounded by harmonious, kind, loving, patient people. But even with all our careful arrangements the conventional world of people and situations, of inner troubles and confusions, of karma fruiting up, is going to push against and into our self-concern, to dislodge our happy fictions of equanimity, throwing our attachments and aversions up in our face. That is in fact our fortunate karma, because we actually need these disturbing companions and appearances—to show us our mind's disordered thought patterns, so we can master them. Fortunately, the world and other beings are generous providers of the necessary disturbances.

What appears to obstruct, threaten, or even hurt us makes it both necessary and possible for us to develop patience, the willingness to meet difficult experiences and conditions without compounding the karma that has given rise to them. Tokme Zangpo says that to the bodhisattva "all harm is like a precious treasure." Precious, indeed, is all that challenges our rigidity, fixation, and self-concern, all that moistens and softens the hard-pack of our minds.

On the bodhisattva path patience is essential: aspiring and acting to liberate all beings, we practice without regard to time or outcome. Love and compassion strengthen patience, and patience nourishes love and compassion. We cultivate patience for the benefit of both ourselves and others: for ourselves because anger-hatred, the actual energy fueling impatience, damages our relative bodhicitta, and for others so that we will not harm those very beings we vow to love and liberate. Patience is an antidote to anger, mild or wild. We could also say that in the perfection practices, the far reaching attitudes, patience is pivotal, building on the necessary foundation of generosity and ethics and making possible the practices that come next: effort, concentration, and wisdom.

Patience can be a stern taskmaster. Requiring us to take genuine responsibility for our minds and actions, patience restrains self-interested, self-righteous hostility and anger in reaction to apparent attack or insult. And patience can be austere, laying bare the burning embers of resentment and anger in the very instant we are incensed, poised and impelled to act. What a patient teacher is patience! Stern, strict, demanding, yes, and also like a parent, holding us tightly, constraining us when we would rail and flail, with wisdom and compassion taming our reckless minds and words and actions.

That impatience is a form of anger points to the essence teaching and practice here: cultivating patience devoid of hostility. What looks like patience can sometimes be its opposite, as when you are being patient not with but *at* a person or situation. That is performative patience, wielded like a weapon. It is when we are confronted with what triggers our impatience that we are able to recognize and take responsibility for the hostility in our reaction.

We speak of three kinds of patience, which are also three methods for its practice: patience as forbearance, patience as endurance, and patience as courage. Forbearing patience is non-retaliation. When someone has hurt your feelings, offended you, harmed someone or something you care about, taking even enough of a pause to think "I don't want to hurt back" is a powerful inner practice of patience. The next thought could be, "I thank that person, my spiritual friend," because in that moment you learn something about yourself: your impulse to retaliate, your ability not to; the importance and power of the inward attention that allows you an instant of delay and thus the possibility of wise choice; and your willingness to restrain yourself for the benefit of another. Going further, in the moment of recognizing hostility we can actually extend compassion and love to the frustrating person or situation, the one we perceive or experience as the harm-doer, the one Tokme calls a precious treasure. Relying upon the one toward whom we experience angry impatience arising, we lift our bodhicitta in the moment of testing. This is the true "wealth of virtue."

Right relationship with circumstance is as important as right relationship with beings, for the condition of our mind is always at stake. I think of the cancer diagnosis to which one might react with outrage and anger: "Why me?"—a rather pitiful indictment of fate, ignoring karmic cause and consequence, and a momentary loss of compassion for those considered not-me: do we really want them to have cancer instead of us? Without some understanding of and confidence in karma, anger is a common reaction to such experiences. Patient forbearance pacifies the childish impulse to refute and refuse what disappoints, hurts, or frightens us, liberating us into willingness and capacity to experience life just as it is.

Exacting discernment is necessary to the practice of patience. Consider, for example, the anger we may feel toward those who harm us, others, the environment, or a cherished cause. We may think of this anger as righteous, and it may well arise along with noble intentions, but anger and rage are self-involved reactions, afflictive emotions. They will compromise the clarity and impeccability of the fierce compassion and love that motivate authentic righteous wrath. Wrath is moral outrage, an authentic and effective expression of love. Moral outrage seeks right relationship; rage destroys it. Restrain the act arising from immediate, impatient, hostile emotion long enough to glance within, to recognize and rest in mind of compassion—then act to benefit all.

Endurance is the second patience. Life for all beings, and certainly life on the path of the bodhisattva, spiritual lover and warrior, can be difficult and demanding, requiring endurance. (We can rejoice when it is also exhausting, because it is supposed to be: progress on the spiritual path actually means that our karmic debts and propensities are being exhausted.) We need patience simply to endure the mundane, as Garchen Rinpoche has spoken of it: to put up with the duties and the trivial, boring, repetitive events and activities of human beings, from brushing our teeth to tolerating the neighbors, not to mention the apparently unending obligations that allow us to practice tax generosity. How will we attain anything noble or even minimally desirable in our lives unless we are able to tolerate the challenges and obstacles in our way, even the simple passage of time between intention and accomplishment? Simply put, patience is required in order to accomplish anything at all. Enduring our needs and difficulties, accepting life's requirements and challenges, we work with our barley flour minds.

Endurance is supported and nourished by remembering the simple facticity of impermanence and interdependence and the truth of emptiness to which they point. Everything changes, comes and goes, including what is hard to bear.

Our mastery of patience takes on impetus when wedded to gratitude. Rejoice in apparent obstacles, which strengthen our resolve, and rejoice in signs of patience increasing. The most important sign will likely not be something dramatic but rather a gradual recognition that in the situations that have usually found you annoyed and impatient you are becoming less reactive.

The third patience is courage. Courage to live in a body; to face and master what is difficult, painful, and frightening in your life; to participate in the world, which is not in your control; to be honest and sincere, to be humble, to be kind, without regard to circumstance or outcome. And, for the bodhisattva aspiring to liberate all beings from ignorance, courage to approach the vast, profound truth of emptiness.

Geshe Jampa has written, "Meditating on emptiness cuts through the layers of our misconceptions, and this can initially be unnerving. We have to be able to bear the fact that all phenomena are empty. . . ."[4] It can be a relief simply to hear these words, this acknowledgement that our own initial trepidation, bewilderment, and even panic at hearing of the void nature of all phenomena is so normal that it takes its place in the high Dharma teachings: don't be afraid, balance alarm and aspiration, keep practicing. Be patient.

Contained in this teaching is also the simple fact that the approach to understanding and directly experiencing emptiness is, for most of us, very gradual, perhaps so gradual as sometimes to bring with it discouragement or despair. This heart of wisdom, the absolute itself—might I fail to realize it? This is fear arising from doubt; it can also be accompanied by shame. I have known these emotions and held them as a secret sorrow over many years, borne only with the patience of aspiration and the armor of faith, so I want to say this to you: Please recognize that this heartache of self-doubt is arising not from incapacity but from your profound longing—a *divine impatience* that can sear like fire. However inchoate, it is a resonance of indwelling truth, arising with your urgent desire for the liberation of yourself and others. This impatience is of compassionate love, not of anger, and instead of destroying your

---

4. Jampa Tegchok, *Transforming the Heart*, 284.

good qualities increases them, when held in patient humility and faith. You will recognize it in the mounting warmth of bodhicitta and in the eager, joyful commitment and effort it arouses in you. In this condition of mind, over and over again we allow doubt to dissolve in longing, impatience to be lifted away by love for all.

Let us take deep into our hearts these words of the great Dilgo Khyentse Rinpoche, calling us to "the deep, inner courage that it takes to be ready, out of compassion, to work over many aeons for the sake of beings and to face without any fear the highest truths of the teachings—that ultimately all phenomena are totally empty by nature, that emptiness is expressed as radiant clarity, that there is a buddha nature, a self-existing primordial wisdom that is uncompounded, and an absolute truth beyond the reach of the intellect."[5]

We need not fear looking into the mirror of reality and recognizing there our own true face, nor need we fear not being able to recognize it—because it *is*. There is nothing that is not of this nature. Let fall away all preconceptions about ultimate truth and practice with joyful patience.

**Verse 28.** Even hearers or solitary realizers, who accomplish only their own purpose, strive as if putting out a fire on their head. Seeing this, practice with diligence—the source of good qualities—for the sake of all beings. This is the way of a bodhisattva.

Diligence, joyful effort, flourishes in soil nourished by clear aspiration and intention, softened regularly with patience. Most things worth doing and even those not so worthy require time and effort, and we are usually quite diligent to secure the mundane things we desire and need. How leisurely we can be, though, in our efforts, day by day and hour by hour, to realize our highest aspirations. Though we have studied and practiced on impermanence, we tend to live as if what matters most are our worldly responsibilities and pleasures, and we will get to spiritual purpose and practice: later, when we have time, soon, some day . . . maybe. Oh, well.

---

5. Dilgo Khyentse, *Heart of Compassion*, 157-158.

Another word for diligence is enthusiasm: enthusiasm for what is important. Whatever your spiritual intention, if you don't place that first in your heart your enthusiasm may seem to rise up one day and flag the next, joyful effort easily drawn to more immediate and immediately gratifying pursuits than liberating all beings. An old friend, faithfully traveling long distances to attend session after session of teachings, was very honest about this, one day saying, "I know this is what I want to do with my whole life, but I'm not sure it's what I want to do with all my weekends."

Lifetime to lifetime, nothing is more important than fulfilling our spiritual potential and the ultimate purpose of ourselves and others, so we need to understand how to further these commitments in every circumstance of our lives. When our wholehearted aspiration articulates through all our activities of body, speech, and mind, diligence and enthusiasm are truly well described as joyful effort: a steady continuity of purpose not only unimpeded by but actually even supported by challenging and apparently adverse conditions. For example, if you think you can't practice because you must care for your sick friend, your caregiving is your practice: holding mind of vast compassion for the many as you minister to the one. This principle can be followed in every moment. There is no obstacle to spiritual practice in any condition or circumstance if our mind is functioning, because the essence of practice is in the mind, in love and compassion.

Even if or when the brain-based mind declines, prior imprints of consistent attention to truth and love can persist. For example, Gar Rinpoche explained to me that a foundation of practice on the clear light nature of the deity (Tara, Chenrezig, or another) can give important spiritual support in later dementia, the deity image stirring resonance and memory traces—most especially as a reminder of the clear light, the true nature of both deity and practitioner.

In some circumstances and conditions it may be that the only practice you can offer is your desire that all beings be free of suffering. That is the compassionate essence of your bodhisattva commitment, so offer that deep-hearted desire, over and over again. The joyous effort required to think that thought is simply to remember and be willing to think it. And to put some energy into it: "On the basis of my own suffering I know what suffering is. I long for all beings to be free of suffering, and I will do everything I can for their freedom." Generate this aspiration until your body heats up and sweating begins—as if a fire is burning on your head. *Stoke* your joyous effort. Regenerate that powerful intention whenever it comes to mind; make it explicit at every opportunity. If that is all you do, and you do it with joy and love, at the end you will find that your whole life will have been transformed, for you will have become one with bodhicitta. Don't take debility as an excuse: in your mind you can be generating the altruistic intention with every breath, even on your deathbed. Just as in tonglen, breathing in and breathing out. No obstacle. And at the end, when that very last breath leaves the body, the great generosity practice: effortlessly, you offer your death for the liberation of all.

Joyous effort will keep us on the path in a conscious, sustained way. There is suffering in life; there is suffering on the path. Shall we wait for a life with no pain and no challenges? How would that work? With no suffering, why would you even think of liberation, for yourself or anyone else? Practice spiritual economy: Life is painful. Love anyway. Love more.

People engaging in spiritual practice for only their own liberation may be among the most diligent of practitioners. And what about those who wish to liberate all beings? Our efforts need to be total, no holds barred; the freedom of all beings depends on us.

I reflect sometimes, in a very personal way, on what would have become of me in this lifetime if I hadn't had the good fortune to meet kind teachers who had themselves formed this great intention, who diligently practiced and trained, who were willing and able to give me the teachings and practices that would dispel my confusion. What if, having met them, I hadn't recognized their kindness or had not taken advantage of the great opportunity, even to the minimal extent that I have? Most of the time I can hardly be said to be practicing at all, much less as if there is a fire on my head, but sometimes I am—and with what my teachers have given me, if I had consistently been practicing with joyful effort I am sure my progress would have been greater. But in this lifetime I have met true teachers, I have taken the teachings, I am practicing, and that makes all the difference to my willingness and effort to penetrate conditioning, to generate bodhicitta. What if someone is relying upon me in the way I rely upon my teachers? Beings are relying on us, in fact, all the time, because we are completely interdependent: we inter-are. There is nothing on this planet or in our universe that is not affected by every other element or event, not the blink of an eye that doesn't register a pulse somewhere in vast space. If you recognize that your happiness depends on others then you can be certain that others' happiness depends on you.

Diligence is the bed in which the river of bodhicitta runs strong, leaving no one stranded on the riverbanks. Joyful, persistent, altruistic effort is *armor-like* diligence, protecting our minds and allowing us to engage in bodhisattva efforts and conduct per-sistently, consistently, until all are free. Without this, the diligence of *application* is sporadic and desultory; with it we are applying the efforts needed to face all obstacles, *insatiable* in our joyous effort to fulfill the ultimate purpose of ourselves and others.[6]

Enthusiastic effort is needed to counter our laziness, which prospers in self-centered indulgence and also in excessive activity, stealing away mind and time not for the ultimate but for the mundane.[7] Loss of heart, discouragement that saps both aspiration and effort, is a particularly slippery and pernicious kind of spiritual laziness, similar to a condition called acedia in early Christian monastic tradition. Pema Sangdzin Khandro referred to this as lethargy, "a dangerous point of complacency in the inner develop-ment," like "the cold water that doesn't move."[8] I have experienced this and also known others who have been caught in it. One of its challenges is that the sufferer can be blind to the condition,

---

6. See Dilgo Khyentse, *Heart of Compassion*, 161.
7. First explained to me by Khenpo Konchog Tamphel.
8. Personal communication. See also Du Bois, *Light Years*, 260, n.134.

refuse to acknowledge it, or reject the means offered to address it. This lethargy, or torpor, is a deep heaviness, an immovability. It is like resistance but more dead-set, more like refusal—refusal to generate the faith that is its cure, the warmth, the ardor, which will open up the ice-cold water to move again. And deep within this refusal can hide a turning against those who offer spiritual help and against the help they offer—a refusal unrecognized by the sufferer as pride.

It is the practitioner's responsibility to generate and regenerate faith. Sometimes diligence is simply this: to blow on the dark, cold ember for as long as it takes to kindle a spark—and then to keep blowing. No one can do this for us, but we can be sure we are well supported by those whose diligent efforts have raised the warmth of faith again and again in their own minds. The key is bodhicitta, love and compassion for all beings and for all of existence, and haste to secure ultimate liberation for all. Let us confidently, eagerly, insatiably take up joyful effort, the source of good qualities, for the sake of all beings.

**Verse 29.** Disturbing emotions are destroyed by insight grounded in calm abiding. Knowing this, cultivate meditative concentration that purely transcends the four formless absorptions. This is the way of a bodhisattva.

We all know some activities where we find it natural and easy to gather and maintain focus and concentration, perhaps in playing music, skiing, bathing your child, making love, and so on. But when you decide to "do" what we call "meditating," have you noticed that often, after the first few seconds or minutes of unforced, relaxed attention, it becomes more like trying to not try? Take heart, because if you have the ability to concentrate in any activity you have the ability to concentrate in the inner activity we call meditating. Concentrating, in general, means sustaining attention to our intended focus, other elements of experience ignored, receding to the background, or dropping below the horizon of conscious attention, our mind thus free to rest with its focus. In a general way, I think this is what is meant by one-pointed attention. In both outer activity and in meditating, over time we experience a kind of ease and clarity in which the concentration is not "holding it together" but instead "letting go." The letting go is what runners call entering "the zone," what potters know as centering. It is an important key to concentration, allowing body and mind to relax in any focused activity, mental or physical, including meditating.

Tokme Zangpo here introduces us to the perfection practice of meditative concentration as the union of two specific meditative practices: calm abiding (shamatha, Skt.) and special or profound insight (vipasyana, Skt.). I think of these two concentrations as relaxing and recognizing.

Concentration in the mundane context points to stability of intention, sustained attention, and clarity of focus. We can recognize the same three elements, in the context of our meditative practice, as aspiration, inward attention, and natural clarity. The present condition of our mind reflects phenomenal reality, filled with the comings and goings of thoughts, emotions, and so on, while the actual nature of our mind, primordially present, is unchanging. Mind grasping at emotions and conceptions is grasping at ephemeral appearances; mind calmly abiding is free from this obscured, agitated, fettered mental condition.

We train the mind in calm abiding through practice with a support, or object, such as breath, visualization, mantra, statue, etc., or without an object, when we are practicing directly on mind itself. The principle is the same in each method: the gradual, steady, consistent encouragement of natural, unforced, attentive awareness of object or of mind. This is an *allowing* of awareness, not a grasping or manipulation of it, in the gradual stilling of impulse to distraction— stilling not through suppressing but through bringing attention gently back to its focus each time it is recognized to have wandered. This is what is meant by abandoning or meditating "without distraction." It is not stasis but process, alert and dynamic. Distractions abound, and if they don't present themselves spontaneously we will make them up. Mind chasing after distraction, seeking or reacting to it, is distracted mind. Undistracted mind is not necessarily empty of content or movement but is not involved with it. In our practice, then, what we are abandoning is not the mental activity itself but rather our reacting to it in grasping, repulsing, and elaborating.

We may hear calm abiding meditation sometimes described as holding our attention on the object of meditation (visual, mental, etc.), although not with fixity. As attention wanders and jumps around, quite naturally you can gently draw it back and let it rest where you place it, even if just for an instant. And then again. Just like that. No grasping, no pushing away—just a certain quality of *attention* registering that mind has wandered, and a certain quality of *intention* allowing us to return it to the object, whether exterior or interior. It is an open, relaxed attention, like gazing rather than looking or staring; like friendliness, receptivity, rather than reaction.

Calm abiding practice allows us to experience some tranquility in and about our state, however that state may appear at a given time. A thought comes, we notice, we gently call our attention back. And again. Gradually body and mind relax; there's a sense of opening into ease, a certain pliancy and spaciousness. We might experience our thoughts as a leisurely flow, or observe that there seems to be more space between them. When one thought has dissolved and the next one has not yet arisen, in that "space between" is the clear, open nature of mind itself.

In the equipoise of calmly abiding, now intentionally sharpening and invigorating the mind, we call forth penetrating clarity, keen perception—always available, now invoked intentionally. Seeing, feeling, hearing. Recalling the empty nature of all appearances and experiences. No bells and whistles, just recognizing experienced, observed reality, empty of ascribed meaning. Perceived in the moment just as it is. Bare attention. In this field arises direct insight into emptiness, the true nature of our mental arisings, liberating them. When this insight penetrates or is invoked in mind calmly abiding, it is called special or profound insight.

Mind resting in equipoise is happy and at ease because not grasping, but this can also be a seductive point in our practice, for one can become attached to this state, desiring, even craving, to return to it again and again. This is why Tokme Zangpo calls us to transcend the "four formless absorptions," which I have heard described as advanced meditative states in which there remains still a subtle clinging to meditative experiences. Subtle clinging is still clinging. You can hang out for minutes or lifetimes in such states. However, as beautiful and expansive as our meditative experiences may be, at our stage of development it is likely that they are experiences, not enlightenment—including the triumphant thought "This is it!"

Don't look for the dazzlies in your practice; if they come let them come and if they go let them go—and if they don't come let them go. We are practicing to liberate beings; we must not lose our way. In all our practices of the six perfections we recognize and release attachment, aversion, and elaboration. In our meditation sessions, as in the run of life, grasp at nothing and neither push anything away. Without fixating on any experience that arises, blissful or painful, just continue practicing, without regard to outcome.

Calm abiding and special insight are foundation methods arising from and naturally expanding into ultimate awareness—because they are never other than that. When we are concentrating in this natural, unforced way, whether in meditating or in throwing a vessel on the potter's wheel, we are "concentering." And what is the center we find when we directly perceive mind's nature? Openness, emptiness.

Calmly abiding, this is shamatha; in this state, mind recognizing its own nature is special insight, vipasyana. The sign that we are not wandering in confused byways but rather cultivating the true path of accomplishment that leads to buddhahood? It is that our compassion and love are increasing. This is the unmistaken sign, Garchen Rinpoche says: "The perfection of meditation is to remain inseparable from the state of love and compassion."9

9. Garchen Rinpoche, Great Drikung Monlam, Prescott, Arizona June 2017.

**Verse 30.** Without wisdom, the other five perfections alone are not enough to reach complete enlightenment. Thus, combined with skillful means, develop the wisdom that does not distinguish among the three spheres. This is the way of a bodhisattva.[10]

The perfection of wisdom, Prajnaparamita—primordial purity, open and empty like space, with neither ground nor substance: of this nature also are all phenomena, vividly appearing while void of inherent existence.

When we begin to understand and eventually to recognize this open, pristine nature, the basis of all delusion begins to dissolve, and thus also our attachment and clinging to things, people, emotional states, to our thoughts and plans and hopes and fears, to our identities and even to our present existence. As attachment based on the mistaken notion of self and selfness loosens, so, too, do the confusion and suffering to which it gives birth. When the root of the tree of ignorance is cut, the branches, leaves, and fruit are no more.

Emptiness: it is just the way it is. Everything that exists is composite, interdependently coming into existence, and impermanent, with beginning and end, while its true nature is unborn, undying, unchanging. "Unborn, yet continuing without interruption, neither coming nor going, . . . present beyond space and time . . . perfect from the beginning," as the Song of the Vajra tells.[11]

It is not an illusion that we exist; here we are together. But we urgently need to apprehend correctly the *manner of our abiding* in the realms of existence. Upon the evidence of sense-based perception, to that which is only appearance we impute intrinsic existence, and thus our world and our experience of it are like illusions, and we are as if deluded. When delusion about the manner of existing disperses in understanding of the nature of being, we see and experience reality just as it is.

---

10. The three spheres: agent, action, object.
11. Song of the Vajra: see Namkhai Norbu, *The Crystal and the Way of Light*, 58.

In the relative, the realm of existence, ruled by karma, everything necessarily comes and goes, while the absolute, the realm of being, nakedly is, each element of appearance and experience radiant with isness, beingness, fresh in its original luster. I simply am, you simply are. When the causes of our meeting in this lifetime meet the conditions that allow us to come together, here we are. Just for this moment. Causes will be exhausted, conditions will change, cherished friends and implacable enemies will part—in the realms of existence. In the wisdom understanding emptiness, no one ever came and no one ever left.

We are continuously lifted by our aspiration to realize ultimate wisdom, we who are impelled and propelled to attain buddhahood in order to establish all in supreme truth. Within this fertile bodhisattva mind flourish all the activities of hearing, reflecting, and meditating that we use to liberate ourselves from ignorance, to render ourselves fit in mind and skillful in methods to benefit others. In following the way of the bodhisattva, we particularly study, ponder, and practice the first five of the six noble paramitas, the perfection practices: generosity, ethics, patience, diligence, and concentration. We develop these ways of being in the world, in circumstances and activities with others, to benefit beings and to generate merit, loosening the stranglehold of self-grasping and freeing our love and compassion. These first five paramitas are relative reality practices, associated with conceptuality and its limits. Even so, they are turning over and amending the soil, readying our minds for practice on their essence: transcendent wisdom.

With language that relies on dualistic categories and contrasts, posits and opposites, we cannot describe or understand the primordial, but we can use our words to point to, or toward, what we call the absolute, the true nature of mind and of all beings, all phenomena. Our great teachers bathe us in its radiance with their beautiful words, distilled from direct experience, and these shine in our consciousness to illumine the way.

The immeasurable, unconditioned, absolute love-wisdom that is reflected in the love and compassion we are able to generate every day of our lives—this is the inner meaning of "method" and "skillful means" as used in the Buddhadharma. And emptiness is the inner meaning of "wisdom."

On the one hand, we continually rouse ourselves to full presence in our actual lives, engaging all the virtues of relationship and activity that align our minds and actions with bodhicitta, right understanding, right action, right speech, and so on. On the other hand, we continue to learn, reflect, contemplate, and meditate to perfect our understanding and experience of the open, insubstantial nature of all appearances and experiences, including ourselves. "Method is like having legs, and wisdom is like having eyes," says Geshe Jampa. "Wisdom supported by method means meditating on emptiness with the compassionate motivation of becoming a Buddha to benefit . . . all beings. Method supported by wisdom is cultivating the virtuous practices [the first five paramitas] . . . accompanied by the wisdom realizing that they are not inherently existent. We meditate on this wisdom by contemplating the emptiness of the three spheres—agent, action, and object."[12] This is the path that unites method and wisdom: love-compassion in union with emptiness.

Even before realizing emptiness, our practice of love and compassion is "held by an echo" of the ultimate, as Geshe Jampa beautifully puts it. Our compulsion to maintain the illusion of selfness weakens as we turn our thoughts, intentions, and attentions to others with care, friendliness, compassion, and love. Duality fixation and its sufferings dissolve in bodhicitta, empty of referent, naturally and universally radiant like the sun. Relative love reflects this, in the selfless, tender, profoundly kind heart of parent for child, for example, or of lover for beloved, teacher for disciple, individual for the world. In such connections there are moments when self-other duality evaporates, moments of union and communion. These are intimations of the emptiness nature inseparable from love. Though at times perhaps uncertain or anxious, once having heard of this ultimate openness that we call emptiness we will continue

---

12. Geshe Jampa, *Transforming the Heart*, 289.

to be drawn to know it directly—because this is the truth of the nature of reality, of both existence and being. As magnet draws the iron filing, truth draws us.

Don't get caught in hoping to "see" emptiness and fearing you won't. Hope and fear: walk between. Try it this way, try it that way, yes, let's try and try until we realize directly that which is not found by effort but to which effort clears the way, most especially our noble effort to *not* do that which we have always been doing. All our trying purifies and refines our mind, generating great merit for us, great increase in love, and softening our grasp to illusion-like appearances—chief among them the appearance of selfness, in us or in any other phenomenal appearance. But it is not the trying that achieves the longed-for result. The trying is like polishing a lens, so we can see directly what already is, that which we think we are looking *for* but which in fact we are looking *at*, seeing without recognizing.

"By meditating upon emptiness in the state of complete tranquil abiding, the nothing-to-see will see that seeing."[13] Ha! Jai Guru! These are the startling, shimmering words of Khenchen Palden Sherab, who emphasizes the importance of finding our own certainty wisdom. No one can do this for us; this we must accomplish ourselves, not just by analyzing and reflecting but most particularly, and crucially, by contemplating, meditating. In Khyentse Rinpoche's words: "A thorough, experiential understanding of emptiness is the only antidote to the belief in an 'I,' in a truly existing self."[14]

We may recognize the true nature of reality at any time, in a glimpse or an extended contemplation. From that moment on our work is to stabilize what that lived experience has revealed to us. We do this by practice, both on the cushion and in normal life activities. Realization is always fresh, occurring in this precise, particular, present moment. What you have seen and known will not unsee or unknow itself. Keep purifying and refining conduct and mind to clear away what obscures recognizing what is, just as it is. Continue to generate the highest aspiration, continue to

13. Palden Sherab, *Prajnaparamita*, 48.
14. Dilgo Khyentse, *Heart of Compassion*, 172.

cultivate bodhicitta—and just keep practicing. As the vajra yogi Traga Rinpoche told me, tapping me sharply on my self-grasping mind, "We practice not for this life but for liberation."

When doubt arises while we are practicing to realize ultimate wisdom, supplicate the blessings of guru and lineage, without acceding to the distractions of disturbing thoughts and emotions. Doubts appear; truth is. Rinpoche reminds us to ignore the mental tugs of "Is this it? Maybe this isn't it. How can I know?" When we cease grasping to doubt, there certainty is.

It is taught that even aspiring to realize emptiness generates great merit and that an instant of suchness destroys a mountain of nonvirtue. With this profound purification comes also an expansion of all one's positive qualities, one's enlightenment qualities. All negative purified, all positive expanded. This is buddhahood.

Radical trust: always fall back upon what you know to be true—even and especially when you don't feel or see it directly. Sensory experience is relative. You are longing for the absolute. The part is longing for the whole while never separate. Your longing is a cry of remembrance. Rely on that, and offer it in every moment for the liberation of all.

## The Six Perfections in the View
*H. E. Garchen Rinpoche*

*When this body dies, my mind has not died.*
*I will continue to remain, pervading the five elements.*

Apart from giving up self-grasping,
there is no other perfection of *generosity*.

Apart from giving up deception,
there is no other perfection of *moral conduct*.

Apart from being fearless of ultimate truth,
there is no other perfection of *patience*.

Apart from remaining inseparable from practice,
there is no other perfection of *diligence*.

Apart from abiding within the natural state,
there is no other perfection of *meditative concentration*.

Apart from realizing the nature of mind,
there is no other perfection of *wisdom*.

*I supplicate Lord Milarepa, Laughing Vajra.*

Garchen Triptrul Rinpoche spoke these words to retreatants in Milarepa's cave in Lapchi Snow Mountain, Nepal, in 2007. [15]

---

15. Christina Lundberg, "For the Benefit of All Beings."

# CHAPTER SIX

# GUARDIANS OF THE GATES (VERSES 31-37)

Having introduced us to the ultimate, Tokme Zangpo is now going to show us how the bodhisattva view is vast view in union with close view: holding mind steady in truth while working tirelessly in the fields of delusion. I think of these next instructions as the guardians of the gates, gates of mind and gates of conduct, that allow our intention and practice to mature this bodhisattva commitment.

**Verse 31.** Unless you examine your own confused ideas, you might look like a practitioner but not be acting like one. Therefore, always examine yourself and abandon confusion. This is the way of a bodhisattva.

"You might look like a practitioner but not be acting like one." A bracing splash of cold water in my face, reminding me that all my high aspirations, my devotion and dedication, my sincere practice and well-intentioned activities, not to mention my pretensions and presumptions, are not enough to shield me from confusion and error if I do not take to heart both the grounded relative reality precepts of the Dharma and its actual essence. If I am still clinging to illusion and still acting contrary to love and compassion, I am still causing harm to myself and others. The illusion and the "contrary" are self-grasping, of course, as we have come to recognize; all our faults and shortcomings trace their root to this fundamental error of understanding. Look for self-grasping when examining your mind. Wherever there is suffering, even the slightest mental tension, there is its root, clear to see: thought of self, concern with self, grasping to the notion of self and its supposed interests. Look for self-grasping when evaluating your conduct. If there is ill action, self-reference and self-concern are in the seedbed.

It might be easy to look the way you think a spiritual practitioner should—right costume, posture, lingo, even the right activities—but what is going on in the mind is what determines whether or not actual practice and progress are occurring. Our mind condition and our conduct are unfailing mirrors, if we choose to look into them. Are we or are we not taking the medicine of Dharma, truly allowing it to cure us of our ills?

Here, with this verse's teaching, we are sharply challenged: Cultivate the inward attention that allows you to see your motivations and behavior; recognize those that are not in accord with the meaning of Dharma, with bodhicitta, love and compassion. Assiduously search out your faults, small and large: faults of omission and commission, faults of unawareness and faults of intention. Examine your own mind and acknowledge your own shortcomings; don't focus on those of others. Be very clear about *why* you are taking your inventory in this way: it is to see what needs to be changed. If we are obsessively examining our faults, over and over, we might be maintaining our intimate involvement and investment in our mind's productions rather than abandoning them. Our negative karmic predispositions thrive on unawareness, laziness, and repetition. Deprive them of sustenance. Abandon them without hesitation.

Cultivating attentive awareness to see our own mind's condition is authentic spiritual practice, as well as a requirement for simply being at choice in our lives. It is how we discern in our own conduct what is good and what is harmful and thus choose between these two pathways. Actively discerning and choosing transforms the mind from doubtful and wavering to certain, certain of both underlying and immediate motivation—and capable of benefitting others.

Garchen Rinpoche urges us to examine our mind especially when we are afflicted by anger-hatred and jealousy. He sometimes speaks extensively on jealousy, bringing it to our attention with some emphasis because it is, he says, virtually ubiquitous in our self-concerned, conditioned mind, and because it is so injurious to our bodhisattva commitment. Jealousy, he says, destroys our merit, our love. It is an often subtle, insidious form of anger-hatred. We may think of it mostly in terms of our own painful emotional state without explicitly acknowledging that within that state is actual animosity toward another. The monster with the creepy green eyes, ever on the alert for its own advantage, is also ever on the alert for the disadvantage of the other, rejoicing in them both. Wise to use your own jealousy as a mirror that shows you the potentials and desires you have denied or ignored in yourself—and then, instead of putting down someone else's accomplishments or good fortune, take your own gifts and capacities seriously and act to fulfill them. Certain of your own positive potentials and your ability to realize them, you will rejoice in the accomplishments of others.

"Examining our own mind and abandoning confusion" can be unexpectedly challenging for those of us at home in contemporary Western culture, which teaches us to examine our experience with the perspectives of psychology, sociology, history, and so forth. These methods and findings can be useful in the relative sphere but they concern conditioning, not causation, so they don't go deep enough to identify and abandon confusion rooted in mis-understanding the actual nature of reality. No matter how many faults lie in the times and in the minds and actions of others, your mind's condition is yours. To think otherwise is to abandon not our confusion but our responsibility, which is also our power and agency. We are cultivating the inward attention to find cause, in the seeds of karma coming to fruition in our own minds—to uproot them and not to sow them again. This is the abandoning. This is how we take responsibility for our own minds.

Our faults and negative habits begin to lose their power over our minds and behavior when we recognize them for what they are: mistaken understanding, self-grasping mind, and actions that cause harm. This insight can occur in an instant, although the abandoning may take time and repetition. We have sown these karmic seeds more than once so we will see their fruits more than once, but each time we do, and recognize them for what they are, our predisposition to these tendencies weakens. Two keys here: One, learn to distinguish clearly and confidently between virtue and nonvirtue, what brings happiness and what brings suffering, for yourself and others. And two, when recognizing in yourself even a germ of what causes harm, abandon it: instantly, in intention; in your mind, each time it arises; and either instantly or gradually, as you are willing and able, in your choices and behavior. As with the potato chip: see craving, recognize the seeing, allow craving to come to rest in empty mind that recognizes—or, see craving, recognize the seeing, and take the potato chip anyway, or the whole bag. Which course of action, taken repeatedly, strengthens the practitioner and which strengthens the habit of craving?

Remember these good words of Geshe Jampa: "Whenever we see one of our faults, instead of feeling despondent, we can rejoice, for now we recognize the enemy—self-centeredness—and can dispel it."[1]

**Verse 32.** If you are driven by disturbing emotions and talk about another bodhisattva's faults, it is actually to your own detriment. So, don't mention the faults of those who have entered the Great Vehicle. This is the way of a bodhisattva.

When we are perceiving the faults of another it is our own view that is faulty. We all have buddha nature, intrinsic perfect essence, so examining the faults of another means we are focusing not on truth but on temporary appearances that are arising from karma

---

1. Geshe Jampa, *Transforming the Heart*, 290.

and afflictive emotions. Counting the faults of others adds fuel to the fires of our own confusion; if we're going to start counting, that is where to start. It is a significant step even to recognize and acknowledge, as a fault in ourselves, our tendency to criticize and pull others down. This shifts the angle of view, freeing us from our useless preoccupation with wanting to change others' minds and bringing our attention to what we can actually do something about—the condition of our own.

It is important for us to understand that in our present condition we ourselves cannot know who is and who is not a bodhisattva or a buddha, so it is wise for us to respect and love all beings as our teachers, friends, and companions on the path. Criticizing a bodhisattva, one who is generating bodhicitta and is vowed to benefit all, is like turning your back on those great qualities, and broadcasting such obscured views further obscures your own pure view and may also impede that of others.

If we are critical of other bodhisattvas because we don't perceive their buddha nature, it is actually our ignorance of our own buddha nature that is at issue. I see that when I have negativity towards others it is that I am somehow suffering in my relationship with myself—holding myself as unworthy or inadequate, or seeing my negative characteristics and taking them as the entirety or the essence of who I am. This is an example of how we pile suffering on top of suffering. Shantideva teaches that bodhisattvas suffer without generating negativity.[2] I remember being stunned by this teaching when I met it very early on. Possible to suffer without generating negativity? I couldn't imagine it, and my research in the Dharma from that point on had this question in view. What I came to understand was that wrong view about ourselves will out-picture: we project that wrong view onto other beings and circumstances in order not to see it in ourselves. It is deeply demoralizing to think we are somehow wrong from the beginning, in our essence not good. Hearing that absolute goodness is in fact our true nature may register as excellent news, but until we attain

---

2. Shantideva, *A Guide to the Bodhisattva's Way of Life*: "Patience," Verse 19.

certainty in this view we are not likely to recognize or have confidence in the absolute goodness of anyone else, either. So, unable to know who is and who is not a bodhisattva or a buddha, respect and praise buddha nature in yourself and all beings.

Two keys here: First, even when not directly recognizing our true nature, we can take profound succor and rest in the sure knowing that it *is*—that within us and all beings lives the indestructible seed of the tathagatagarbha, the Thus Gone Ones: our true nature, from which we are inseparable. This is how we rely on what we know to be true when we do not, in that moment, see, feel, or recognize it— creative intelligence and faith working together for wisdom. Second, suffering without generating negativity relies, in mind, on the intention to have compassion and love for all, including ourselves. In practice, it relies on clarifying and stabilizing our view, our understanding of emptiness and bodhicitta, so that our own confusion is allowed to arise, abide, and pass away, as moment-to-moment experience, empty in nature. Our suffering is not a confirmation of all our worst thoughts about ourselves but rather the absolutely trustworthy, intimate relationship of specific causes we have set and their precise and temporary results. Neither cause nor consequence is possessed of inherent existence. This understanding, at first conceptual and then, through experience, clearly held, swiftly erodes the tendency to blame others and circumstances. We are gradually learning to be certain of our own minds. Such a person has no need to find fault with others or with circumstances.

This verse is also conveying important teachings about how we perceive and speak of those on whom we and others rely. As we have discussed in verse 6, when teachers are giving Dharma our good fortune and responsibility are to take the medicine of the teachings and to support others in doing so. We all have faults, and spiritual teachers are no exception. There is nothing wrong with recognizing a teacher's faults, or even, when necessary, speaking of them with others, but there is neither need for nor benefit to dwelling on them or using your catalogue of them to cause harm. This tendency clouds your mind and damps down faith, and publicizing your doubts or criticisms can have the same effect on others and the sangha.

Pure perception is the key here. We train in pure perception by viewing everything and everyone with the understanding that all beings and all phenomena are of the same essential nature, the nondual union of emptiness and love. Mind practicing this view becomes open and vast. It is not spiritual censorship that the teachings in this verse are directed to: they are directed to preserving our own minds in impeccability. This is what allows us to see things as they are, love and compassion and creativity to flourish in us, and bodhicitta to increase in our minds. Our purpose is to love and liberate beings. With pure view, seeing things as they are rather than through the obscured lens of self-reference and conditioning, we see the goodness, even the sublime qualities, in all we meet, reflections of their true nature seen through the lens of our own.

**Verse 33.** Concern for gain and respect causes conflict and a decline in the activities of learning, reflecting, and meditating. So abandon attachment to your circle of friends, relations, and benefactors. This is the way of a bodhisattva.

To seek gain and respect requires great efforts, in a worldly sense, and these achievements can come at high cost. The wealthy and powerful may be regarded with admiration but also with envy and fear, and while some with wealth and power use it to benefit others, many are continuously striving and grasping for still more of what they already have, propelled by their own envy and fear. Also, material wealth and worldly power require constant vigilance by those who possess them: you have to count the money, protect the boundaries, massage the relationships that sustain status and goods, manage infighting among dependents and contenders, and defend against competitors. What a life of ease! The spiritual costs are manifest and dangerous: ever active self-reference and self-concern. Preoccupied with our own position and goods and the relationships and activities that sustain them, how can we devote ourselves to others' wellbeing? Better to be content with what we have, use our power and resources to benefit others, and seek neither admiration nor a return on our investment.

To abandon attachment to our circle of friends, relations, and benefactors doesn't mean we shouldn't have friends, relations, and benefactors; it means abandon the grasping, the craving for others to take responsibility for us, to provide what we want or think we need, and so on. That mind of attachment and grasping will spoil the positive potential of even the relationships that start out unencumbered and high-minded. Gar Rinpoche emphasizes the important role jealousy plays in such dynamics, even in relationships of teachers and students. The student vying for recognition, approval, to be special, the "best" student, and so on, is confused about what aspiration and devotion really mean, as is the jealous, possessive, ambitious teacher.

It is very beneficial for teachers and serious practitioners to have benefactors who support their Dharma activities by supplying their basic needs, to free them for study, practice, and teaching, and by providing lodging, transportation, and facilities where many can gather to receive teachings and engage in practice. These generosity practices, undertaken with bodhicitta rather than with desire for respect and admiration, generate merit for the sponsor, as it is said that enabling another to practice or teach generates the same merit as if you are doing it yourself. The teacher or practitioner who receives such support, however, needs to be keenly aware of her own mind's condition. We can generate unselfish love and appreciation for our donors, rejoicing in the merit that generates and increases their good fortune, or, perhaps without realizing, we may find that our afflictive emotions are stirred in such relationships and that in our own minds pridefulness, craving, jealousy, competitiveness, and conceit are growing. Helpful here is to recall that we are, literally, all in this together; with mind of gratitude and generosity, what one receives benefits all.

Thinking our supplies, spiritual or material, must come from others, from sources outside ourselves, may express a subtle sense of oneself as being in deficit or unable to access some mysterious source of blessings and support. This is a mindset, a karmic pattern, not a fixed reality. As we know, it is generosity that creates wealth. Seeing the generosity of others, rejoice in and aspire to their goodness, not to their goods. Pinched oneself, give away. Literally. Nothing in the garden but nettles? Place some on the ground for the aphids. Give away, give away, even your very last bite. Rejoice in the good fortune of others and find the inner source of all goodness freshened, amplified, flowing freely. Cultivate within yourself the source of authentic sufficiency: bodhicitta, care for all beings. Understand the open, spacious, effulgent, ceaselessly and creatively manifesting nature of reality and be at home wherever you are, whatever you have or have not.

**Verse 34.** Harsh words disturb others' minds and thus diminish the practice of a bodhisattva. Therefore, abandon harsh speech, which is unpleasant to others. This is the way of a bodhisattva.

We speak of the doors of the senses. The doorway of hearing is the one that we have perhaps the least ability to control; we are like unguarded receptor sites for whatever sounds happen to float through our environment. For many, it is particularly challenging to be helplessly or unwillingly exposed to the speech of others. But the door of our own speech, where we should be able to exercise clear intention and responsibility, is often just swinging back and forth like the loose old gate in grandma's garden, is it not? Many of us, including me, exercise far too little mastery over the gate of speech, with results that can be disturbing and sometimes seriously damaging. Words can precipitate pain and anger, division and conflict, sometimes with life-changing and life-destroying effects. On the current world stage we see devastating results of harsh speech taken all the way to murderous speech: beautiful, intelligent young people adopting beliefs and desperate acts of destruction based on false teachings of what is noble and virtuous;

suffering and suicides of fragile people receiving bullying speech, racist speech, misogynist and xenophobic speech, homophobic and transphobic speech; incitements to hatred and violence in the public sphere, even from those at high levels of responsibility in politics, government, education, religion, and society, with power to influence many for good or for ill.

Though the sound of a word is dissolving even as it is being uttered, its traces in the memories of both speaker and hearer can be long lasting, hard to silence, hard to forget, hard to forgive, hard to live with. That old saw, "sticks and stones may break my bones but words will never hurt me," is far from true. The wounds of hurtful, hateful speech, oral and written, can damage lives and minds and families and nations in the present and far into the future.

For us as practitioners, as bodhisattvas, the obvious fact about our harsh speech is that it can hurt others. Simple as that. And that is the very definition of nonvirtue. For bodhisattvas who are committed to relieving suffering, causing more suffering is a sad and sometimes tragic dereliction. Even speaking truth to another in a harsh way—from which the hearer recoils protectively, pulls away, closes up a little bit, or strikes out to hurt back—may limit our capacity to be of benefit to that being.

People will usually recover from hearing us say something harsh; in fact, they will often recognize it, correctly, as a fault in us rather than in themselves. But not always. Childhood memories of harsh words from parents and teachers, for example, are sometimes even more painful than memories of actual physical abuse. Sentient beings, all sentient beings, are highly sensitive and tender, and we are utterly interdependent. *Nous entre-sommes*: we inter-are.

As we all have buddha nature, spiritually we are indissolubly one at the root, while even in the most material sense we are completely interdependent, mutually affecting and affected. We are interchanging our molecules all the time, breathing in and out together, co-resonant; anything that one thinks or says or does affects all. To use speech for harm is to misuse sound, one of the sacred elements of existence. Right speech arises in truth, stirring truth in the minds of beings.

Sometimes our harsh speech is casual and subtle, easy for us and others to ignore. Harshness resides not only in our words but also in our tones, so we can pretend to ourselves and others that we didn't really mean to be mean. But too often, we did. As you come to know the condition of your own mind you may recognize rivulets of negative thoughts about self, others, events, and situations. If so, and if you carefully observe your patterns of thought and speech, you will also note that even when your speech patterns appear innocuous there can be underlying tones of voice, little inflections, moments of silence where there might be speech, speech where there could be silence—many ways of making known your negativity, whatever it may be.

Harsh speech expresses harsh mind. What could be more obvious? But we don't usually think of it that way. We think, "Oh, I have a bad speech habit." No, it is a bad mind habit. Hearing that habit made overt in the words and tones you use in speaking to others, or to yourself, can be the moment in which you actually recognize their underlying harsh motivation. This is always the gift of our faults and wrongdoing: they are our mirrors, showing us where we need to—and can—align more finely with our good-hearted intentions.

If you find yourself engaging in harsh speech, you probably know, as I do about myself, that you actually have a tendency to that. It doesn't just pop out from time to time; there is a leaning in that direction. Turning to harsh speech can function like a default position. We must and can become conscious of this tendency and its almost imperceptible activation—almost imperceptible but perceptible, nonetheless, to the inward attention. As always, best to catch the harsh impulse at the first possible moment, and redirect both intention and words; failing that, catch the harsh thought and words as they form and express; and failing that, catch them once they have flown forth, and swiftly acknowledge and generate regret. Sometimes an almost mechanical action of the mind, like closing a sluice gate, will prevent the speech from going down its habitual channel, giving us a pause in which to direct our speech more consciously, or to choose silence instead of speech.

For those of us who have the tendency to harsh speech, let us be clear and courageous in confronting and correcting it. At the same time, let us be extremely kind, compassionate, and loving in our speech to ourselves about it. When you make a mistake, how do you treat yourself, in your own mind or in your private mutterings? We may be aware of the harsh speech that we direct outwardly, but are we aware of the harsh speech that we direct toward ourselves? We tend to treat others the way we treat ourselves, so when we begin to see this pattern of unkind, unskillful, harmful expression we can understand that it manifests our hurtful thoughts about ourselves—arising, as does all confusion, from misunderstanding of our true nature.

Words leaping out of our mouths before we see them coming are often glib, glittery, and superficial, in the kind of repartee that people sometimes think is chic and smart. What an edge there often is on that kind of verbal "play." It is not just meaningless chatter (also a form of negative speech); it often has a sarcastic, belittling, caustic quality. For example, the comment channels in online media are sometimes beyond shocking in their casual, vicious cruelty. As well, many so-called comedies include verbal cruelty; the comedic situation is often a put-down, the ostensible joke taking its laughs at the expense of others. Observe what is seen as humorous around you and in your own mind, note what is considered funny and why, and in your own life look not for the easy laugh at another's expense, the humor that divides, but for what makes you laugh with warmth. Find the things in the culture and in your own mind and relationships that bring laughter with understanding and empathy, laughter with fellow-feeling and compassion, laughter with love. Find what brings us closer through humor. If we were all laughing together over our own follies we would be rolling around on the floor, holding our bellies, laughing and laughing, just loving each other, so light-hearted, so warm-hearted, because we all share so many follies together—and the wisdom nature in which they all dissolve.

**Verse 35.** When disturbing emotions become habitual, it is difficult to reverse them with antidotes. Thus, the soldier of mindfulness wields antidotes as weapons and destroys disturbing emotions such as attachment the moment they start to arise. This is the way of a bodhisattva.

Gar Rinpoche frequently reminds us that a single instant of our own awareness is exactly the same as the primordial wisdom awareness of all buddhas of past, present, and future. How is this possible?

*Thought : mind :: wave : water.*
*Thought is to mind as wave is to water.*
*Water and wave: one nature. Thought and mind: one nature.*

Our ongoing experience of mind and emotions is not usually one of continuous awareness; instead, we experience thoughts appearing and disappearing, sometimes catching our attention (more often not), and reinforcing our habituated reaction patterns, sometimes quite primitive, in which the I-me-mine is ascendant. Sometimes vivid and easy to see, but more often subtly flickering and fluttering, coming and going out of conscious awareness, obscuring thoughts and emotional reactions are continuously creating karmic cause—so we train in mindfulness and alertness to recognize and liberate them before they inevitably grow and multiply. It is much more difficult to dispel aversion, for example, once it has become a roaring inferno of rage; the same is true of all our harmful mental arisings. This is why we need the many and diverse methods Dharma provides, practices such as meditations, mind training instructions, ways to sit and ways to see, visualizations and recitations, and so on.

Such practices can work as antidotes to our confusions and afflictions, when we are mindful enough both to recognize the need and to reach for a good remedy. Reciting mantra, even just loudly enough for your collarbone to hear, engages body, speech, and mind simultaneously in Dharma. Silent recitation, too, can profoundly seclude your mind from disturbing thoughts and emotions. A meditation as simple as quietly, invisibly, counting your breaths can gently, steadily calm agitation and emotion. When feeling threatened, frightened, or angry, remembering compassion for others redirects troubled mind from confusion to clarity. These are examples of how to draw on teachings and practices during occasions of forgetting, distraction, and disturbance, even in the very instant you are aware of being knocked off balance by your mind's reactivity to inner and outer phenomena. In this way, mind of clarity returns mind of confusion to orderly pathways. Applying these antidotal methods as soon as possible is best, to interrupt the process of habituating negative patterns, but they can be brought to bear at any and every time needed.

As we apply antidotes of practice, it is good to be reminded by Dilgo Khyentse Rinpoche that "Whatever practice you are doing, it has to work as an effective antidote to your negative emotions and to your belief in substantial existence."[3] However heavy, overwhelming, tormenting, and pervasive they may seem, our negative thoughts and emotional reactions are arising from causes and dependent on conditions, so their appearance is just that: appearance. No solidity, no durability. Appearances are of the same nature as the awareness that recognizes them, and when recognized directly by awareness they naturally subside into the nature of mind itself: open, empty, luminous, clear. Awareness reveals mind's nature as wisdom.

Thought is to mind as wave is to water. Wave arising in water is transitory appearance as wave while its unchanging nature is water, behaving as water behaves under specific conditions. Wave subsiding in water is water changing in appearance, not in nature. Same with thought and mind. Thought arising in mind is transitory appearance, while its unchanging nature is nature of mind itself.

---

3. Dilgo Khyentse, *Heart of Compassion*, 186.

Our thoughts are in essence free and unfettered, simply and naturally, because empty of selfness. Any fettering happens with us: we grasp at, push away, and elaborate our mental arisings as if they are real. And this is how we ourselves are fettered, over and over again, caught in habit, caught in delusion.

When we discern a thought in the instant of its arising and with the inward attention recognize it—not engaging, simply perceiving, seeing—that scarcely emergent thought vanishes. In that moment we create no karma. Let it go just a little bit further, engage however subtly, and karma is in effect. The moment at which awareness recognizes a mental arising is the moment that arising is liberated, simply by recognizing, in non-reaction. This is the mindful awareness that destroys affliction the instant it arises—the single antidote for the countless disturbing emotions.

Our thoughts are not really *in* our mind, they *are* our mind: the natural, effervescent play of limitless, effortless, creative essence—the dynamic nature of emptiness. As thought is not in any instant separate from mind, so momentary mind condition is not in any instant separate from primordial mind, the absolute nature. Unmoving primordial awareness recognizes conditioned mind's appearances of movement, and in that recognizing, apparent movement comes to rest.

This awareness must be habituated, becoming so familiar and natural to us that easily, spontaneously our thoughts self-liberate as they arise. With calm abiding and vipasyana practice we train in mental stability and clarity and on this basis gradually develop an ongoing continuity of awareness. Continuously cultivating the inward attention, we will come to see our mental arisings beginning to self-liberate, dissolving in their very arising, without our having to do anything or not do anything.

As my spoken words are vanishing in space and soundlessness even as I utter them, so do the thoughts arising in our minds vanish in their empty nature—unless we in some manner involve ourselves with them. Then they appear to reify, become a "something" with selfness, momentum, impact, consequence, and effect, and we reach for them, push them away, or follow them. We might liken this dynamic to the behavior of energy, which can appear as wave or particle—in free flow until interfered with, touched, manipulated, or merely thought of, and then behaving like a particle, a something.

On the baseball diamond, the first umpire says, "I call 'em as I see 'em." The second umpire says, "I call 'em as they are." The third says, "They ain't nothin' till I call 'em."

In the free, unconditioned flow, claim nothing, see all.

**Verse 36.** In brief, wherever you are and whatever you are doing, always examine the state of your mind. Act to accomplish the purpose of others through constant mindfulness and awareness. This is the way of a bodhisattva.

In brief, indeed. "Wherever you are and whatever you are doing" means any and all conduct of body, speech, and mind. And when we are examining the state of our mind we are turning our attention within, inquiring inwardly, to see our mind state in this precise, particular, present moment. What are we really up to, right here, right now? Is our intent to benefit beings or to pursue our self-interest? If it is the latter, clearly seeing this makes possible an instant correction, easily accomplished: "I offer this action for the benefit of all." Self-fixation diminishes even in formulating this conscious intention, as self-grasping mind, source of all troubles, relaxes into and is thus transformed by altruistic mind, source of all benefit and happiness. So that is our starting point in this mind-condition inventory.

Second, in the inner inquiry it is important, at times even urgent, to discern clearly the activity of negative thoughts and emotions in our mind in this specific moment. Recognized at the moment of arising, they are rendered powerless over your mind, your speech, and your behavior. With an anger reaction, for example, sometimes simply stop yourself on the spot, mid-sentence, if necessary. Sometimes, over and over again in a short space of time, see the thoughtform, rest in mind; see the thoughtform arising again, rest again in mind; and when clear, proceed.

Third, only through continuous practice does our attentive awareness become strong and stable enough to recognize our present condition when it matters most, and particularly when our afflictive thoughts are emotionally laden and heavily habituated. As the "soldier of mindfulness [wielding] antidotes as weapons," through stable, clear intention and continuous practice you develop a strong capacity to recognize the current condition of your mind—and to hold steady in that recognizing, so you are not caught up in reactions to your own thoughts and emotions. While we are developing this capacity we make use of the many antidotes, the remedies, that Dharma and our other wisdom traditions give, as well as those that come to us in our ordinary lives, like counting to ten, as your mother taught you.

Motivation is everything, determining the ultimate positive or negative value and effect of any action, word, or thought. To speak of motivation is to speak not only of over-arching aspiration but specifically, and repeatedly, of the actual present condition of our own mind in this very moment, and the next one, and the next one.

If you dedicate all your activities to the wellbeing and liberation of all, your *bodhicitta* will deepen and expand without limit. If you understand that all your words and actions arise first in your mind, and develop a strong, clear capacity to recognize in your mind the roots of everything you say and do, then your *mindful alertness* will grow and grow. If you engage this practice in the knowledge that appearances and mind are not separate but one in their essential open and empty nature, then your *mindful awareness* will expand naturally in primordial awareness, which is wisdom.

In this way, without reserve, for this entire lifetime and all lifetimes to come, taking full responsibility for this present embodied existence and abiding in pure bodhicitta, vast, empty, timeless, limitless love and compassion for all, we will swiftly accomplish the two purposes, bringing oneself and all beings to ultimate wisdom and love, the heart of enlightenment.

This is the essence of Dharma. This is what it means to be a bodhisattva.

## Dedicating the Merit

**Verse 37.** With the wisdom of threefold purity, dedicate all the virtue gained from having made such effort toward enlightenment. Dedicate it to clear away the suffering of infinite beings. This is the way of a bodhisattva.

The Buddhadharma teaches that throughout countless lifetimes, inconceivably diverse in forms and circumstances, we sentient beings are acting sometimes with good intent and sometimes with ill, thus bringing to ourselves and others both wellbeing and harm. On the way to ultimate realization, we practice the two accumulations. As the great Patrul Rinpoche has taught, "It is impossible to attain the twofold purity of Buddhahood or to realize fully the truth of emptiness without completing the two accumulations of merit and wisdom."[4] Merit is love; wisdom is emptiness realization. Their primordial, nondual union is ultimate bodhicitta: enlightenment.

At the relative level, even to conceive of and long for one's own freedom is the fruit of accumulated merit. How vast, then, is the merit of those dedicated to the freedom of all? This dedication is called the mind of enlightenment, bodhicitta, and once having generated this mind, bodhicitta is shaping our every moment, every thought, word, and act—even while sleeping, our teachers say. Altruistic love, like the outflowing tide, washes away the detritus of our self-grasping, and, because all minds are of the same essence, the great love in one pervades all.

The act of love that we call dedicating the merit means giving away to all beings the merit we have generated through our positive thoughts, speech, and actions. To give away our merit is like adding our own small drop of nectar to the limitless effulgence

4. Patrul Rinpoche, *Words of My Perfect Teacher*, 283; see also 391, n.200.

that is ultimate bodhicitta, pervading all space, all minds. Once dedicated in this way, merit is indestructible.

The "wisdom of threefold purity" is primordial, nondual wisdom, recognizing the purity, —the emptiness—of the three spheres: agent, action, and object. Conceptualizing self is the innocent misapprehension that blinds us and binds us. No selfness to protect, no otherness to react to, so also no my merit or your merit, no my buddhahood or yours. Being and existence: one taste.

# TOKME ZANGPO'S CONCLUDING WORDS

In accordance with the words of the holy ones regarding the meaning of the sutras, tantras, and their commentaries, I have written these thirty-seven verses on the ways of a bodhisattva for those who wish to train on the bodhisattva's path.

This composition will not be admired by the learned because my intellect is poor and my education is limited. However, I have followed the sutras and the words of holy ones, so I believe these ways of a bodhisattva are not mistaken.

Still, because the vast deeds of bodhisattvas are difficult to grasp by simple-minded beings like myself, I beg the forgiveness of the holy ones for the mass of my errors such as contradictions and inconsistencies.

By the virtue arising from this, may all beings give rise to relative and ultimate bodhicitta and thereby become like the Protector Chenrezig, who does not abide in the extremes of existence or peace.

The monk Tokme, a proponent of scripture and reasoning, composed these verses in the Precious Cave of Ngulchu, for his own and others' benefit.

In composing this profound, luminous compendium of timeless wisdom, Tokme Zangpo drew upon the deep roots of Buddhadharma, the sutra teachings attributed to Buddha Shakyamuni, and the strong trunk and branches and their flowering in the works of countless teachers and practitioners grounded in scholarship and practice and expanded in wisdom. Tokme's gift to those, like us, who wish to train on the bodhisattva path, is to give the essence of the tradition into our very hands. His accomplishment and its benefits, throughout the centuries, are incalculable. His final words bespeak humility and certainty in perfect harmony, and at the end, dedicating to all beings the merit of this work, we see the graceful, empty gesture that points to the gracious, empty nature and the vast, empty love—the two that are not two.

# AFTERWORD

Wisdom recognizing that beings neither come nor go, one with the love that must free them all from ignorance and suffering—this is bodhicitta. Bodhicitta is unborn and undying, timeless and unchanging, illumining and transforming appearances that come and go. In this vast embrace, rescue, and celebration of all, we come to love even situations, eras, harms, and harm-doers as if they are our own dear relatives. Empty and all-pervading, essence of impermanence and interdependence, bodhi love is free and freeing for all.

Bodhicitta liberates us completely from every kind of suffering because it frees us from our illusions of selfness. No matter the circumstance, we abide in unwavering commitment to full presence in life for the benefit of all. It is in no way a withdrawal from life to be a bodhisattva. It is an ever more profound and transforming engagement, taken up in certainty and devotion: certainty in truth and devotion with beings. These bodhisattva qualities are made manifest in mind generating universal, infinite love for beings and existence, in full awareness that all phenomena are indivisibly one with the ultimate while vibrantly, exuberantly, astonishingly, powerfully displaying as our present material reality.

We are brave to step out on the bodhisattva way, to walk these thirty-seven steps, fully exposed. We are generous even to consider trying to live this, and transcendentally generous actually to do so. And we walk undefended the entire bodhisattva path in order to realize truth itself, naked and radiant—our natural mind. This is our offering to all our relations.

# APPENDIX A

# TONGLEN: A TEACHING BY HIS EMINENCE GARCHEN TRIPTRUL RINPOCHE

KATHMANDU, NEPAL, 2007[1]

The main practice I did in prison was tong-len (giving and taking). Khenpo Munsel gave me many special oral instructions on tong-len that were not in the text.

In tong-len, we generally say that we are sending happiness out to others and taking others' suffering in. But for the actual meaning of tong-len, you have to understand the inseparability of self and other.

The ground of our minds is the same. We understand this from the View. In this context, even if there are many different types of suffering, there is really only one thing called "suffering." There is only one suffering, he taught.

If there is only one suffering, then at this time when you, yourself, have great suffering, you should think, "The minds of the sentient beings of the three realms and my mind have the same ground."

However, the essence of the suffering of the sentient beings of the three realms and your own suffering is the same. If you see them as the same, if you see them as being non-dual, and then

---

1. Christina Lundberg, "For the Benefit of All Beings."

meditate on that suffering in the mind's natural state, that suffering goes away.

At that moment, you have been able to lessen the suffering of all sentient beings of the three realms, all at once.

The "len" of tong-len means "taking." First, take in this way. "Tong" means "giving." If you understand mind's nature, then you recognize the essence of whatever suffering and afflictive emotions there may be to be emptiness.

When suffering does not harm you anymore, the mind has great bliss. If at that time you meditate, making self and others inseparable, then that bliss can diminish the self-grasping of all sentient beings. It can lessen the self-grasping.

The happiness that is being given is the bliss that comes from the practice of giving and taking. This is how you should practice.

This is very special. Others do not explain it this way.

# APPENDIX B
# THE FOUR OPPONENT POWERS

*To purify negative actions of body, speech, or mind*

- **Regret.** Generate sincere, profound remorse and regret for the specific negativities of body, speech, or mind which you need to purify. The practice of regret can at first be painful, as we recall our harmful acts. Offer your own pain to relieve the pain of others, and as you practice, the pain of regret transforms into gratitude. Do the practice of regret *gently*. It is a gift, not a punishment. As you feel able, you may also, over time, recall your negativities of this and all lifetimes, generating regret for them as well as for all those you cannot now recall. Bodhisattvas generate sincere regret also for the negativities of all sentient beings, offering this practice of the Four Opponent Powers for their merit and liberation.

- **Reliance.** Rely on the wisdom being or the wisdom in which you have great faith and devotion. Make offerings (mental and/or physical) and supplications. With sincere remorse and strong confidence and faith, confess your thoughts, words, and actions that now give you the heartache of regret. Relying and practicing on this spiritual friend or spiritual truth is relying on a pure support, to purify your negative deeds of body, speech and mind.

- **Remedy.** In a general sense the remedy is the opposite of the negativity to be purified—e.g., for anger, practice "patience devoid of hostility"; for grasping, practice generosity; for harming others, practice harmlessness and benefitting others; and so on. Since all negativities of body, speech, or mind involve one's own confusion rooted in self-grasping, remedy in all cases calls for generating bodhicitta, the altruistic intention. Specifically, there is the remedy of the particular practice you are doing and the particular support upon which you are relying in the second instruction above, Reliance.

- **Resolve.** Make firm resolve and commitment to abandon these negative actions of body, speech, and mind. In the event of lapse, repeat these four steps—and especially, supplicate the lama (or that in which you have great faith) for the courage and commitment born of great love and compassion.

H. E. Garchen Rinpoche says that practicing the Four Opponent Powers will purify even the greatest negativity. He also says that we can purify by giving rise to bodhicitta and by realizing the true nature: "In an instant all can be purified."

# APPENDIX C
# STUDYING *THE 37 BODHISATTVA PRACTICES*

- Once a day, recite the entire root text by Tokme Zangpo, preferably aloud, then sit quietly for a bit, allowing the words and meanings to permeate your mind.

- Starting at the beginning of the text, take one verse each week for study and practice. Every day, contemplate that verse, drawing on teachings, commentaries, conversations with others, your own experience, and so on, to expand and deepen your understanding. Bring the verse and its meanings into your awareness over and over again throughout the coming week.

- Each verse contains an explicit, specific instruction for practice. Apply this practice every day throughout the week.

- At the end of the day and whenever you remember, dedicate the merit of your study, reflection, and practice to the well-being, happiness, and liberation of all.

- Meeting with others to study and discuss the text can be very helpful, increasing the range of experience and perspectives to draw on. We all have wisdom to share with one another. Sometimes it comes in the form of questions, doubts, and confusion, for when these are brought to light and acknowledged and shared they can be clarified—and where confusion was and clarity now is there is wisdom of both content and method.

In working with the root text and the commentary texts you choose to study, it is your sincere motivation and energetic approach that bring you into active relationship with them. Your understanding and insights, your questions and uncertainties: this is what will make your study dynamic, powerful, and personally meaningful to you. Spiritual teachings, study, and practice are not academic exercises. There is nothing theoretical about the teachings and the truth to which they point, and nothing theoretical about their benefit for each one of us. The Dharma is universal, but your work with it is very personal, as you seek to free your own mind from confusion and suffering, for the benefit of all beings.

# APPENDIX D
# BIOGRAPHICAL NOTES ON PERSONS MENTIONED IN THE COMMENTARY

**Avalokiteshvara (Lokeshvara, Chenrezig)**—Buddhist deity of compassion whose thousand eyes are said to see and whose thousand arms are said to ease all the sufferings of beings. Counted among his manifold emanations is His Holiness the Dalai Lama.

**Buddha Shakyamuni (c. sixth century BCE; chronologies vary)**—an Indian prince who, having become aware of the inevitability of suffering and death, left behind the seeming certainties of his privileged existence to seek the true nature of reality. After some years of study and practice he attained complete awakening and spent the remaining decades of his life giving the teachings that form the basis of the Buddhadharma.

**Dilgo Khyentse Rinpoche (Tashi Peljor; 1910¬–1991)**—scholar, lineage holder, Dzogchen master of profound and penetrating accomplishment, revealer of treasure texts, teacher of teachers, mountain of Dharma, who traveled throughout the world transmitting the teachings of all the major Tibetan traditions.

**Dudjom Rinpoche (Kyabje Dudjom Jigdral Yeshe Dorje; 1904–1987)**—one of the greatest Tibetan scholars and meditation masters of this age, considered the second Padmasambhava. Dudjom Rinpoche was a revealer of Padmasambhava's hidden treasures, revered for his sky-like realization, pristine teachings, and profound scholarly, historical, and doctrinal works on the vast Nyingma tradition. He taught throughout Tibet and, in the last years of his life, in the West, where he established major centers in the United States and France.

**Garchen Rinpoche (Konchok Gyaltsen, His Eminence the Eighth Garchen Rinpoche; b. 1936)**—beloved Drikung Kagyu lama known for his profound realization and bodhicitta. Imprisoned for more than two decades in a Chinese labor camp during the turmoil of the Chinese Cultural Revolution, there he met, studied, and practiced secretly with his root lama, Nyingma master Khenpo Munsel. Since his release he has worked tirelessly to reestablish the Dharma in Tibet and to spread the teachings in the West.

**Geshe Jampa Tegchok (1930–2014)**—a monk and scholar in the Gelug tradition of Tibetan Buddhism, who taught for many years in India and the West before being appointed abbot of Sera-je monastery in India by His Holiness the Dalai Lama in 1993.

**Khenchen Palden Sherab Rinpoche (1942–2010)**—yogi and teacher of the Nyingma school of Tibetan Buddhism who, with his brother, Khenpo Tsewang Dongyal Rinpoche, composed scholarly works and compilations of teachings both profound and very accessible to Westerners. He founded Padmasambhava Buddhist Centre International.

**Khenpo Munsel (1916-1993)**—a great Tibetan Dzogchen master who gave teachings in secret while imprisoned for twenty-two years in a Chinese labor camp and, after his release, taught widely in Tibet. He became the root lama of His Eminence Garchen Rinpoche during Rinpoche's incarceration.

**Khenpo Tsewang Dongyal Rinpoche (b. 1950)**—scholar, translator, and poet, who worked closely with his brother, Khenchen Palden Sherab Rinpoche, and with Kyabje Dudjom Rinpoche. He leads the Padmasambhava Buddhist Centre International, with teaching and retreat centers in Europe, India, and the United States.

**Milarepa (Jetsun Milarepa, Mila-je, Shepa Dorje, "Laughing Vajra"; 1052-1135)**—consummate yogi saint of Tibet, whose songs of realization convey the highest teachings: trenchant, joyous, and unadorned. After committing evil deeds in his youth he sought out Marpa Lotsawa, the Great Translator (Marpa Chokyi Lodro, 1012-1097), for whom he endured great hardships; steadfastly cultivating pure perception of his rigorous guru, Milarepa realized total awakening in one lifetime.

**Nagarjuna (150–250)**—a great philosopher, head of Nalanda University in India, a founder of the Madhyamaka (Middle Way) school of Mahayana Buddhism, and revealer of the Prajnaparamita Sutras. His commentaries are said to explain all the Buddha's teachings.

**Padmasambhava (Guru Rinpoche, Pema Jungne/"Lotus Born," Guru Pema; eighth century)**—Indian pandita who brought Buddhism from India to Tibet and is revered as a second Buddha. The founder of the Nyingma school, he left many teachings concealed for later generations to discover. These are the treasures referred to as terma, revealed by tertons, or treasure revealers, such as Dudjom Rinpoche and Dilgo Khyentse Rinpoche.

**Palden Gyatso (1933–2018)**—Gelug monk who spent more than three decades in Chinese prisons, enduring severe torture, and drew international attention to the atrocities committed there in his *Autobiography of a Tibetan Monk*.

**Patrul Rinpoche (Dza Patrul Orgyen Jigme Chokyi Wangpo; 1808–1887)**—Tibetan scholar, meditation master, teacher, and author of the renowned and beloved *Words of My Perfect Teacher*. He taught frequently and profoundly on Shantideva's *Bodhisattvacaryavatara* (*The Way of the Bodhisattva*) and on Amitabha.

**Pema Sangdzin Khandro (Ven. Dhyani Ywahoo)**—North American spiritual teacher in her Cherokee Ywahoo lineage, of which she is the twenty-seventh generation lineage holder, and in the Tibetan traditions of the Nyingma and Drikung Kagyu schools. A teacher worldwide and founder of Sunray Meditation Society in the United States, Venerable is the author of *Voices of Our Ancestors: Cherokee Teachings from the Wisdom Fire*.

**Shantideva (685–763)**—an apparently undistinguished student at Nalanda University, in India, who startled his colleagues when he revealed that he had in fact composed a text of great brilliance, the *Bodhisattvacaryavatara* (*The Way of the Bodhisattva*), a cornerstone of Mahayana Buddhism.

**Tenzin Gyatso, His Holiness the Fourteenth Dalai Lama (b. 1935)**— spiritual leader of the Tibetan people, Nobel Peace laureate, venerated and beloved around the world. His Holiness has lived in exile in India since leaving Tibet in 1959, traveling the globe to give teachings and engage in humanitarian activities.

**Tokme Zangpo (also Gyalse or Ngulchu Tokme Zangpo; 1295–1369)**—scholar and monk, revered author of *The 37 Bodhisattva Practices* and other works in the Tibetan Buddhist mind training tradition (*lojong*). He served as abbot of Bodong E monastery in Tibet before entering a retreat that would last more than twenty years.

Compiled with the kind assistance of Jordan Kirk, drawing on these sources: The Treasury of Lives (https://treasuryoflives.org/); Rigpa Wiki (https://www.rigpawiki.org/); Wikipedia (https://en.wikipedia.org/)

# READER'S GUIDE TO CONTENTS
# CONCEPTS AND THEMES BY CHAPTER AND VERSE

# ACKNOWLEDGEMENTS

My deep respect, gratitude, and love to:

Kyabje Dudjom Rinpoche, His Holiness Chetsang Rinpoche, His Eminence Garchen Rinpoche, Khenchen Palden Sherab Rinpoche, Khenpo Tsewang Dongyal Rinpoche, Ven. Traga Rinpoche, and Pema Sangdzin Khandro (Ven. Dhyani Ywahoo). Exemplars and inspirations to countless beings, I bow to you.

The lamas, staff, and volunteers at the Garchen Buddhist Institute in Chino Valley, Arizona, H.E. Garchen Rinpoche's seat in the West—including Ina Trinley Wangmo, Rinpoche's precious translator—who lovingly, devotedly, tirelessly, cheerfully serve Rinpoche and his worldwide sangha, and whose support and kindness help me in all my Dharma activities.

The dynamic, energetic, goodhearted sanghas who have gathered with me over the years, notably the Garchen Assembly of Kindness and Love (Garchen Prescott Sangha, Prescott, Arizona); Strong Heart Sangha (Sacramento, California) and my kind hosts there, Nelson Feldman, Jeri Petersen, Donna Hoenig-Couch, Patrick Couch, and Diane McVicker; Angel Canyon Sangha, (Kanab, Utah) and Cyrus and Anne Mejía; Sofie Velander (Stockholm); Sofia Sarquis and Juan Carlos Gil Vargas (Mexico City); and all those meeting in various places and circumstances over many years, calling forth teachings, practice, and bodhicitta by their sincere desire to benefit all.

Dear sangha companions, esteemed practitioners, supporters, helpers, and friends on the way, too many to name so I name these few in homage to you all: Sue Favia, Robert and Linda Ewing, Tsering and Paljor Thondup, Trisha Lamb, Amy Fry-Miller, Moon Teitel, Taryn Kennedy, Kim Agullard, Katharine Davis, Kiel Hemenway, Meiling Pulmones, Christina Lundberg, Juanita McCarron, Pam Powers, Ven. Khenmo Nyima Drolma, Regina Sara Ryan, Paula Sarvani, and Jordan Kirk; the many, many enthusiastic, generous donors who supported the publication of this book, privately and through GoFundMe; Steve Scholl, surely the most supportive publisher ever, elegant designer Christy Collins, and all at White Cloud Press; Clelia Lewis, our pristine copy editor; and the kind Boyd family at the base of Granite Mountain, where this book was written.

I bow to and thank all beings in the realms of existence, beloved companions and relatives, upon whom I rely for necessity, inspiration, and accomplishment on the bodhisattva way. Holy, holy, holy. Praise, praise, praise.

# BIBLIOGRAPHY

Berzin, Alexander. *Relating to a Spiritual Teacher: Building a Healthy Relationship*. Ithaca, NY: Snow Lion Publications, 2000.

Bhakha Tulku and Steven Goodman. "The Prayer of Kuntuzangpo," in *Quintessential Dzogchen: Confusion Dawns as Wisdom*. Hong Kong: Rangjung Yeshe Publications, 2006.

Cantú, Francisco. *The Line Becomes a River: Dispatches from the Border*. New York: Riverhead Books, 2018.

Chang, Garma C. C., ed. *The Hundred Thousand Songs of Milarepa*. Boston: Shambhala Publications, 1999.

Chökyi Dragpa. *Uniting Wisdom and Compassion: Illuminating the Thirty-seven Practices of a Bodhisattva*. Boston: Wisdom Publications, 2004.

Dharmarakshita. *The Wheel of Sharp Weapons: A Mahayana Training of the Mind*. Commentary by Geshey Ngawang Dhargyey. 2nd rev. ed. Dharamsala, India: Library of Tibetan Works and Archives, 1994.

Dilgo Khyentse. *The Heart of Compassion: The Thirty-seven Verses on the Practice of a Bodhisattva*. Boston: Shambhala Publications, 2007.

————. *The Wish-fulfilling Jewel*. Boston: Shambhala Publications, 1988.

Du Bois, Barbara. *Light Years: A Spiritual Memoir*. Prescott, AZ: Laughing Vajra Press, 2011.

Dudjom Rinpoche. *Extracting the Quintessence of Accomplishment: Oral Instructions for the Practice of Mountain Retreat Expounded Simply and Directly in their Essential Nakedness*. Corralitos, CA: Vajrayana Foundation, 2000.

Dunnington, Jacqueline. *The Tibetan Wheel of Existence: An Introduction*. New York: Tibet House, 2000.

Gampopa. *The Jewel Ornament of Liberation*. Khenpo Konchog Gyaltsen Rinpoche, trans. Ithaca, NY: Snow Lion Publications, 1998.

Garchen Rinpoche. *Commentary on the 37 Bodhisattva Practices by Ngulchu Thogme Zangpo*. Hamburg: Sept 2007; unpublished transcript.

_____. *Thirty-seven Bodhisattva Practices: Teachings by H. E. Garchen Rinpoche*. Taiwan: Taipei Drikung Kagyu Center, 2001; unpublished monograph.

Jamgön Kongtrul (Jamgon Kongtrul Lodrö Thayé). *The Teacher-Student Relationship*. Ron Garry, trans. Ithaca, NY: Snow Lion Publications, 1999.

Jampa Tegchok. *Transforming the Heart: The Buddhist Way to Joy and Courage, A Commentary to the Bodhisattva Togme Sangpo's* The Thirty-seven Practices of Bodhisattvas. Ithaca, NY: Snow Lion Publications, 1999. (2005 reissued as *Transforming Adversity into Joy and Courage: An Explanation of the Thirty-seven Practices of Bodhisattvas*.)

Khandro Rinpoche. *This Precious Life: Tibetan Buddhist Teachings on the Path to Enlightenment*. Boston: Shambhala Publications, 2005.

Khunu Rinpoche. *Vast as the Heavens, Deep as the Sea: Verses in Praise of Bodhicitta*. Boston: Wisdom Publications, 1999.

Lhalungpa, Lobsang P., trans. *The Life of Milarepa*. New York: E. P. Dutton, 1977.

Lhundub Sopa. *Peacock in the Poison Grove: Two Buddhist Texts on Training the Mind, attributed to Dharmarakshita*. Boston: Wisdom Publications, 2001.

Lifton, Robert Jay. *Home from the War: Vietnam Veterans—Neither Victims nor Executioners*. New York: Simon & Schuster, 1973.

Lundberg, Christina. "For the Benefit of All Beings: The Extraordinary Life of His Eminence Garchen Triptrul Rinpoche." A film from Garuda Sky Productions, 2013. See also www.FortheBenefitofAllBeings.com.

McLeod, Ken. *Reflections on Silver River: Tokmé Zangpo's Thirty-Seven Practices of a Bodhisattva*. Sonoma, CA: Unfettered Mind Media, 2014.

Namkhai Norbu. *The Crystal and the Way of Light: Sutra, Tantra and Dzogchen*. New York: Routledge & Kegan Paul, 1986.

_____. *The Song of the Vajra: An Oral Commentary*. Arcidosso, Italy: Shang Shang Edizioni, 2004; restricted distribution.

Ngawang Dhargyey. *Tibetan Tradition of Mental Development*. Dharamsala, India: Library of Tibetan Works and Archives. 1974.

Padmasambhava. *The Tibetan Book of the Dead [The Great Liberation through Hearing in the Bardo]*. Francesca Fremantle and Chogyam Trungpa, trans. Boston: Shambhala Publications, 1975.

Palden Gyatso. *The Autobiography of a Tibetan Monk*. New York: Grove Press, 1998.

Palden Sherab Rinpoche. *Prajnaparamita: The Six Perfections*. Khenpo Tsewang Dongyal Rinpoche, trans. Highland Beach, FL: Sky Dancer Press, 1990.

Palden Sherab Rinpoche and Khenpo Tsewang Dongyal Rinpoche. *The Prayer of Kuntuzangpo: Text and Commentary*. New York: Dharma Samudra, 1996.

Patrul Rinpoche. *The Words of My Perfect Teacher*. Boston: Shambhala Publications, rev. ed., 1998.

Samten Chhosphel. "Biography of Khenpo Munsel." https://treasuryoflives.org/biographies/view/Khenpo-Munsel/9929. Accessed June 12, 2019.

Scales, Sandra. *Sacred Voices of the Nyingma Masters*. Junction City, CA: Padma Publishing, 2004.

Shantideva. *A Guide to the Bodhisattva's Way of Life (Bodhisattvacharyavatara)*. Stephen Batchelor, trans. Dharamsala, India: Library of Tibetan Works and Archives, 1979.

Sonam Rinpoche. *How Karma Works: The Twelve Links of Dependent Arising*. Ithaca, NY: Snow Lion Publications, 2006.

_____. *The Six Perfections*. Ithaca, NY: Snow Lion Publications, 1998.

_____. *The Thirty-seven Practices of Bodhisattvas*. Ithaca, NY: Snow Lion Publications, 1997.

Sue-Sue (Tâm Bào Đàn). *The Lama of Many Lifetimes: Touching the Living Heart of Garchen Rinpoche; Book One, The Early Years (1937-1958)*. Irvine, California: Milam Bardo Publications, 2013.

Tenzin Gyatso, His Holiness the 14th Dalai Lama. *Commentary on the Thirty Seven Practices of a Bodhisattva*. Dharamsala, India: Library of Tibetan Works and Archives, 1995.

_____. *A Flash of Lightning in the Dark of Night: A Guide to the Bodhisattva's Way of Life*. Boston: Shambhala Publications, 1994.

Thich Nhat Hanh. *Interbeing: Fourteen Guidelines for Engaged Buddhism*. Berkeley: Parallax Press, 1987.

Thogme Zangpo (Acharya dNgol-Chu Thogs-Med bZangpo). *The Thirty Seven Bodhisattva Practices*. Acharya Rigzin Dorjee and Bonnie

Rothenberg, trans. 2nd ed. Central Institute of Higher Tibetan Studies, Nyingma Students Welfare Committee. Sarnath, Varanasi, India: 1988.

Thrangu Rinpoche, *The Twelve Links of Interdependent Origination*. Boulder, CO: Namo Buddha Publications, 2001.

Thubten Chodron. *Don't Believe Everything You Think: Living with Wisdom and Compassion*. Ithaca, NY: Snow Lion Publications, 2013.

Tokme Zangpo. *37 Practices of the Bodhisattva's Way of Life*. Ina Trinley Wangmo, trans. Chino Valley, AZ: Garchen Buddhist Institute, n.d.

# ABOUT THE AUTHORS

 HIS EMINENCE GARCHEN TRIPTRUL RINPOCHE is renowned and beloved worldwide for his vast wisdom and universal love and for his profound, precise, and eminently practicable teachings of Buddhadharma. Born in Tibet in 1936 and traditionally trained as a lama in his youth, Garchen Rinpoche was caught up in the Tibetan resistance to the 1958 Chinese take-over of Tibetan and imprisoned for twenty years in a Chinese labor camp during the Cultural Revolution. In prison he was taught and trained in secret by his root guru, the great Khenpo Munsel. When released from prison in 1979, he took it upon himself to rebuild the Drikung Kagyu monasteries, re-establish the Buddhist teachings, and build schools for local children in eastern Tibet. Rinpoche first came to North America in 1997. He is the founder and spiritual director of the Garchen Buddhist Institute and other Dharma centers in the United States, North America, Asia, and Europe. Rinpoche is now residing at his Western seat, the Garchen Buddhist Institute, in Arizona.

 BARBARA DU BOIS, Ph.D., sharing Buddhadharma for 35 years, is known for the clarity, freshness, humor, and fearless love with which she shines a frank Western light on the path. Her principal gurus in this lifetime are H. H. Dudjom Rinpoche and H. E. Garchen Rinpoche. Barbara's lifetime of service includes work with the United Nations, disarmaent, refugees from colonial regimes and genocide, and initiating an indigenous women's peace movement during an active civil war in Africa. She holds the doctorate from Harvard University and has taught at undergraduate and graduate levels. She is the author of *Light Years: A Spiritual Memoir* and *Brave, Generous, & Undefended: Heart Teachings on the 37 Bodhisattva Practices* (White Cloud Press, 2020); she has also compiled and edited works by contemporary Western spiritual teachers Dhyani Ywahoo, *Voices of Our Ancestors*, and David Chethlahe Paladin, *Painting the Dream*. Barbara currently resides in Arizona.